Biased

Biased

Uncovering the Hidden
Prejudice That Shapes
What We See, Think, and Do

JENNIFER L.
EBERHARDT, PhD

Viking

VIKING
An imprint of Penguin Random House LLC
penguinrandomhouse.com

Illustration credits appear on page 327.

Library of Congress Cataloging-in-Publication Data
Names: Eberhardt, Jennifer L. (Jennifer Lynn), author.
Title: Biased : uncovering the hidden prejudice that shapes what we see, think, and do / Jennifer L. Eberhardt. PhD.
Description: New York : Viking, [2019] | Includes index.
Identifiers: LCCN 2018051011 | ISBN 9780735224933 (hardcover) | ISBN 9780735224940 (ebook)
Subjects: LCSH: Prejudices. | Discrimination. | Racism.
Classification: LCC BF575.P9 E34 2019 | DDC 303.3/85--dc23
LC record available at https://lccn.loc.gov/2018051011

Printed in the United States of America
10 9 8 7 6 5 4 3 2 1

Book design by Daniel Lagin

Names of certain individuals have been changed to protect their privacy.

For my love, Rick, who inspires me to do more
and to move further than I ever thought I could

CONTENTS

Part III

The Way Out

A journey is called that because you cannot know what you will . . . do with what you find, or what you find will do to you.

—James Baldwin

Introduction

I walked in through a sea of navy-blue uniforms. The auditorium was filled to capacity, with 132 sworn members of the Oakland Police Department sitting motionless with perfect posture: erect, arms crossed. As I walked down the aisle to take the stage, I could not see their faces, but I already knew what they were thinking.

The road to this particular presentation was a long one. The police force was still recovering from a major scandal that had left a legacy of distrust in the community. I was just wrapping up a two-year report that was about to be released to the public—one of the final steps required by the federal oversight team brought in to investigate extensive civil rights violations by members of this department—and I didn't want the police to be blindsided by our findings. Many in the community were calling for an end to racial profiling. They wanted fair treatment. They were demanding justice. Many in the police department felt they were delivering that justice every day—sometimes at great sacrifice. I wanted to help the officers to understand the insidious ways in which implicit bias could act on human decision making, despite the officers' noble intentions and deliberate efforts.

Reporters were pressuring me to discuss our findings before the report was released, but I couldn't; there was too much at stake. I first wanted the department to be prepared and to be willing to work with our team as they crafted solutions to any problems the report would reveal.

I was tired—exhausted, really—from working on the report around the clock for months, to the neglect of my teaching, my husband, and our three sons. As I marched up the aisle, I could feel a chill in the room.

I made it to the stage. Although not exactly as modern or as high-tech as the classrooms at Stanford where I normally taught, the auditorium—with its wood-paneled walls and rows of cushioned red metal chairs—seemed familiar enough. I looked out at the faces in the crowd, searching for a connection. I found every face expressionless, their eyes distant. Each officer wore a crisp, clean uniform over a bulletproof vest. At the waist was a duty belt holding the essential tools of their trade: handcuffs, Taser, OC pepper spray, and Glock 17 9 mm firearm. The officers looked ready for duty, but no one seemed ready to engage with me.

For the first time in my career, I was facing a hostile crowd. There was no booing or yelling. There were no verbal complaints of any kind—just a steely silence that was more eloquent than any words. I tried to make a few jokes. Nothing landed. I led them through an interactive "shoot–don't shoot" simulation, which was always a crowd-pleaser. The exercise fell flat. I showed a few movie clips that in other places triggered bursts of laughter. Still nothing.

Finally, I caught the eye of LeRonne Armstrong, a captain whom I'd worked with before on trainings designed to improve police-community relations. I knew he understood the importance of delivering this message to law enforcement. I was relieved to see his face, until I realized that his expression was one of concern for me. He was looking around the crowd with the same worry I was trying not to let show onstage. I saw him shifting uncomfortably in his seat. *How, I wondered, can I possibly deliver this training ten more times to units across the department when I'm not really sure whether I can make it through this first session?*

Eventually, I stopped with the lessons, and the data graphs, and the images, and the jokes, and the movie clips. I decided to veer off my usual script and share a personal story.

I explained that some years ago my son Everett and I were on a plane. He was five years old, wide-eyed, and trying to take it all in. He looked around and saw a black passenger. He said, "Hey, that guy looks like Daddy." I looked at the man, and truth be told, he did not look anything like Daddy—not in any way. I looked around for anyone else Everett might be referring to. But there was only one black man on the plane.

I couldn't help but be struck by the irony: the race researcher having to explain to her own black child that not all black people look alike. But then I paused and thought about the fact that kids see the world differently from adults. Maybe Everett was seeing something that I missed. I decided to take another look.

I checked the guy's height. No resemblance there. He was several inches shorter than my husband. I studied his face. There was nothing in his features that looked familiar. I looked at his skin color. No similarity there either. Then I took a look at his hair. This man had dreadlocks flowing down his back. Everett's father is bald.

I gathered my thoughts and turned to my son, prepared to lecture him in the way that I might inform an unobservant student in my class. But before I could begin, he looked up at me and said, "I hope that man doesn't rob the plane."

Maybe I didn't get that right. "What did you say?" I asked him, wishing I had not heard what I heard. And he said it again, as innocently and as sweetly as you can imagine from a bright-eyed boy trying to understand the world: "I hope he doesn't rob the plane."

I was on the brink of being upset. "Why would you say that?" I asked as gently as I could. "You know Daddy wouldn't rob a plane."

"Yes," he said. "I know."

"Well, why did you say that?" This time my voice dropped an octave and turned sharp.

Everett looked up at me with a really sad face and said very solemnly, "I don't know why I said that. I don't know why I was *thinking* that."

Just telling that story reminded me of how much that moment hurt. I took a deep breath, and when I looked back out at the crowd in the auditorium, I saw that the expressions had changed. Their eyes had softened. They were no longer uniformed police officers, and I was no longer a university researcher. We were parents, unable to protect our children from a world that is often bewildering and frightening, a world that influences them so profoundly, so insidiously, and so unconsciously that they—and we—don't know why we think the way we do.

With a heavy heart, I continued with my point: "We are living with such severe racial stratification that even a five-year-old can tell us what's supposed to happen next. Even with no malice—even with no hatred—the black-crime association made its way into the mind of my five-year-old son, into all of our children, into all of us."

I finished the training and invited the audience to come up to ask questions or share their stories. I had been warned that no one would, but one officer did stay behind in the emptying auditorium. As he approached the stage, I stepped down to meet him. "Your story about your son on the plane reminded me of an experience I had on the street. It's something I haven't thought about in a long time," the officer told me.

"I was out one day, working undercover," the officer said, "and I saw a guy, at a distance, who didn't look right. This guy looked similar to me—you know, black, same build, same height. But this guy had a scruffy beard, unkempt hair, ripped clothes, and he looked like he was up to no good. The guy began approaching me, and as he was getting closer, I had a feeling that he had a gun on him. *Something's off with this guy*, I thought. *This dude ain't right.*

"So the guy is coming down a hill, near the front of a nice office building—one of those big office towers with glass walls. And as the guy is approaching, I couldn't shake the feeling that he was armed and dangerous.

"As I got closer to the building, I lost him for a second and I began to feel panicked. Suddenly I see the guy again, but this time he is *inside* the office building. I could see the guy clearly through the glass wall. He was walking inside the building—in the same direction and at the same pace as I was walking.

"Something was wrong. When I quickened my pace, I could see him quicken his pace. And finally, I decided to stop abruptly, turn, and confront the guy.

"He stops too, and I look at him face-to-face," the officer said to me. "And when I look in his eyes, a shock went through me. I realized that I was staring at myself. *I* was the person I feared. I was staring at my own reflection through the mirrored wall. That entire time, I was tailing myself; I was profiling myself."

The stories kept coming. At *every single session*, someone came up and told me a story—stories that enriched my understanding not only of police-community relations but also of our human predicament.

This book is an examination of implicit bias—what it is, where it comes from, how it affects us, and how we can address it. Implicit bias is not a new way of calling someone a racist. In fact, you don't have to be a racist at all to be influenced by it. Implicit bias is a kind of distorting lens that's a product of both the architecture of our brain and the disparities in our society.

We all have ideas about race, even the most open-minded among us. Those ideas have the power to bias our perception, our attention, our memory, and our actions—all despite our conscious awareness or deliberate intentions. Our ideas about race are shaped by the stereotypes to which we are exposed on a daily basis. And one of the strongest stereotypes in American society associates blacks with criminality.

This stereotypic association is so powerful that the mere presence of a black face, even one that appears so fleetingly we are unaware of it, can cause us to see weapons more quickly—or to imagine weapons that are not there. The mere thought of violent crime can lead us to shift our eyes away from a white face and toward a black face. And although looking black is not a crime, jurors are more likely to deliver a death sentence to black felons who have stereotypically black facial features than to those who do not, at least when their victims are white.

Bias can lead to racial disparities in everything from preschool suspensions to corporate leadership. And the disparities themselves then bolster our biases. For example, knowing that a disproportionate amount of violent crime is committed by young black men can bias judgments about black people more generally. That affects how blacks are seen in all manner of situations—whether sitting in a classroom or a coffee shop, whether leading a Fortune 500 company or fighting a California wildfire. The stereotypes shadow them.

In this book, I'll show you the many surprising places and ways that racial bias affects all sorts of decisions we make during the normal course of our lives—the homes we buy, the people we hire, the way we treat our neighbors. Bias is not limited to one domain of life. It is not limited to one profession, one race, or one country. It is also not limited to one stereotypic association. This book grew from my research on the black-crime association, yet it is not the only association that matters and blacks are not the only group affected. Probing the role of implicit bias in the criminal justice arena can teach us broader lessons about who we are, where we've been, and what we can become, regardless of our social group or the groups toward which we may be biased.

People can hold biases based on all sorts of characteristics—skin color, age, weight, ethnic origin, accent, disability, height, gender. I talk a lot about race, specifically about blacks and whites, because those two groups have been studied the most by researchers investigating bias. And because the racial dynamics between blacks and whites are dramatic, consequential, and enduring. In the United States, those tensions over centuries have even set the tone for how other social groups are regarded.

Confronting implicit bias requires us to look in the mirror. To understand the influence of implicit racial bias requires us to stare into our own eyes—much as the undercover police officer who found that he had been tailing himself had done—to face how readily stereotypes and unconscious associations can shape our reality. By acknowledging the distorting lens of fear and bias, we move one step closer to clearly seeing each other. And we move one step closer to clearly seeing the social harms—the devastation—that bias can leave in its wake.

Neither our evolutionary path nor our present culture dooms us to be held hostage by bias. Change requires a kind of open-minded attention that is well within our reach. There are successful approaches we can learn from and new ways of thinking that we can build upon, whether we are trying to change ourselves or the settings where we live, work, and learn.

This book is a representation of the journey I have taken—the unexpected findings I have uncovered, the stories I have heard, the struggles I have encountered, and the triumphs I have been buttressed by. I invite you to join me.

Part I

WHAT MEETS THE EYE

CHAPTER 1

Seeing Each Other

I spent the first twelve years of my life in Cleveland, Ohio, in an all-black world. My family, my neighbors, my teachers, my classmates, my friends—every person I had any meaningful contact with until that point was black. So when my parents announced we were moving to a nearly all-white suburb called Beachwood, I was excited about living in a bigger house but worried about how I would be greeted by my new middle school classmates.

I worried they would make fun of me—my brown skin, my wiry hair, my large dark eyes. I worried about my way of speaking—my cadence, my word choice, my voice.

Yet when I arrived that fall, white students went out of their way to welcome me. They introduced themselves. They invited me to eat with them at lunch. They showed me around the school and loaded me up with details on the dizzying array of activities now open to me. It was what my parents had always dreamed of. I could sing in the choir or act in a play. I could study sign language or learn gymnastics. I could try out for the volleyball team or run for a seat on the student council.

My classmates seemed genuinely interested in helping me transition to this new place. I was grateful, and yet I struggled to make new friends. I'd call students by the wrong name, walk past a classmate in the hall without speaking, fail to remember the girl I'd shared a lunch table with in the cafeteria the day before. They didn't seem to hold it against me. They understood that I was meeting people every day and it was a lot to take in. But I knew there was something more going on. Every day I was confronted with a mass of white faces that I could not distinguish from one another. I didn't know how to do it or even where to start.

I'd had no practice recognizing white faces. They all looked alike to me. I could describe in detail the face of the black woman I happened to pass in a shopping mall. But I could not pick out from a crowd the white girl who sat next to me in English class every day.

I found myself constantly seduced by the easiest way to sort people. I would hold on to the fact that the girl in the red sweater said this and the girl in the gray sweatshirt said that. This helped me to track a conversation in the moment, but I would be at a loss again the very next day.

I tried training myself to pay attention to features that I'd never needed to notice in my black neighborhood—eye color, various shades of blond hair, freckles. I tried remembering the most distinctive feature about each person I encountered. But all the faces would ultimately blend together again in my mind.

As time went on, I worried that my new friends would begin to drift away. Who would want to be friends with a girl who had to be reminded to whom she was talking from one day to the next?

Stripped of this most basic skill, I became a different person in my new neighborhood—awkward, uncertain, hesitant, withdrawn. I was afraid of making a mistake, of embarrassing myself or hurting the feelings of people I'd grown to like.

By springtime, whenever I saw girls whispering among themselves, I'd wonder whether their patience was finally wearing thin. *Are they talking about me?* I'd sidle over to try to join the conversation, but they'd fall silent whenever I showed up.

I was relieved when one of the popular girls invited me to lunch at a restaurant one weekend. When I walked in, she was sitting at a table with a group of girls I didn't recognize, until they all yelled out, "Happy birthday!" I scanned their faces and realized that these were the classmates I'd seen whispering in the hall, planning a surprise party for the new girl who still hadn't managed to get their names right.

They'd brought gifts that reflected touchstones in their lives, including albums by musicians I'd never heard of: Bruce Springsteen, Billy Joel. I was moved beyond words by the gesture; no one had ever planned a surprise party for me. But when we finished the cake, hugged good-bye, and parted ways, I still was not confident I could tell those faces apart.

The irony of that school year always troubled me. I worried about being ostracized because I wasn't one of them. But I was the one stumbling over our racial differences. They wanted to connect, and so did I. But I had suddenly acquired a deficiency that they were not aware of and that I did not understand.

Decades later, I would realize that I was not alone.

THE SCIENCE OF RECOGNITION

For nearly fifty years, scientists have been documenting the fact that people are much better at recognizing faces of their own race than faces of other races—a finding dubbed the "other-race effect."

It's a universal phenomenon, and it shows up in different racial groups across the United States and in countries all over the world.

It appears early and intensifies over time. By the time babies are three months old, their brains react more strongly to faces of their own race than to faces of people unlike them. That race-selective response only grows stronger as children move into adolescence, which suggests it is driven, in part, by the circumstances of our lives.

We learn what's important—the faces we see every day—and over time our brain builds a preference for those faces, at the expense of skills needed to recognize others less relevant. That experience-driven evolution of face perception skills remodels our brains so they can operate more efficiently.

Scientists see the other-race effect as a sign that our perceptive powers are shaped by what we see. That cringe-worthy expression "*They all look alike*" has long been considered the province of the bigot. But it is actually a function of biology and exposure. Our brains are better at processing faces that evoke a sense of familiarity.

I'd struggled to recognize my white classmates' faces because black faces were all I'd been routinely exposed to in the twelve years before I moved to the suburbs. My adolescent brain took some time to catch up to the new world I was navigating, but I would soon develop new skills to function in that world.

Race is not a pure dividing line. Children who are adopted by parents of a different race do not exhibit the classic other-race effect. For example, researchers in Belgium found that white children were better at recognizing white faces than Asian faces. But Chinese and Vietnamese children who'd been adopted by white families were equally good at recognizing white and Asian faces.

Age and familiarity with various age-groups can also be factors. In England, a study of primary school teachers found that they were better at recognizing the faces of random eight- to eleven-year-olds than were college students who spent most of their time around other college students. And scientists in Italy found that maternity-ward nurses were better at telling infants apart by looking at their faces than were people from other professions—a proficiency that helps to ensure "mix-ups don't happen in the nursery," the researchers suggest.

Our experiences in the world seep into our brain over time, and without our awareness they conspire to reshape the workings of our mind.

IMAGING RACE

I couldn't have known back in middle school that my own brain development played a part in my struggle to connect. But I was convinced that skin color had a role in the dislocation I felt. That's ultimately what drew me to the field of social psychology. It offered the perspective I needed to address a question fundamental to my own adolescent experience: *How does race shape who we are and how we experience the world?* That question is the starting point of bigger questions about identity, power, and privilege that have molded our country and roiled the world for centuries.

Today, I am a professor and a researcher at Stanford University, a campus nestled in Silicon Valley, the heart of the start-up economy and a magnet for bright, energetic young people eager to tap the rich vein of technology for scientific solutions to social problems. When I arrived at Stanford, I was enticed by the tools of neuroscience research and began exploring the ways that race might influence basic brain functioning.

The brain is not a hardwired machine. It's a malleable organ that responds to the environments we are placed in and the challenges we face. This view of the brain runs counter to what most of us learned in science class. In fact, the whole idea of neuroplasticity runs counter

15

to what scientists believed to be true about the brain for centuries. Only fairly recent advances in neuroscience have allowed us to peek inside the brain and track its adaptation over time. Slowly, we're beginning to understand the many ways the brain can be altered by experience.

For example, in the last several decades, we have learned that when someone becomes blind, the occipital lobe, typically dedicated to processing visual stimuli, can dedicate itself instead to processing other types of stimuli, including sound and touch. When someone has a stroke, they might be able to learn to speak again, despite massive damage to specific areas of the temporal lobe that are dedicated to processing language. We don't know yet the extent of this neuroplasticity. And some of the most intriguing lessons come not only from studying damaged brains but also from watching people with normal brain function acquire unusual skills.

Research has shown that something as simple as driving a taxi can offer lessons in how basic practice and repetition can retrain our brains to function differently. In 2000, not long after I arrived at Stanford, a team led by Professor Eleanor Maguire published a paper that caused quite a stir in the neuroscience community. They'd scanned the brains of London cabdrivers in an effort to examine how the hippocampus—a horseshoe-shaped structure in the medial temporal lobe—might grow in response to demands placed upon it by the taxing experience of driving through the London city streets day in and day out.

Maguire's team found that the brains of taxicab drivers—who had by necessity learned the structural layout of more than twenty-five thousand London streets—showed significant differences in the hippocampus, the part of the brain that plays a critical role in spatial memory and navigation. The taxi drivers' navigational expertise was associated with increased gray matter. They had enlarged posterior hippocampal regions, in comparison with a control group of people who didn't drive cabs for a living. In fact, the longer the drivers had been on the job and the more experience they had, the larger their posterior hippocampus.

I found this all remarkable because it seemed to show not only how powerful our experiences must be to fundamentally change our brain but also how swiftly the transformation can take place. In the case of the taxi drivers, developing a deep structural knowledge of their environment forced a striking structural change in their brains. And that change happened not over hundreds of thousands of years but within a few years of an individual's life. Individual expertise, as it turns out, has its own neurobiological signature.

That revelation led me to pose another question, driven by both scientific curiosity and personal memories of my own adolescent lapse: *Because our experiences in the world are reflected in our brains, might our expertise in recognizing faces of our own race—and failing to recognize those of others—display its own neurobiological signature as well?*

Neuroscientists were initially skeptical about the prospect of race having an influence on something as basic, ancient, and important as how faces register in our brains. The act of perceiving faces is both critical and complicated, which may be why the task is distributed across multiple areas of the occipitotemporal region, stretching across two of four major lobes of the brain. The superior temporal sulcus—a trench-like structure in the temporal lobe that's vital to social competence—helps us to read the many different expressions that can suddenly emerge on someone's face, signaling us to approach, to smile, to share, to flee, or to quickly arm ourselves. A region known as the fusiform face area, buried deep near the base of the brain, helps us distinguish the familiar from the unfamiliar, friend from foe.

The fusiform face area, known as the FFA, is widely thought to be both primitive and fundamental to our survival as a species. Affiliation is a basic human need. Without the ability to track the identity of those around us, we are left alone, vulnerable, and exposed.

The FFA has been studied extensively, yet despite decades of research there had been little attention paid to whether race might influence FFA functioning. From the narrow perspective of brain science, the primary function of the FFA is to detect faces. Race, most scientists felt, should have nothing to do with that.

Against that backdrop, I began working with a team of Stanford neuroscientists who specialized in human memory to look further into the matter. Together, we recruited dozens of white and black volunteers and subjected them to functional magnetic resonance imaging (fMRI) scans that allowed us to track the blood flow changes in the brain that illustrate neural activity.

As is common, our study participants had giant coils wrapped around their heads to transmit the images. We slid them into a tube-like scanner (a giant magnet, actually) and showed them a series of faces of black and white strangers. We monitored the process from a control room nearby, taking whole-brain pictures as each face appeared before their eyes. The stronger their response to a face, the more oxygen flooded the targeted part of their brain and the brighter our measuring sensors shined.

By tracking the activation of the FFA over multiple displays of strangers' faces, we found that the FFA was responding more vigorously to faces that were the same race as the study participant. That finding held true for both the black and the white people we scanned. We also found that the more dramatic the FFA response to a specific face, the more likely the study participants were able to recognize that stranger's face when they were shown the photograph again later, outside the scanner.

Ours was the first neuroimaging study to demonstrate that there is a neural component to the same-race advantage in the face-recognition process. It offered support for the emerging notion that the brain tunes itself to our experiences as we move through life. And we learned that race can serve as a powerful interpretive lens in that tuning process. Race, as it turns out, could exert influence over one of the brain's most basic functions. The FFA, with its bright colors on our imaging scans, provided us with a clear picture of how in- and out-group distinctions—set in motion by our relationship to the world around us—are mapped onto the inner workings of our brains.

THE PURSE SNATCHERS

Call it scientific progress or streetwise knowledge. But what it took me decades to learn about the role of race in face recognition turned out to be common knowledge among an opportunistic band of young men on a crime spree in Oakland.

It was 2014 and I had just begun analyzing racial disparities in policing with the Oakland Police Department when the story made its rounds: Despite a substantial decline in crime across the city, the shopping district in Chinatown had registered an alarming rise in strong-arm robberies. Apparently, black teenage boys were roaming the streets, snatching the purses of middle-aged Asian women.

The police developed leads, made arrests, and even recovered some stolen property. But the cases fell apart before the suspects could be prosecuted, because even if a victim had seen the robber's face as he grabbed her purse and ran, none of the women could pick the culprits out of a police lineup.

"We would make stops on the suspect," recalled Captain Le-Ronne Armstrong from the police department. "Yet the victim could not ID. Absent the ID, you couldn't charge the case. This made it impossible to prosecute."

As the young men began to figure out that Asian women couldn't tell them apart, it turned into a license to steal, Armstrong explained to me years later, after some of the crimes were solved and the robbers who were bound for jail had confessed the details. "When we'd ask, 'Why'd you focus in on this particular woman?' they'd say to us very openly, 'The Asian people can't ID. They just can't tell brothers apart.' They'd tell us, 'Like, this is our dream. That's why we go.'"

There was a clear pattern to whom the teens targeted and where and how they struck. They focused on a neighborhood crowded with female, middle-aged Chinese shoppers. They approached from behind, grabbed the purses, and fled, so the victim didn't have much time to study their faces. And sure enough, Armstrong said, in nearly 80 percent of the cases tracked by Oakland police, the Asian victims could not identify the young men who robbed them. Black women, on the other hand, could identify black robbery suspects at a much higher rate, even after a mere glance.

The challenges of cross-racial identification are as well known to law enforcement officials as they are to scientists. Research and real-life experience have shown that the chance of false alarms—of identifying someone as the culprit who is not—goes way up when the suspect is of a different race from the victim. That's the practical fallout of the other-race effect.

Oakland investigators worked to minimize the possibility of misidentification. They followed scientific guidelines on how to construct and use lineups with textbook precision. They even tried offering the victims training, directing them "to focus on anything at all that was distinctive," Armstrong told me. *Was his skin dark or light? Did he have gold teeth? Was his hair in dreadlocks or braids?* "We needed them to move beyond the generic 'male black' description." But for the most part, the Asian women couldn't move beyond it. Even with all the training, they were still unable to distinguish one black teenager's face from another.

Ultimately, what did help put an end to the crime spree was technology. When cameras were placed outside the businesses that lined the busy streets of Chinatown, the risks of being caught suddenly shot up. The camera could capture what the women could not. The boys knew the jig was up.

Captain Armstrong's description of the situation led me to recall my own as a newcomer to Beachwood. I too tried the "remember what's distinctive" strategy. I failed and the Asian women failed, despite our strong desire to get it right. Yet the women's inability to remember those black male faces went beyond awkward moments and insecurities about conversations held in hushed tones. Their inability to remember those faces stymied the police and spread fear across the Chinatown community for months and months before the cameras were installed. These teenagers could rob them at will—even in broad daylight. They needed no mask. Their face was their mask.

CHAPTER 2

Nurturing Bias

T he Asian women were easy targets. They were a group the robbers predicted would not resist: middle-aged, frail, unfamiliar with English, and unable to identify the black teenagers who snatched the purses from their arms. As a category, that made them ideal crime victims. To the women, the thieves became a category too. The women didn't know whether they were being robbed by Michael or Jamal; they knew only they were being robbed by a constant stream of young black men. And for these women, the robberies had a cost beyond the contents of their purses or the loss of their sense of safety in Oakland's insular Chinatown. Each frightening encounter with a lone black youth amplified an ambient stereotype the women might have previously felt free to ignore: black men are dangerous. This is how a toxic association is born.

The sort of categorization that allows such broad generalizations to somehow seem reasonable is a product not only of our personal experience and social messaging but also of our evolution as human beings. Categorization—grouping like things together—is not some abhorrent feature of the human brain, a process that some people engage in and others do not. Rather, it is a universal function of the brain that allows us to organize and manage the overload of stimuli that constantly bombard us. It's a system that brings coherence to a chaotic world; it helps our brains make judgments more quickly and efficiently by instinctively relying on patterns that seem predictable.

But categorization also can impede our efforts to embrace and understand people who are deemed not like us, by tuning us to the faces of people who look like us and dampening our sensitivity to those who don't.

Our awareness of racial categories can determine what we see, and not just in the research laboratory but in the settings we find ourselves in every day. My college friend Marsha is African American and has a sister who is so fair-skinned she passed for white for much of her life as a young adult. Sometimes that sister worried that Marsha's presence might ruin her charade. She didn't want her friends or co-workers to realize she was black, so when she and Marsha were spotted together, she never mentioned they were related. And no one ever caught on. Marsha was always amused by the look of panic on her sister's face whenever a co-worker saw them simply standing near each other, but she never thought to "out" her. She understood the social dynamics that motivated her sister's choice. Because the co-workers thought of Marsha as black and presumed her sister was white, they were oblivious to the many physical resemblances—the same eyes, forehead, and nose—between the two women. To be honest, I don't know if I would have pegged them as sisters if I hadn't already known. Once we've decided on the category, our perceptual reality adjusts to suit the label we've settled on.

The effect is so strong that we can look at the same face and respond to it differently, depending on whether we believe that person to be one of us or an out-group member. In one study conducted by researchers at the University of Texas in El Paso, Latino participants were shown a set of computer-generated faces designed (using a facial composite construction kit) to be racially ambiguous. The researchers displayed the same faces with hairstyles typically worn by African Americans or hairstyles typically worn by Latinos. When asked later which faces they recognized, the participants were better able to remember the ones with the Latino hairstyles—those faces that they perceived as belonging to their own group. Simply presenting them as in-group members allowed the study participants to remember their faces more readily than they remembered those same faces when the hairstyles suggested those people were black.

The impact categorization has on us is so strong that it too makes its mark on our neurons. For example, in one study I conducted with Brent Hughes, Nicholas Camp, and other colleagues at Stanford, we found that white participants exhibited less brain activity in brain areas that specialize in processing faces when shown black faces than when shown white faces. I was struck by the dampened response to black faces because it suggests the brain registered those faces in categorical terms.

When participants were presented with a series of different white faces, the neurons fired away, responding vigorously to each face. It was only when the participants were presented with the same white face over and over again that the neural response began to weaken. That's because the brain begins to disengage when confronted with stimuli that are not novel. It's as if our brain were telling us that because we have already seen this, there is no need to pay attention again. This weakened response to repeated exposure is known by neuroscientists as repetition suppression.

What is remarkable is that we observed repetition suppression even in response to black faces that the participants had never seen before. Although we were exposing the participants to faces of different black individuals one at a time, the white study participants appeared to be processing the faces categorically, as though they were all the same stimulus. Their brains were responding to the type of category that was being presented—a black face, another black face, another black face, the same thing, over and over again—rather than the individual, unique identity of each face. And once faces are categorized as out-group members, they are not processed as deeply or attended to as carefully. We reserve our precious cognitive resources for those who are "like us."

To form categories is to be human, yet our unique cultures play a role in determining what categories we create in our minds, what we place in them, and how we label them. A fair-skinned person could be considered white in Brazil but black in the United States. People from Japan and China are lumped together as Asian in the United States but seen as distinctly different elsewhere. In some countries, people consider religion or social class a more important way to sort people than race. And even within one country, the rules for who is in what social category can change across decades.

In the United States, racial categories are so significant that knowing a person is black or white, for example, can shape how we see that person's facial features. Some years ago, my colleagues and I got interested not only in categorization but in the lay theories people use to explain others. From decades of research conducted by Carol Dweck and others, we know that some people believe human traits are fixed (people are either smart or dumb, they are responsible or irresponsible, they are mean or nice) whereas other people believe these traits are malleable (over time, a mean person can become nice). My colleagues and I wanted to know whether people's theories about others might affect how they perceived not only personality traits but physical traits as well.

If you are presented with a face that is racially ambiguous—the face could be that of a black or a white person—does knowing that the person identifies as black change how you see that person's face? And how might your own theories about others influence what you see?

To answer these questions, we had white Stanford undergraduates complete a survey designed to examine the extent to which they viewed the traits of others as fixed (for example, you can't teach an old dog new tricks) or malleable (for example, people can change even their most basic qualities). Later in the academic term, we invited those students to our lab to participate in a study individually. Each student viewed a computer image of a face that was racially ambiguous. Half of the study participants were told that the person was black, and the other half were told the person was white. We then asked them to take four minutes to draw the face they saw while the face remained on their computer screen to reference.

We found that study participants who believed that human traits are fixed were wedded to the racial label when they tried to duplicate the face. If they'd been told the person was black, they drew a face that looked "more black" than the face on their computer screen. Likewise, those who had been told that the person on the screen was white drew a face that looked "more white" and was later recognized by other participants as white. Their perceptions moved to line up with the label assigned to the face.

But among the participants who thought of traits as malleable, the opposite occurred. Those who had been told the face was black drew a face that appeared more recognizably white. And if they had been told that the face was white, they drew a face that appeared more recognizably black. These people reacted against the stereotypical image the label suggested. Our findings show that what we perceive is influenced not only by the labels we are provided but by our own attitudes about the rigidity of categories. Although we tend to think

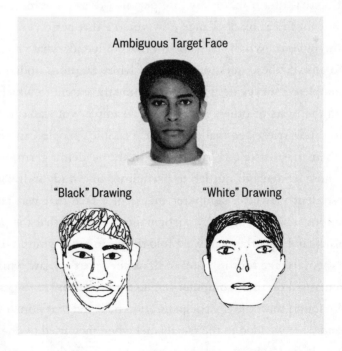

Ambiguous Target Face

"Black" Drawing   "White" Drawing

about seeing as objective and straightforward, how and what we see can be heavily shaped by our own mind-set.

In fact, the swirl of social judgments that flow from categorization is so strong it affects not only how we see others but how we perceive ourselves. That's the premise of one of my favorite novels. The renowned playwright Arthur Miller wrote *Focus* in 1945. It was his first novel and one of the first books to focus on American anti-Semitism—in the wake of the Nazi regime's systematic murder of European Jews. The story is set in New York City. World War II is drawing to a close. The protagonist, Newman, is a white Christian man charged with making sure that Jews who are attempting to pass as Christian are not hired at his company. He takes great pride in protecting the company from the scourge of Jews. In fact, he is one of the best in the business.

Then his eyesight begins to fail, rendering him less able to categorize people efficiently. At the urging of his boss, he purchases eyeglasses and gets back to work immediately. Yet the glasses create a much bigger problem for Newman: To the people around him, he suddenly resembles the sort of person he's supposed to protect them from. His neighbors, his co-workers, people on the street—all begin to suspect that *he* is Jewish. He is mortified at the thought and responds by letting people know in every way he can that he certainly is not Jewish, not even a little bit. Yet the suspicion lingers. There is nothing he can say to dissuade people from how he is seen.

In fact, when he catches a glimpse of himself in the bathroom mirror with his glasses on for the first time, he sees the face of a Jew looking back. Alarmed, he snatches the glasses off, but he cannot undo what's already been decided. Rumor has spread, and no one can un-see the Jewish identity that's now assigned to him.

Newman's life becomes unhinged. He's forced to leave his job. He becomes a target of anti-Semitism at home, where neighbors and passersby throw garbage on his lawn and smear his house with racial epithets. His treatment by others eventually begins to affect how he views himself. The loathing he had for Jews turns into self-loathing. He has become the person he once prided himself on keeping out.

The novel shows the power of the gaze of others to define how you're seen in the world; it can shape the scope of your life and influence how you see yourself. But the story also illustrates the redemptive power of personal connections to break through the bias that categorization seeds. In the end, Newman's experience forces him to develop a nuanced understanding of and appreciation for Jewish identity. He sees Jewish people for the first time unaided by the stereotypes and attitudes that surrounded them, and thus breaks free from the narrow, negative imagery that had begun to define him.

It's been fifteen years since I read this story, but it continues to shape the way I approach thinking about all sorts of stereotypes and prejudices. The plague and power of bias are too consequential to let them go unacknowledged and unchecked. They can affect us in surprising ways.

THE MECHANICS OF BIAS

The social categories we use to sort people are filled with beliefs and feelings that may direct our actions. This is what Newman learns. Once he is categorized as Jewish, people make assumptions about him, they experience an aversion to him, and they begin to act on those assumptions and feelings. At its core, Newman's story shows us how categorization can be a precursor to bias.

But at the same time, categorization is a fundamental tool that our brains are wired to use. And the categorization process applies not just to people; it works on all things. Just as we place people into categories, we place other animals into categories. We place food into categories. We place furniture into categories. And we fill every category we develop with information and imbue it with feelings that guide our actions toward it.

Take the category "apples." This category contains our beliefs about how apples grow, where they grow, what varieties exist, what colors they come in, how large they are, what they feel like, what they taste like, when we should eat them, whether we should cook them or eat them raw, how healthy they are for us, and so on. We also may like or dislike apples, depending on our experience with them and what we've been told about them. And this feeling, along with the beliefs we have about apples, can dictate whether we will eat an apple that is offered to us, buy an apple in a grocery store, or pick an apple off a tree. Simply seeing one apple can bring to mind the feelings and thoughts associated with the entire category. In fact, the stronger those associations are, the faster those feelings and thoughts are brought to mind.

The categories we have about social groups work in a similar way. But in this instance, we label the beliefs we have about social groups "stereotypes" and the attitudes we have about them "prejudice." Whether bad or good, whether justified or unjustified, our beliefs and attitudes can become so strongly associated with the category that they are automatically triggered, affecting our behavior and decision making. So, for example, simply seeing a black person can automatically bring to mind a host of associations that we have picked up from our society: this person is a good athlete, this person doesn't do well in school, this person is poor, this person dances well, this person lives in a black neighborhood, this person should be feared. The process of making these connections is called bias. It can happen unintentionally. It can happen unconsciously. It can happen effortlessly. And it can happen in a matter of milliseconds. These associations can take hold of us no matter our values, no matter our conscious beliefs, no matter what kind of person we wish to be in the world.

The concept of stereotypes dates back to the time of Plato, whose dialogues explored the question of whether one's perceptions correspond to the actual state of affairs. But the term didn't enter the popular discourse until the 1920s, introduced not by a scientist but by a journalist concerned that the news coverage of important issues was being filtered through the "preconceived notions" of both reporters and the public—a problem we still wrestle with today.

Walter Lippmann was considered one of the most influential journalists of the twentieth century. He spent more than fifty years as a newspaper columnist in New York and Washington, D.C., chronicling war, politics, social upheaval, and demographic change.

He applied the term "stereotype" to what he called "the pictures in our heads"—impressions that reflect subjective perceptions but stand in for objective reality. The word comes from the old typesetting process, in which a mold of a message is cast on a metal plate and replicated in the printing process again and again—mimicking the unchecked spread of ideas that we only presume to be true. Those ideas then dictate how we interpret what we see.

The stereotyping process was at work when the Oakland undercover officer mistook his own reflection for an armed-and-dangerous dude. To do his undercover work, the officer had to fit in with the criminals he pursued—scruffy and unkempt in raggedy clothes. But that image was so at odds with his own sense of himself—valiant emblem of order and safety—that when he spotted himself in a mirrored window, he could not process the dichotomy. The picture in his head didn't match the image he saw.

Lippmann understood the role and influence of stereotypes. "For the most part we do not first see, and then define, we define first and then see," he wrote in his 1922 book, *Public Opinion*. "In the great blooming, buzzing confusion of the outer world we pick out what our culture has already defined for us, and we tend to perceive that which we have picked out in the form stereotyped for us by our culture."

His work led him to worry that Americans might make rash and illogical civic and political choices if stereotypes blinded them to information that didn't conform to what they already believed. And that is exactly what is happening now.

Psychologists today dub what worried Lippmann "confirmation bias." People tend to seek out and attend to information that already confirms their beliefs. We find such information more trustworthy and are less critical of it, even when we are presented with credible, seemingly unassailable facts that suggest otherwise. Once we develop theories about how things operate, that framework is hard to dislodge.

Confirmation bias is a mechanism that allows inaccurate beliefs to spread and persist. And these days there is no shortage of venues offering confirmation for whatever you believe. In the twenty-first century, we have access to more information than ever before through online sources shaped by specific perspectives and aimed at people who share the same views. This segregation of information removes from view those facts that are uncomfortable, inconvenient, and incongruous to what we already believe and leaves us susceptible to "fake news" that supports our preconceived notions.

In Lippmann's era, the problem was not too many sources of information, but so few that ignorance flourished. He opens *Public Opinion* with a story of British, French, and German men living peaceably on an island in 1914, unaware that their countries were at war. They were technically enemies, but they were living side by side comfortably because the pictures in their heads hadn't evolved to match the progression of events in real time. The world had changed dramatically, yet these isolated men could live only according to their existing mental representations of the world.

Lippmann was not concerned with the idea of stereotypes as a precursor to prejudice nor as a rationalization for it. In fact, the attitudes he expressed toward racial and ethnic intolerance would brand him a bigot today. He seems to have been a hostage of his own stereotypical thinking: In 1919, he belittled upwardly mobile blacks who aimed to blend into white America, labeling them victims of "the peculiar oppressiveness of recently oppressed peoples." He advocated for the "mass evacuation and mass internment" of Japanese Americans in California after the bombing of Pearl Harbor. And his advice to other Jews wrestling with anti-Semitism was to lie low, blend in, and not call attention to their own "sharp trading and blatant vulgarity." The son of German Jewish émigrés, Lippmann was a Phi Beta Kappa graduate of Harvard who would later applaud a plan limiting Jewish admission and suggest that "too great a concentration" would be "bad for the immigrant Jews as well as for Harvard."

Still, he clearly understood both the practical function that stereotypes serve and the power they hold to taint certain groups and protect the status quo.

"There is economy in [stereotyping]," he wrote. "For the attempt to see all things freshly and in detail, rather than as types and generalities, is exhausting. . . . We are not equipped to deal with so much subtlety. . . . [W]e have to reconstruct it on a simpler model before we can manage with it."

The elements of that simpler model tend to rest on concepts of "us" and "them" and are driven by cultural, political, and economic forces to protect the status quo. Stereotypes help prop up the existing social order by providing us at least with the illusion of "an ordered, more or less consistent picture of the world," Lippmann observed. It may not be the actual world, but we are comfortable there.

So comfortable that we ultimately adapt to and embrace stereotypes, rooting them so deeply that they're passed along unquestioned to each new generation, over decades and centuries. Without our permission or even awareness, stereotypes come to guide what we see, and in so doing seem to validate themselves. That makes them stronger, more pervasive, and resistant to change.

The "fictions and symbols" they represent are the thought paths that lead to expressions of implicit bias. Yet, as Lippmann contends, we continue to "hold to our stereotypes when we might pursue a more disinterested vision" because they have become "the core of our personal tradition, the defenses of our position in society."

Just like categorization, the process of stereotyping is universal. We all tend to access and apply stereotypes to help us make sense of other people. However, the content of those stereotypes is culturally generated and culturally specific. In the United States, blacks are so strongly associated with threat and aggression that this stereotypic association can even impact our ability to accurately read the facial expressions of black people. For example, a black man who is excited might appear angry. Fear can be misread as outrage. Silence taken as belligerence.

To explore the power of those associations, social psychologists Galen Bodenhausen and Kurt Hugenberg asked white participants to sit at a computer screen and evaluate the expressions on a black face displayed over multiple frames, moving gradually from angry to friendly. Attitudes about race shaped participants' perceptions. When the face was black, they found that those participants who were high in racial prejudice perceived the angry expression as lingering longer than did those participants who were less prejudiced. Even as the black face settled into neutral, those high in prejudice were poised to see the facial expression as threatening. That result held true even when they were shown a racially ambiguous face and told it was black. The label exerted enough influence to shape their perceptions to conform to the stereotype.

I THINK IT'S FEAR

Stereotypes do not need to be explained to be understood or reproduced. My oldest son, Ebbie, reminded me of this one Thanksgiving when he was just six years old. I was busy preparing the turkey, pumping it up with fluids and spices, while he sat at the kitchen table. Out of the blue he asked, "Mommy, do you think people see black people as different from white people?" I was taken aback and asked him why he wondered about that. "Oh, I don't know. I just feel like there's something different." I prodded him on: "What do you mean?" He scrunched his forehead, as if to help himself think it through. "I don't know," he finally said. "I just feel like there's something different. Like there is something extra special in how people see black people."

I asked him for an example, and he sat quietly, deep in thought. He recalled an episode from our recent shopping trip: "Do you remember the other day when we were in the grocery store?" His tone had moved from uncertain and hesitant to eager and confident. "I remember there was a black guy who came in. It was like he had an invisible force field around him." My son was in his *Star Wars* period back then. "So when he walked in, people kind of stayed away from him a little bit. It was like they didn't want to get too close to him. And I remember when he stood in line, his line was the shortest line for a long time."

At the time, we lived in San Mateo, in a mostly white neighborhood midway between San Francisco and Stanford. Even at six, my son could recognize that shoppers in a neighborhood where few black people live were responding to this man as if he weren't one of them. I decided to probe further.

"What do you think it is?" I asked, in a voice I hoped was level and calm. I was bracing myself for what might come. He scrunched his forehead again. His confidence seemed to evaporate. But he continued to think it through. After a few minutes, his eyes widened, and he turned to look at me. And just as I was sliding the turkey into the oven, he said in a voice deeper than I had ever heard him use before, "I think it's fear." I was so startled that I burned my hand on the oven rack.

How could a first grader pick that up? It wasn't anything we ever discussed. I didn't think it was anything he'd heard or seen on television. That conversation led me to more fully appreciate how good children are at making sense of the world from the many signals they're given as they move through their days—at home, at school, on the playground, in the grocery store.

That is basically their job, to make connections and to see correlations: What goes with what? They're making meaning from things that might appear random and looking to adults to help them figure it all out. They watch us, how we move through the world, to make a determination of how we feel about each other, how we see our own social standing, how we evaluate others.

The scar from that burn stayed on my hand for over a year. And every time I looked at it, I thought about what my son said to me and wondered about the lessons he was learning, unbeknownst to me. That conversation would leave a mark long after the scar was gone.

THE TRANSMISSION OF BIAS

Even preschoolers are able to pick up on how adults view other people, and quickly too. Researchers from the University of Washington showed Seattle preschoolers videos of one adult greeting and engaging with two others. She greets one of the other adults by smiling, leaning toward her, using a warm tone of voice, and happily sharing a colorful toy. She greets the other adult by scowling, leaning away, using a cold tone of voice, and reluctantly handing over the colorful toy.

After watching the video, the preschoolers are asked to point to the adult they prefer. The researchers found that 75 percent of the time the children point to the adult who was treated well. They prefer her. When asked to whom they would like to give the toy, 69 percent of the time they chose the adult who was treated well. The calculus these preschoolers are using seems straightforward: if you are treated badly, you are a bad person. Upon watching just one thirty-second clip of a negative interaction, preschoolers have seen enough to hold the target of bias responsible rather than the holder of bias. And these children make this known not only in their negative view of the adult treated less favorably but also in their desire to see that adult receive fewer resources.

The power of adults to shape that lens is heavily vested in parents. Unsurprisingly, studies confirm that biased parents tend to produce children who are biased as well. In one study, researchers measured bias in a group of mostly white parents in a midwestern town, using a survey gauging the extent to which they agreed with items like "African Americans are a physical threat to the safety of most Americans" and "African Americans get more from this country than they deserve." Then they asked the participants' fourth- and fifth-grade children to complete a survey aimed at measuring how strongly they identified with their parents. Finally, the researchers administered an implicit association test (IAT) to these children at a computer lab in their school.

The IAT is more involved than a standard survey. It is more sensitive and designed to measure associations that we don't even know we have. To administer the IAT, the researchers asked each child to sit in front of a computer screen where they were presented with a series of faces and words one at a time. The faces were of black and white people, and the words were good (for example, "joy," "peace") or bad (for instance, "nasty," "evil"). The IAT measures bias by tracking the speed at which study participants can categorize the faces as black or white and the words as good or bad.

Sometimes the children were told to push one computer key if they saw black faces or bad words and a different key if they saw white faces or good words. Other times the children were told to push one key if they saw black faces or good words and a different key if they saw white faces or bad words. Their responses were timed. What researchers typically find is that people are faster to categorize the faces and words when they are using the same key to respond to faces that are black and words that are bad. But if they are using a single key to respond to faces that are black and to words that are good, their brains seem to bog down. It takes more effort to connect black and good, because black and bad are more strongly associated in our minds. The speed of response is a measure of that association.

In this case, researchers found that the more antiblack bias the parents exhibited on the survey, the more antiblack bias their children exhibited on the IAT. But only for children who identified more closely with their parents—children who reported that they frequently do what their parents tell them to do, want to grow up to be like them, want to make them proud, and enjoy spending time with them. As it turns out, their parents are not just sharing their time, love, and resources with their children; they are also sharing the bias they carry around in their heads.

Even dogs are exquisitely attentive to the behavior and emotions of the families they live with. Dogs are considered "best friends" to humans because of their unique ability to connect to us. They register the reactions of their owners to figure out how to read the social environment. Consistent with this idea, canine researchers in France found that dogs seize upon the subtle movements of their owners to determine how to react to approaching strangers. The researchers instructed the owners to take three steps forward at the sight of the stranger, take three steps back, or remain in place. When the owners stepped back, the researchers found that the dogs behaved in a more protective manner: They looked more quickly at the stranger, hovered around the owner more, and were more hesitant to make contact with the stranger. With three small steps, the owners were telegraphing a message to their dogs: Beware.

Well-meaning human adults can also be influenced by the nonverbal behavior of others. Let's take media as an example. People typically assume that having black characters play more powerful, positive roles on television and in the movies will curb bias. Yet researchers have found that even in popular television shows that feature black characters playing such roles, white actors tend to react more negatively to black actors than to other white actors on-screen. This bias is exhibited through subtle, nonverbal actions—a squint, a slight grimace, a small shift of the body—yet it still has impact. It leads those viewers who tune in to those shows to exhibit more bias themselves.

The researchers—Max Weisbuch, Kristin Pauker, and Nalini Ambady—chose eleven popular television shows that have positive representations of black characters—shows like *CSI* and *Grey's Anatomy,* where black characters are doctors, police officers, and scientists.

They showed study participants ten-second clips of a variety of white characters interacting with the same black character, but with the sound muted and the black characters edited out of the frame.

Participants who were unfamiliar with the shows were asked to watch a number of these clips and to rate how much each unseen character was liked and was being treated positively by the white characters on the screen. Sometimes the unseen character was black, and sometimes the unseen character was white.

A consistent pattern emerged when the researchers pooled the ratings: participants perceived the unseen black characters in these popular shows to be less liked and treated less positively than the unseen white characters.

And the television viewers were affected by this: The more negative the nonverbal actions directed at the unseen black characters, the more antiblack bias the study participants revealed on an implicit association test following the showing. That is, there was evidence for a type of "bias contagion." The researchers found this to be the case even though the study participants were unable to identify any consistent pattern in treatment of the white and black characters when asked to do so directly.

While this study was going on, more than nine million viewers tuned in to each of these shows across the United States every week. Altogether, the shows were viewed more than five billion times in a single year. It's easy to get absorbed in a story line and invest in characters. But even as we come to connect with the characters and their lives, we are absorbing their biases as well. Increasing positive representation of blacks in the media may be a step forward, but then again, it could wind up reflecting and spreading implicit bias rather than defusing it.

And just as bias leaks out between the words of scripted dialogue, it seeps out of all of us in our everyday lives, in ways that are difficult to name and evaluate.

Is clutching your purse when you see a black man a reflection of prejudice? Is presuming a Latino doesn't speak English logical or ignorant? Is it bias speaking when you ask a young black woman who was just admitted to Harvard whether "that's the one in Massachusetts"? Or when you compliment an Asian student on those high math scores? When you think a teenager's music is louder than it is, is that bias? What about asking for a different nurse because yours has tattoos?

How do we know when we are being insensitive or unfair? How much of who we are and how we feel is dictated by things outside our awareness or control? How often are we really the tolerant, fair-minded person we want to be? And how can we learn to check ourselves and mute the negative impact that bias can have?

Part II

WHERE WE FIND OURSELVES

CHAPTER 3

A Bad Dude

For nearly fifteen years now, I've been teaching police officers to recognize and understand how implicit bias can shade their interactions with the communities they protect and serve. My presentations are part of a law enforcement training movement that I helped to start. The effort had been building behind the scenes for many years but was thrust into the limelight more recently by a flurry of questionable police shootings and the protests that ensued.

Some departments embrace this kind of training. They see it as exactly what is needed to improve police-community relations. Others sign on grudgingly, waiting for this approach to be replaced by another that is more comfortable and familiar. Some departments have sought me out because implicit bias training has become mandatory through a negotiated settlement agreement or a federal consent decree. Yet even when I know why a particular law enforcement agency has signed on, I never know how the individual officers who fill the room will react.

On this morning in September 2016, I was in Sacramento with fellow trainers, rehearsing for a two-day train-the-trainer course that we would soon begin delivering across the state. My fellow trainers included people from local police departments, the California Department of Justice, community organizations, and a colleague from Stanford. We were a mixed group convened by the then California state attorney general, Kamala Harris. My role in all of this was to help prepare hundreds of trainers in waiting to take this message back to their departments: *Bias, even when we are not conscious of it, has consequences that we need to understand and mitigate. The stereotypic associations we carry in our heads can affect what we perceive, how we think, and the actions we take.*

On this morning, everyone was talking about the just-released video of an unarmed black man shot to death by police in Tulsa, Oklahoma—the latest in a two-year string of high-profile shootings. The video showed Terence Crutcher walking slowly with his hands in the air, followed by a group of police officers. Moments later, a shot was fired, and Crutcher crumpled to the ground.

My fellow presenters couldn't stop talking about the video. "Did you see it? Have you heard about it?" I was asked again and again. "It's so relevant to your research." Here was a real-life example of the situations police officers face, an encounter that can suddenly turn deadly and quickly become racialized.

Yet not everyone was nudging me to discuss it. The trainers and trainees from police departments did not seem eager to focus on this at all. I imagined the video left them feeling demoralized. They might have felt sympathy for the victim, but they also worried about the blowback. Every shooting that hits the news provides another opportunity to vilify police, adding another burden to the baggage they carry as they patrol the streets. For them, this was not just about policies or attitudes or tactics. It was a moral crisis that by their very choice of profession they could not avoid.

I was feeling pinched by that moral crisis too. I dreaded watching another police-shooting video. The steady stream of tragic scenes led me to question the value of what I was doing. I've tried to sustain myself through years of research, trainings, and community meetings by believing that change is possible. But each new incident offers damning evidence of just how entrenched the problems are. It's painful, it's discouraging, it's a reality I'd rather avoid. But it's also a reminder of why I can't let up.

In 2016, nearly a thousand people were killed in the United States by police officers. Other cases had also generated outrage, but nothing seemed to change. Two months before Terence Crutcher died, Philando Castile was killed during a traffic stop in Minnesota, after politely informing a police officer that he was legally carrying a gun. The moments after the shooting were live streamed by Castile's girlfriend and witnessed by her four-year-old daughter. More than three million people would watch social media footage of Castile bleeding to death in the front seat of his car while the officer who'd fired seven shots at point-blank range emotionally melted down.

Two years before that, twelve-year-old Tamir Rice had been shot to death at a Cleveland park while playing with a toy gun. It took a rookie cop just two seconds to decide that Tamir posed a lethal threat. He fired the fatal shot before his patrol car had even come to a stop. Then, as Tamir lay unattended on the snow-covered ground—with a wound so severe his intestines were poking out—the officer who shot him retreated to his patrol car to tend to the ankle he'd twisted in the rush to fire his gun.

It fell to an FBI agent who'd been in the area and heard the shooting call to provide medical aid to the injured boy. The agent told investigators that he couldn't tell at first if Tamir was still alive. Then he leaned in, and Tamir "looked at me and he like reached for my hand," he said. The agent went to work clearing his airway and pressing hard on the wound to stanch the flow of blood. But within moments Tamir began losing consciousness.

The agent knew Tamir would die if he wasn't rushed to a hospital: "The reality is [with] an injury like that, he needs bright lights and cold surgical steel." But he didn't know that the wounded "suspect" was still in elementary school—until he heard Tamir's sister screaming that he was just twelve years old. After the ambulance pulled off, the agent tried to comfort the girl, who'd been handcuffed and placed in the back of a patrol car. Ten hours later, her brother died at the hospital. Thirteen months later, the local prosecutor said no criminal charges would be filed against the police officer, calling the tragedy simply "a perfect storm of human error, mistakes and miscommunications."

The Cleveland encounter, like dozens of others, was a visual reminder of the unfettered power that police officers have to decide who lives and who dies. These shootings, caught on video by bystanders or officers' patrol cars and body cameras, have sparked protests and vigils that focused new attention on issues like racial bias, the militarization of police, and inadequate hiring and training practices. It was incidents like these that led communities of color around the country to begin demanding that police officers undergo implicit bias training.

As the pressure built, community leaders and law enforcement officials alike began to seek guidance from me as well as others around the country. Yet with each video release of a high-profile shooting, I was working to calm a sense of my own helplessness. I worried (and I still worry) that people put too much faith in the power of these trainings, which can educate but not eradicate the forces that keep officers primed for trouble and communities on edge.

I've been giving talks for years to community groups, and I can feel a growing sense of urgency, a shift in the energy surrounding the issue of police shootings. Now I have to brace for emotional entreaties from mothers who stand up in tears and ask me, "*What can we do to keep our sons safe?*"

They used to know what to tell their boys: Be respectful if you're stopped by police. Keep your hands on the wheel. Don't run away. They believed that if they followed this script, their children would be safe. But these days they're at a loss for what to say. "You put your hands up," you could still be shot. "You be respectful," you can still be shot. There's a real fear that if you have a black son, he could die at the hands of the state and there's no way you can prevent that.

The relentless loop of police-shooting videos leaves some people angry and introduces others to the challenges faced by police. But for these mothers, the constant exposure evokes a sense of fear and panic that goes well beyond what's probable. We've lost the tempering and are only seeing the extremes; people are thinking that at any moment this could happen to me, my son, my family, my friends.

I'm never sure how to respond to the questions posed to me. I try to answer first with facts and statistics: more than 99 percent of police contacts happen with no police use of force at all, let alone deadly force.

But ultimately I also have to answer as a mother, with three sons and fears of my own. It's hard to tell people not to worry. Black people are stopped by police at disproportionate levels and are more likely to have force used upon them. I know how our sons are perceived in society generally, and that can affect how they're perceived and treated by police.

I knew it was my responsibility to bear witness, but I couldn't afford to wade into emotional terrain in Sacramento on that day. I went ahead with the presentation I'd planned, slogging through my lesson plans and PowerPoint slides with no mention of the man who had just died.

I did not summon the nerve to watch the video on my laptop until the following week. Alone in my office, I see Terence Crutcher with his hands stretched high in the air, heading toward his SUV. Several police officers are clustered behind him, with guns or Tasers pointed toward the figure lumbering away from them. Above them a helicopter hovers, carrying officers and videotaping the scene. I hear the voice of someone in the chopper describing Crutcher: "Oh, he's got his hands up there for her now." And moments later, "I got a feeling what's about to happen." And then, "That looks like a bad dude."

What I can see is Crutcher placing his hands on the roof of his car and leaning toward it. Then suddenly his body slumps toward the ground. Officer Betty Shelby yells out, a hint of panic in her voice, "Shots fired!," as if the officer and the act were somehow detached. Crutcher, hit by a bullet from Shelby's gun, has collapsed and is lying still on the street alongside his car.

A clutch of officers surrounds and comforts Shelby. The figure of Crutcher recedes, becoming part of the background. The camera is focused on the group. But my eyes are fixed on the man behind the officers, lying untended on the pavement, bleeding to death.

I know that even unavoidable shootings take an emotional toll on police officers—a toll that can be felt decades later. Still, it was hard to watch those officers huddling around Shelby while the life was seeping out of a man who seemed more dazed than dangerous when she approached him.

The shooting was considered egregious enough that she was charged a week later with felony manslaughter for "unlawfully and unnecessarily" shooting Crutcher—a rare outcome in a police-shooting incident. "Officer Shelby reacted unreasonably by escalating the situation," the prosecutor's affidavit said. The "defendant's fear resulted in her unreasonable actions."

At trial the next year, Shelby testified that Crutcher's death was his own fault. She'd ordered Crutcher to kneel on the ground and show his hands. He should have just followed her orders, she said. She fired her gun because she feared for her life, she told the jury at trial. The jury would deliberate just nine hours before finding her not guilty of a crime.

After the acquittal, the jury foreman composed a letter, conveying the anguish the deliberations involved. "The jury wonders and some believe that she had other options available to subdue Mr. Crutcher," he wrote. Many jurors "could never get comfortable with the concept of Betty Shelby being blameless for Mr. Crutcher's death."

One month later, the officer on trial for shooting Castile in Minnesota was also found not guilty of manslaughter. Officer Jeronimo Yanez cried on the stand, telling the jury he fired into Castile's car because he feared for his life. The jury took a week to agree on acquittal. "What happened to [Castile] is not OK to any of us," one juror later said. But they believed that the officer "was an honest guy," he said. "In the end, we had to go on his word and that's what it came down to."

Only a tiny fraction of officers involved in questionable shootings are prosecuted, and it's rare to get a conviction. Jurors tend to sympathize and identify with the officers on the stand. They believe the officers are genuinely afraid. They're reluctant to second-guess the choices a police officer must make in the daily life-or-death calculus of keeping order and staying safe. They don't feel the law allows them to penalize officers for what their departments have trained them to do. And they are not immune to the same perceptions and attitudes that some officers unconsciously carry along on patrol.

Still, I wanted to better understand why jury verdicts so often belie what we think we've seen. And how that breach impacts families and communities. So I contacted Ben Crump, a civil rights attorney who has a client list of more than forty families across the country who have lost loved ones to police shootings.

I learned from Crump that Terence had a twin sister, Tiffany, who had become the family's voice. Tiffany Crutcher has a doctorate in physical medicine and works in a clinic in rural Alabama where residents have limited access to health care. Her brother's death had upended and refocused her life. A year after Terence was killed, I headed to Montgomery to meet Tiffany and learn more about her family's ordeal.

I wanted to understand the private anguish behind the public spectacle. The families of people killed by police inhabit a peculiar and painful niche. Their loved ones become caricatures, object lessons, faces on T-shirts. They are saddled with unsavory labels that suggest they are to blame for their own demise: drug addict, robbery suspect, belligerent black man. But they are also brothers, fathers, cousins, sons—men who were living full and meaningful lives.

DINNER WITH TIFFANY

Tiffany and Terence were born just three minutes apart. They were inseparable as kids. Their father was a pastor, their mother a drama teacher. They had two brothers, one older and one younger. "We were in church almost every day of the week," Tiffany recalled. She and Terence sang in the choir and played in a traveling junior orchestra,

Terence on cello and Tiffany on violin. "He was just a big teddy bear, soft heart, very laid-back, mild-mannered."

Terence came from a family of high achievers: All of his siblings graduated from college, and both parents have graduate degrees. He'd found his niche as a gospel singer and imagined a career in music. But he hit a few bumps that complicated his course. In his early twenties, Terence was robbed and beaten so badly that he lost his right eye and the hearing in his right ear. "He was never the same again," Tiffany said. "He would have these spells of depression, and then that's when he turned to drugs." At times, those drugs led him to rehab programs and landed him in jail. But he still traveled with a gospel troupe, worked when he could, and cared for his four children.

In the summer of 2016, Terence found a new sense of purpose. He enrolled in community college. His first class—music appreciation— was scheduled to meet the day he died. After he was shot to death, police searched his car looking for a gun. All they found, his sister said, were his Bible, his collection of gospel CDs, and the textbooks for his college class.

Tiffany was in Montgomery when the news came, through a cousin in Texas, that her brother had been shot. She willed herself not to believe it. If the news was true, her father would surely call. She waited out the next hour at the home of a friend, praying non-stop. Then her phone rang and she saw "Daddy" on the caller ID.

Her parents had been in church, leading a concert rehearsal, when they got the news. Her father was hysterical when he called Tiffany from the hospital. "He said, 'They killed my son. They killed my son. He's gone!'" "Who killed him?" she asked. "The police," her father said. "We're at the hospital, and they won't let me see my son." The circumstances of Terence's death had suspended his body in limbo. An investigation would be required, and his body was evidence—either as suspect or as victim. But that explanation did nothing to ease the family's pain.

The Crutcher family had a ritual for whenever a loved one died: They'd pray over the body and sing the gospel classic "Till We Meet Again." But in this case, "they denied us our right to see my brother, to pray over my brother," Tiffany said. "That hurt my parents so bad. They treated us like we did something wrong."

Two days later, the family was asked to join the mayor and police officials to privately watch the official video—not yet released—of the shooting. Tiffany's parents refused to attend, but she steeled herself and went, with a few of her cousins supporting her.

When they arrived, Chief Chuck Jordan offered his condolences and acknowledged that the video was "quite disturbing." "Your brother was belligerent and out of control," Tiffany recalls him saying. He informed them that police had found a vial of PCP in the car, but said "we're not going to put that in the newspaper [or] demonize your brother."

The very notion that her brother was a "demon" had Tiffany reeling. She'd gone prepared to face the searing image of Terence dying on the street, but she couldn't stomach listening to the police trying to justify his death or refusing to answer her questions about whether they had alternatives to killing him. "I'm not going to sit here and watch my brother be murdered," she told them. As she headed for the door, she heard the mayor announce, "I'm going to get up, and I'm going to go sit with Dr. Crutcher." A young white police officer rose with the mayor and followed them out of the room.

Mayor Dewey F. Bartlett had tried to be a stabilizing force in the shooting aftermath. A white man and the son of a former Oklahoma governor, Bartlett addressed the city the day after Crutcher's death, calling on Tulsans to bridge the racial divide, recognize the role that racism played in the city's history, and embrace the Crutcher family.

As Bartlett left the group and took a seat alongside her, Tiffany was struck by his gesture of compassion. "The mayor, he looked at me, his eyes were watering," she recalled. "He said, 'I have so much respect for your dad.'" Terence and Tiffany's father, the Reverend Joey Crutcher, is in the Oklahoma Jazz Hall of Fame. He and the mayor had played together before. "I'm so sorry," he told Tiffany. "I have grandsons and sons. I'm just sorry."

She met his eyes, grateful for the unexpected comfort. Then she glanced at the young white officer sitting across from them. That police officer had tears in his eyes too.

THE SCIENTIFIC LENS

Watching the video and listening to Tiffany's story, I felt the findings of years of research on implicit bias assume new clarity and gain new meaning. As I examined the circumstances of the shooting, it seemed clear to me that bias—implicit or not—could have played some role in the encounter, from beginning to end. There was a study appropriate to each critical act, from Officer Shelby's decision to make contact with Terence, until Terence lay dying untended on the ground. Of course, we cannot know what went on in Officer Shelby's mind during her encounter with Terence. Neither can we say what Terence was thinking. There are so many factors that could have influenced them both that it is impossible to decipher the extent to which one element—race—was the key driver of choices that were made.

Yet the value of science is that it allows us to pull back from the isolated case and examine larger forces at work. Researchers can place people under conditions that are relevant to one small aspect of a situation, and do so with precision and control. For instance, by creating two situations, identical but for race, we can measure the difference in how study participants respond to that particular variation. This lets us look beyond the lone individual and the isolated case and toward the average response across many cases. Science, then, allows us to make discoveries about human behavior more generally, to see trends and patterns develop. What happens in our homes, in our classrooms, and on our streets can be analyzed and understood in the laboratory.

So what are some of the broader questions scientists could ask that might shed light on fatal police-community encounters and on human behavior more generally?

Act 1: A Visible Man

First, we could ask whether the association between black people and crime is so powerful in the minds of Americans that it can influence what we see and what we ignore. Can this association determine what draws our attention? To what extent does thinking about violent crime lead us to turn our attention toward black faces?

These questions are at the heart of a series of studies I have conducted with colleagues on attentional bias. These are also the very questions that have been raised in the Terence Crutcher case. What drew Betty Shelby to approach Terence Crutcher on the night his car stalled on the road? Why did she abandon her rush to a domestic violence scene to focus on Terence instead? How did he end up at the center of a scene involving several officers on foot with guns drawn as officers in a helicopter above recorded his every move?

Years before the Crutcher case, my colleagues and I were in search of answers. We set up shop at a local police department where we invited officers to participate in a study in groups of two to five people. We seated them each in front of their own personal computer screen for the purposes of the study, and informed them they were about to engage in an "attentional vigilance task." We asked that they keep their eyes on a focus dot at the center of the screen. We told them that flashes of light would appear around that focus dot and their goal was to indicate—as rapidly as possible, using a button push—where on the computer screen each flash of light appeared.

This task was actually a subliminal priming task. It is a standard technique used in psychology to measure the extent to which people are influenced by words or images that are beneath their conscious awareness. For this particular study, we exposed half of our study participants to words relevant to crime, such as "apprehend," "arrest," "capture," "shoot." These participants were in the "crime condition" of the study. Each word flashed on the screen for just seventy-five milliseconds; the officers could not consciously detect it, yet nevertheless had been prompted to think of crime. The remaining officers were in the "control condition," and we exposed them to a series of jumbled letters instead of words.

Next, we showed all of the participants two faces (a black face and a white face) simultaneously. We found that those in the control condition, who had not been prompted to think of crime, looked

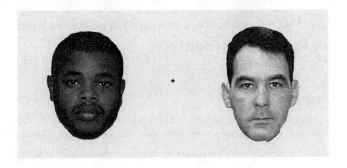

more at the white face. However, as predicted, those in the crime condition looked more at the black face. Thinking about apprehending, arresting, and shooting pulled their attention in the direction of the black face. And the power of this black-crime association is not limited to police officers. We conducted a similar study with undergraduates at Stanford, and we got the same results. Whether we are college students or crime fighters, our attention can be driven by stereotypic associations that we are not even aware are operating on us.

The increased visual attention to black faces that the "crime prime" generates is reminiscent of the phenomenon of "high visibility," a theme in Ralph Ellison's 1950s American classic, *Invisible Man*. Ellison described the black American predicament as one where black people are visually registered only with the aid of cultural stereotypes that function to distort their image. These stereotypes lead blacks to be the subject of gaze, then block them from being fully seen. It's a paradox of peril: High visibility is accompanied by invisibility. Applying science to Ellison's observations, we've shown that black faces are much more likely to capture the attentional systems of those who have been induced to think about crime than of those who have not. It is as if the existing stereotypic association between blacks and crime renders these faces more perceptually relevant and therefore worthy of being seen.

That's what Tiffany Crutcher believes drew the attention of officers to her brother, whom they perceived as a "fleeing felon" rather than as a citizen in need of help.

Act 2: Larger Than Life

Once Terence came into view that night, the police characterized him as if he were a giant, estimating his weight to be at 300 pounds.

Terence actually stood at five feet nine and weighed 255 pounds. Might race distort people's perception of body size? And if so, to what extent might such distortions influence police use of force?

Humans have evolved to detect threat. And assessments of the physical stature and strength of others help us to determine what kind of threat they pose to us and what kind of force would be required to subdue them. Although there are reams of studies demonstrating that blacks are perceived as threatening, we have relatively little understanding of how race could warp people's perceptions of physical stature. Three researchers, John Paul Wilson, Kurt Hugenberg, and Nicholas Rule, sought to correct this.

In a series of studies, they asked people to rate the height, weight, and strength of young black and white men from photographs showing only their faces. Study participants consistently rated black men as taller, heavier, and stronger than white men. Sometimes they asked people to look at photographs of young men's bodies only (that did not depict their faces). The skin tone was racially ambiguous, which allowed the researchers to indicate to some participants that the bodies were of black people but to others that the same bodies were of white people. Participants rated the bodies as taller and heavier when they believed they belonged to black men. Race influenced the judgments of black and white study participants alike.

The researchers also examined whether this racial bias was related to the capacity to do harm. Here, the study participants' race mattered. White participants rated black men as more capable of doing harm than white men of the same physical stature and size. Black participants exhibited no such bias. They then showed nonblack study participants a series of faces and asked them to imagine that the person depicted had "behaved aggressively toward a police officer but was not wielding a weapon." Study participants thought that the police officer would be justified in using more force to subdue the black men in this situation compared with the white men.

Act 3: Race in Motion

If people perceive black bodies as more threatening than white bodies, might they perceive black body movements as more threatening than the identical movements made by whites? Research suggests that they do.

In a classic study conducted in 1976, social psychologist Birt Duncan measured the responses of ninety-six white college students to a mock altercation between two people in a laboratory setting at the University of California–Irvine. The students, enlisted to participate in "interpersonal behavior research," believed that they were watching two strangers having a discussion about a topic that suddenly got heated and led one of them to shove the other. The students didn't know that the argument was scripted and the behavior staged, and that the person who did the shoving was intentionally either black or white.

When the students were asked to rate the behavior of the two on a variety of dimensions, Duncan found striking differences based on race. When the person doing the shoving was black and the victim was white, 75 percent of the participants rated the behavior as "violent." But when the person doing the shoving was white and the victim was black, only 17 percent of the students considered that same behavior "violent." In fact, 42 percent of whites who shoved blacks were deemed to be simply "playing around"—but only 6 percent of blacks who shoved whites were categorized in that benign light. Duncan found that the students used a much lower threshold for labeling black actions as violent.

How might a study conducted more than forty years ago relate to current-day police-community interactions? My colleague Rebecca Hetey and I asked that same question. We were interested in the relevance of those old findings to how police officers interpret the body movements of blacks whom they suspect of criminal activity.

To get at this, we began analyzing data collected by the New York City Police Department on its "stop, question, and frisk" practices. Each time officers stop someone on the streets of New York City, they are required to complete a form indicating why they made the stop. For years, there were ten reasons listed from which officers could select, including wearing clothes that are commonly used in the commission of a crime and having a suspicious bulge that might indicate a weapon. In addition, there was a check box for what they label "furtive movement"—with no further indication about why the movement counts as suspicious or furtive.

In our study, we looked at how race might relate to officers' perception of furtive movement. We examined data from 2010 and 2011, during the height of the NYPD "stop, question, and frisk" crime-fighting campaign. In those two years, officers made nearly 1.3 million pedestrian stops. We found that half of those were based on "furtive movement." It was by far the most common reason police gave for stopping potential criminals on the streets of New York City. And of all stops made for furtive movement, 54 percent were of blacks, in a city that is only 23 percent black.

We next looked at black and white pedestrians who were stopped for furtive movement in those years and examined racial disparities in treatment during the stops. We found that blacks were much more likely than whites to be frisked, and also more likely to be subjected to physical force. Yet blacks were less likely to have a weapon than whites. In fact, less than 1 percent of those stopped for furtive movement were found to have a weapon. So a practice initiated to take guns off the streets turned into a dragnet that swept up hundreds of thousands of black men whose most common offense was moving suspiciously. Furtive movement is no longer considered a legitimate reason to make a stop in New York City. Perhaps as a consequence of this action (along with a series of other reforms), the number of stops NYPD officers make per year has fallen dramatically.

When we step back to look at the high-profile shootings across the country over the past two decades, we see that body movement is often at the center of the case. The act of reaching down to retrieve his wallet led to the shooting of Philando Castile in 2016; the officer thought Castile might be reaching for a gun. An unarmed Oscar Grant was shot to death at an Oakland transit station in 2009, after an officer yelled out "GUN!" when he saw Grant's hands move near his waistband. In Cincinnati, Timothy Thomas had unpaid traffic tickets and was trying to evade an officer who stopped him in 2001, when he was shot to death because he made a quick movement that "spooked" the cop into pulling the trigger. And in what's become the most infamous case, Amadou Diallo was shot forty-one times by NYPD officers in 1999 as he stood unarmed in the vestibule of his Bronx apartment. The officers said Diallo was looking up and down the street and moving suspiciously, "like he was trying to hide from us." The gun they thought he had in his pocket turned out to be a wallet.

And Officer Shelby said she had never been so afraid in her life as she was during that night she encountered Terence Crutcher—a black man walking away slowly with his hands stretched high above his head in the universal sign of surrender.

Act 4: Unarmed but Dangerous

But where was he walking? Officer Shelby was afraid that Crutcher was headed to his car to retrieve a gun. She needed to be ready to protect herself before that gun emerged and was fired at her. This raises yet another set of questions. Typically, we think of stereotypes as influencing how we see people. Could stereotypes also influence how we see objects?

Long before the Crutcher incident, I worked with a number of colleagues at Stanford to understand how the black-crime association could affect the perception of weapons. In a laboratory study, we used a subliminal priming procedure to expose undergraduates to either a series of black male faces, a series of white male faces, or no faces at all. Next, we asked those undergraduates to participate in an object-recognition task. We exposed them to a series of objects that appeared on the computer screen one at a time. The image of each object started out as grainy, and in forty-one frames the object became less and less grainy.

We told our study participants that their goal was to indicate (with a button push) the moment at which they could detect what each object was. Some of these objects were related to crime (for example, guns and knives), and others were completely unrelated to crime (for instance, staplers and cameras).

We found that the face priming had no impact on participants' ability to detect the objects that were unrelated to crime. Those participants

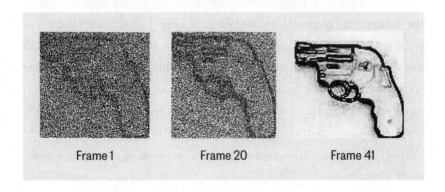

Frame 1   Frame 20   Frame 41

who were exposed to black male faces, for example, were no better or worse at detecting staplers than those who were exposed to white male faces. However, face priming did have a striking impact on participants' ability to detect the crime objects. Those who had been exposed to the black faces needed fewer frames—they needed less clarity—to detect the crime objects than those who had not been exposed to faces. And those who had been exposed to the white faces needed significantly more frames—they needed more clarity—before they could recognize the crime objects.

So mere exposure to black faces—even subliminal exposure—facilitated the detection of the crime objects, while exposure to white faces inhibited the detection of those very same crime objects. As we predicted, the stereotypic association between blacks and crime influences not only how we see black people but how we see guns. Stereotypes can determine which objects we see in the world and which we don't.

Act 5: Shoot–Don't Shoot

Is it just our perceptions that can be hijacked by racial bias or can race exert an influence on our behavior—and in particular, a person's decision to pull the trigger of a gun? This question comes closest to the actions and motivations of Officer Shelby. Joshua Correll and his team at the University of Colorado, Boulder, designed a shoot–don't shoot computer simulation to examine this. On their computer screens, study participants are shown an image of a person who is holding either a gun or a harmless object. Participants are told that if they see somebody holding a gun, they should press a button labeled "shoot." If they see someone holding a harmless object, they should press a button labeled "don't shoot."

They found that participants were quicker to press "shoot" when there was a gun present than they were to press "don't shoot" when there was no gun present. Yet they also found a race effect. Participants were even faster to respond "shoot" to a black person holding a gun than they were to a white person holding a gun. They were also more likely to mistakenly "shoot" a black person with no gun. That is, racial bias was found both in the speed of response and in the decision whether to shoot. Bias was found with both college students and community members. It was found with both white and black study participants.

But when the researchers later conducted the study with a sample of police officers from around the country, the story got a bit more complicated. They found that police officers are faster to shoot blacks with guns than whites with guns, which demonstrates that police officers associate blacks with crime and danger just like everyone else. In fact, those officers who work in bigger cities, with larger black populations and higher crime rates, tend to exhibit the greatest racial bias in reaction time. Yet the police were no more likely to mistakenly shoot a black person with no gun than they were to mistakenly shoot a white person with no gun. What explains this result? Training. The more interactive use-of-force training officers have, the better able they are to discern when a gun is present and when it is not, and the less likely they are to show racial bias in whom they decide to shoot.

These results are illuminating not just because they provide us with a way to combat bias. They also demonstrate that sometimes the way to curb bias is not by attempting to quickly rid people of a racial association that they have practiced throughout their lives but by simply training them to do their jobs better—such that the skills they develop through goal-driven, repetitive practice can override the effects of bias on their actions.

SAYING GOOD-BYE

Officer Shelby's decision to shoot tore a massive hole in the Crutcher family. A year after Terence died, his parents, siblings, children, and friends were still going to counseling, still mired in suffering. And the community that surrounded them was still struggling to deal with a death that seemed to make no sense.

When Terence's children returned to school after their father's death, the staff understood that the children and their classmates needed a safe space to talk about what happened and to grieve the loss. Teacher Rebecca Lee shared their process and their pain with a public Facebook post.

She gathered the fifth graders around her, and they read a news article about the shooting together, "so we can all be informed," she wrote. "As I read, the students busily highlight and underline parts that stand out to them: Fatally shot. Hands raised. 'Bad dude.' Motionless. Affected forever. I finish and I ask them, 'What are your thoughts?'

"They answered with questions: 'Why did they have to kill him? Why were they afraid of him? Why does his daughter have to live life without a father? Who will take her to the father-daughter dance? Why did no one help him after he was shot? Hasn't this happened before? Can we write her cards? Can we protest?'

"As the questions roll, so do the tears," she wrote. "Students cry softly as they speak. Others weep openly. I watch 10 year olds pass tissues to each other, to me, to our principal as he joins our circle. One girl closes our group by sharing: 'I wish white people could give us a chance. We can all come together and get along.' . . . I tell each of them that I am white and I love them."

When she gathers the sixth-grade girls, they surround her red-eyed and withdrawn. "They sit next to Mr. Crutcher's daughter in class. They are her friends. Nearly every student has a tissue as we read the article together. When I open the floor for discussion: silence. It hurts to talk about. It hurts to think about. It hurts. I fight the urge to fill the dead air with my voice." A few quiet words are whispered about sadness and unfairness, but the rest of the time is spent wiping eyes and hugging one another. "I give them the space to process silently. Then I tell them, 'We have different skin colors. I love you. You matter. You are worthy. You are human. You are valuable.' Shoulders shake harder around the circle. I realize that this is the first time all year I have affirmed my love for them. . . .

"I share this story, because Mr. Crutcher's death does not just affect the students at my school. I share this story because we are creating an identity crisis in all of our black and brown students. (Do I matter? Am I to be feared? Should I live in fear? Am I human?) We are shaping their world view with blood and bullets, hashtags and viral videos. Is this how we want them to feel? Is this how we want them to think?"

The teacher's question is one mental health professionals are asking as well. When the police kill unarmed black suspects, those deaths are associated with a significant dip in the mental health of blacks across the entire state where those killings occurred.

Using a large, nationally representative sample, public health researchers Jacob Bor, Atheendar Venkataramani, David Williams, and Alexander Tsai examined respondents' self-reported survey responses regarding their mental health and compared responses before and after a police encounter where a black or white civilian was killed in the respondents' state of residence. When the person killed was black and unarmed, researchers found that black respondents reported feeling more depressed and stressed up to three months after the incident occurred. When the person killed was black and armed, there was no mental health decline. By contrast, white respondents experienced no mental health change whether the civilian was white or black, armed or unarmed.

The researchers point to a variety of factors that could drive the drop in mental health status for blacks who have been exposed to news regarding the killings of unarmed black men, including "heightened perceptions of systemic racism and lack of fairness, loss of social status and self-regard, increased fear of victimization and greater mortality expectations, increased vigilance, diminished trust in social institutions, reactions of anger, activation of prior traumas, and communal bereavement."

• • •

Nearly a thousand people turned out for Terence's funeral. Folks from every phase of his life—from his community college instructors to classmates from his kindergarten class—filled the church sanctuary, crowded the overflow room, and spilled out onto the sidewalk along Martin Luther King Jr. Boulevard. "People were lined up on the street like a parade," Tiffany recalled. "Little kids, white kids and black kids, and families. And they had signs saying, 'We Love You All.'" Inside the church, "it was just wall-to-wall. People were just up singing and praising God."

The mood and spirit were "just beautiful to see," she said. The loss still felt unbearable, but the outpouring of love would fortify Tiffany for the next weeks and months as strangers threatened her, mocked her family, and lambasted her brother in cruel social media posts. "Comply or die" was the common refrain: suggesting that because Terence hadn't obeyed the officer, he deserved to be killed.

To help her cope, Tiffany even reached out to an all-white group dedicated to understanding and addressing racial bias. She was searching for a positive role to play in this new life that was thrust upon her. She was desperate to make sense of it all. "I just went into the meeting, and they were all in a circle, and they just said, 'Welcome.' I introduced myself and I told them who I was and what had happened." Tiffany decided to join, and for months she drove to enter their circle every day after she completed her work at the health clinic.

"My brother was a victim of this implicit bias," she told me as our time together wound down. "He was somebody who was not suspected of committing a crime, and—I'm going to keep saying it—he was not a fleeing felon. . . . Did he have a lot of struggles, like a lot of other millions of Americans? Yes, he did. Did he deserve to die? No, he did not. No, he did not."

CHAPTER 4

Male Black

I arrived at the meeting in the Oakland Public Library prepared for the barrage of complaints. The state attorney general had barely finished addressing the crowd when the first speaker stepped to the microphone and the fusillade began.

"People are damaged. People are heartbroken. People have fear," the dark-skinned Oakland native said, his voice amplified by outrage and pain. "People are scared of the same people that's supposed to protect them."

Like the others sitting with me at the long table in front of the crowd, I was part of an advisory board tasked by the California attorney general with helping to quantify and address racial profiling by law enforcement. Every board meeting was held in a public space so that community members could not only hear our deliberations in the open but offer their input. We listened as speaker after speaker shared hurtful and humiliating stories: traffic stops turned ugly, calls for help ignored, teenage boys hassled by cops for no discernible reason, rude encounters with officers who mistook victims for criminals. For them, these were painful, personal experiences. For us, they were another reminder of how fraught police-community relations had become.

California's Racial and Identity Profiling Act of 2015 requires each of the nearly five hundred law enforcement agencies in the state to collect demographic data on every pedestrian and traffic stop. California is one of a handful of states across the country to make this type of data collection mandatory. Access to police-stop data has been hailed by activists in California as a way to validate what residents in black communities have long suspected: that police stop minorities disproportionately and treat them with less dignity. There were fifteen people on our board, including police executives, lawyers, and community leaders. I sat as the lone academic. Our role was to offer recommendations to the attorney general on what kind of data to gather and how to collect, store, and use it.

Everywhere we held these meetings—in Northern California, Southern California, the Central Valley; in bustling cities and in struggling rural communities—scores of blacks and Latinos turned out to support an effort they believed would finally hold law enforcement accountable.

I often left the meetings feeling exhausted by the raw wash of emotions: the anger, fear, hopelessness, and resentment that so many people feel. They're frustrated because they believe officers don't bother to build relationships with them. They're frustrated that they feel they can't call the police for help without worrying that they'll be handcuffed and hauled off to jail. They feel abandoned, belittled, demonized.

Listening to these stories made one thing painfully clear to me: To understand police-community relations, we need to consider not only basic facts about how our minds are designed to work, but our history and our culture as well. Every encounter police officers and community members have with each other happens in a larger societal context that shapes how each responds. Their behavior is influenced by the history of police relations in the local community and in the country more generally. Their behavior is affected by broader racial disparities in violent crime and in police treatment.

The session in Oakland was particularly intense. The public's complaints were grounded in the present but set against a backdrop of brazen misconduct in a police department that had historically treated the mostly black areas of Oakland like a no-man's-land, where any black face could be an enemy.

The Oakland Police Department had been plagued with scandals for decades. The most notorious involved a band of vigilante cops who called themselves "the Riders" and roamed the streets of Oakland from the late 1990s to 2000, planting drugs on innocent people, physically assaulting them, then falsely accusing them of criminal activity.

Their victims ran the gamut from ex-cons on parole to hardworking single mothers to high school kids running family errands or riding home from a basketball game with dad. The officers were often undercover, driving by bus stops, convenience stores, and street corners, trying to set up drug buys. They seemed to target folks indiscriminately—rolling up in patrol cars and laying siege with flashlights and batons, slipping drugs into pockets, cars, or purses, and later testifying against their victims in court. Few of the people they arrested could afford to fight even fabricated charges. Some spent months in jail, often on the advice of public defenders who knew no one would believe that they had been framed by cops.

I felt ill when I learned of the victims' accounts: A father taking his young son on his first barbershop visit had his nose broken and teeth knocked loose by a cop. A woman was forced to strip in the street while one officer searched her and another planted a rock of co-caine in the trunk of her car. A minister leaving a funeral service was stopped and searched by a cop who slid a crack pipe into his pocket, then hauled him off to jail. A man double-parked outside his girlfriend's house was choked, punched, and beaten with a flashlight; his girlfriend was punched in the face as she tried to call the police department to complain. A seventeen-year-old basketball player riding home from a tournament with his dad was framed by an officer who claimed to have found a rock of cocaine wrapped in a napkin in the boy's pocket. And more than once, officers bragged about shooting and killing their vic-tims' dogs, to send a clear message about who was in control.

The criminal charges in their cases—and more than a hundred others—were ultimately dismissed after the police misconduct was revealed by a rookie officer unwilling to go along with the reign of terror he had witnessed.

Former Oakland police captain Ronald Davis recalls a city at war with itself—under siege by gangs and drug dealers and ripe for the sort of cruel and overzealous policing the rogue band of Riders de-livered. The emergence of the Riders was "completely predictable," said Davis, who spent twenty years with the department and later headed the President's Task Force on 21st Century Policing, created by Barack Obama in 2014.

Like other urban areas across the country, Oakland was experi-encing an unprecedented level of violent crime in the 1990s, much of it related to the drug trade. The police department's battle strategy was "simply to take everything that walks in the street to jail," Davis said. The officers who tallied the most jail bookings "were the kings of the castle." That cultural mandate was communicated in many different ways: "At roll call, their supervisors would be telling them,

'Take the gloves off. . . . Sometimes, you got to bend the rules.' . . . They would talk about . . . how many arrests you made, and that would be the big thing."

"You set this thing in motion, and then it starts to go south," Davis explained. "Then you're looking at the Riders as though you don't even know them, but they're part of this culture. They didn't come out of nowhere. . . . Everything was tied to it from the leadership, to the messaging, to the strategies, to the tactics, to the lack of accountability."

The four officers who led the terror campaign were fired and criminally charged in 2000 with kidnapping, assault, conspiracy, and obstruction of justice, but not one of them was ever convicted. The ringleader fled the country, escaping before he could be tried; juries for the others either acquitted or couldn't agree on a verdict.

A class-action lawsuit was filed, with 119 plaintiffs, all but one of them black. Collectively, they had spent more than 14,665 days (approximately 40 years) behind bars for crimes that never occurred.

Their declarations detailed abuses that cost them jobs, homes, families, businesses, and life savings. And their suffering went beyond the physical and the financial. Their encounters with the Riders left them depressed, anxious, and fearful of police. Some had no idea what they were even arrested for until their arraignment in court. The fallout would ripple through their lives for years. Marriages broke up, children lost faith in parents accused of drug dealing, relatives ostracized family members they wrongly believed had gone back to old criminal ways.

In the end, the lawsuit, filed by civil rights lawyers John Burris and Jim Chanin, led to a $10.9 million settlement for the plaintiffs and federal oversight of the Oakland Police Department.

The oversight agreement required the department to collect data on police stops by race. But it took nearly ten years for the department to collect the kind of reliable data needed to figure out who was being stopped. In the spring of 2014, I was brought in as a subject matter expert to help analyze the data, determine whether there were significant racial disparities, and suggest ways to improve police-community interactions.

I soon recruited a group of researchers at Stanford to assist in the cause. Together, we analyzed over twenty-eight thousand police stops that occurred in 2013 and 2014. We found that roughly 60 percent of the stops officers made in Oakland were of black people, although blacks made up only 28 percent of the Oakland population at the time. Blacks were disproportionately stopped even when we controlled for factors like the crime rate and the racial breakdown of residents in the areas where the stops took place.

We found that not only were blacks significantly more likely than whites to be stopped but blacks were significantly more likely to be searched, handcuffed, and arrested. In fact, while 65 percent of Oakland police officers had conducted a discretionary search on a black person, only 23 percent had conducted such a search on a white person across the same thirteen-month period. And 72 percent had handcuffed a black person during the course of a stop—even when no arrest was made—whereas only 26 percent of officers had handcuffed a white person who was not arrested.

Stop-data collections have been occurring in police departments around the country for years. From Los Angeles to Boston, from Milwaukee to New Orleans, researchers have found evidence for racial disparities of the same sort we discovered in Oakland. In fact, when researchers track police stops by race in other countries—

including England and Canada—the results are quite similar to what studies have shown in the United States.

Many people in black communities hope that these revelations will prod officers to own up to long-standing practices of discrimination and acknowledge community concerns. "Just know this is real pain," said a woman at one of our public hearings as she scanned the faces of law enforcement officials at our table.

"When we come here and speak to you, it's from our hearts. It's not because we're angry that you're . . . police officers. We're angry because nothing is being done and we want to see real change."

THE POLICE RESPONSE

But institutional change requires looking beyond data on traffic stops. As clear as the racial disparities in policing were, we could not say that the differences were due solely to the racial biases of individual officers, which is what many in the community wanted to hear. There were too many cultural and procedural forces within the department that could influence officers' choices on the streets including department policies, enforcement strategies, and supervisors' direct commands to their officers.

In fact, relying on racial disparities to gauge the quality of policing can be a double-edged sword. The same disparities that community leaders view as proof of racial profiling can be cited by police officers as proof of who is most likely to commit crimes. In Oakland, for example, 83 percent of violent crime was attributed to black people in 2014. That sort of racial imbalance appears in the crime rates of almost every large, racially diverse city in the United States. From a law enforcement perspective, the extreme racial disparities that show up in police stops are aligned with those crime rate stats, validating the focus and scope of their crime-fighting tactics.

As a researcher, of course, I support the gathering of data as a means to isolate and identify problems. But in cases like this—with two diametrically opposed interpretations of what the same numbers mean—data collection alone, without additional levers to access, cannot close the breach. The personal experiences on either side of the profiling debate shape what people see. While data collection efforts will give some communities the voice they desperately desire, they may also render their cries less audible. Because it's hard for statistics and summaries to compete with what officers see and hear every day as they patrol the streets.

"MALE BLACK." "MALE BLACK." "MALE BLACK." "MALE BLACK." This is what officers in Oakland hear, booming from their police radios, hundreds of times every day. It's the inescapable background track to the chaos of crime-saturated streets. On a typical day, an officer on patrol might hear that dispatched description three hundred times—or twelve hundred times a week, fifty thousand times each year.

I can only imagine the impact of that constant refrain over time. It would be far more powerful than the onetime ten-minute priming experience that study participants receive in my laboratory on a college campus. It forces officers as they patrol the streets to constantly pair blackness with criminal activity. That repetitive pairing can easily lead to an association of blackness with crime that becomes automatic, expected, routine.

But even beyond the priming process—which I understand as a scientist—the implication of the "MALE BLACK" drumbeat rankles me as a person. The label feels unforgiving, sweeping everyone under it into the same narrow space. It is what sociologist Everett Hughes, back in the 1940s, called a "master status": the primary way in which one is seen. It elevates that aspect of the self above all others.

Indeed, when "MALE BLACK" is broadcast over the police radio, it is seldom followed by substantial descriptions. Sometimes members of the public who call the police may offer a rough estimate of the age or height or weight of the suspect, or possibly a vague description of his clothing. But virtually every description that police on patrol receive includes a basic gender-race pairing: "MALE HIS-PANIC." "FEMALE WHITE." "MALE ASIAN." And most frequently, in cities like Oakland at least, "MALE BLACK."

It's implausible to believe that officers—or anyone else—can be immersed in an environment that repetitively exposes them to the categorical pairing of blacks with crime and not have that affect how they think, feel, or behave.

•   •   •

After one of the police department training sessions I delivered years ago on implicit bias, a young white officer in the class approached me to share his story. He had grown up in Germany, moved to the United States, and joined the police department in a midsized urban center that had more than its share of crime. He'd been an officer for just a few years, but already the experience had altered his way of seeing the world.

Day after day, the "male black" descriptor blared from his police radio, directing his gaze and priming him to act. On patrol, he felt compelled to scrutinize every black man he saw. Even innocent gestures—lighting a cigarette, reaching into a pocket—could register reflexively as a prelude to a criminal act. The black–crime association became so strong that the sight of a random black man wearing baggy pants triggered an avalanche of precautions: His eyes would linger.

He would search for the person's hands and assess the probability that he might have a gun. He would imagine engaging with the person and would quickly run through various scenarios of engagement in his mind—all of which required him to react to some imagined danger the person might pose.

The mere presence of a black person placed the officer on high alert. And that vigilance was relentless. Before long, he'd begun enacting that ritual even when he was off duty, even when he didn't intend to, even when he wasn't aware of the mental gymnastics his mind was performing.

The friends he had before he joined the force noticed and called him on it: *Why are you acting like that? Why are you looking at black men as if they were all suspicious? What's wrong with you?*

He couldn't answer in a way that made sense to them. He *had* begun to presume that every black man posed a threat. And unlike his law enforcement buddies—who probably perceived things the same way he did—his friends outside the department were jarred by the change they'd seen in him.

The revelation was jarring for him too, the officer told me. He'd joined the force with little sense of the racial dynamics that drive American thinking. Now it seemed as if his brain had been seized by those forces; that his mind had begun to work in ways outside his control: *I have this association. It's clear and I'm acting on it. If you're a black man, I'm looking hard at you.*

That automatic response didn't match the way he saw himself and thought of others. He valued having an open mind, one that registered people as individuals, not suspects. He was amazed that such a profound change in his mind-set had happened so quickly and realized that he'd have to work to keep alive a part of him that police work might kill.

Since then, the officer has begun to question himself. *Is this who I need to become? Is this something that is still within my control? Is this the person I want to be?*

PROCEDURAL JUSTICE

Most officers want to see themselves as a force for good. They don't want communities to consider them the enemy. Yet somehow along the way—at least from some community members' perspective—they can begin to act the part. That's where procedural justice training comes in. It is a type of restorative training that many departments have come to embrace. The focus is not on tactics but on building healthy relationships with the public. The goal is not to tally up as many stops as possible, but to improve the quality of each interaction once a stop has occurred.

It's a method being used around the country to help officers stay connected to why they joined the profession: to protect and serve the public. The training aims to override a reflexive reliance on bias by encouraging officers to consider how they talk and how they listen to everyone they encounter on the job. It prods officers to behave in ways that are more in line with their ideal selves. This means that when they stop someone in a car or on the street, they allow that person to have a voice. They give members of the public a chance to tell their story. They listen and consider community members' concerns. They apply the law fairly and impartially. They act in a manner that the public will find respectful. They present themselves as authorities who can be trusted. And they do this not just at community meetings but every day, on every street, in every encounter.

Decades of research have shown that across a variety of professions people care as much about how they are treated during the course of an interaction as the outcome of that interaction. In the policing context, this suggests that people stopped by police care as much about how police officers treat them as they do about whether they got a ticket. In fact, both research and real-life experience have shown that if officers act in accordance with four tenets—voice, fairness, respect, trustworthiness—residents will be more inclined to think of the police as legitimate authorities and therefore be more likely to comply with the law.

The purpose of the training is to remind officers just how important these everyday interactions are. At the end of the day, officers want to feel valued for putting their lives on the line, they want to feel as if they have chosen a profession that people respect, and, most important, they want to stay safe.

Yale law professors Tom Tyler and Tracey Meares have worked together to develop a model for training police officers on the principles of procedural justice. But why do officers need to be reminded of these principles? Because one of the primary barriers to good policing is the cynicism that officers develop while working the streets.

It's easy for officers to get beaten down by fighting crime. Over time, they come to feel as if they were just foot soldiers in an unwinnable war. They become bitter about putting their lives on the line for people who do not seem to respect them or appreciate their efforts. They become frustrated about attempting to protect victims who later become perpetrators, or trying to solve crimes when witnesses refuse to talk. They become jaded as they bear witness to horrific acts of violence. They get worn down by living in a constant state of hypervigilance, not knowing where the next threat will emerge. And that leads to a vicious cycle that can sabotage communication and escalate even the slightest provocation.

As that cynicism grows, it also narrows their vision. The 3 percent of people who are actively engaged in violent crime in the city they police dominate the stage. The other 97 percent go dim. They begin to see all the residents of the communities they serve and protect through this tiny window.

That sort of selective attention is not something limited to the police; it is a basic feature of brain functioning. In fact, just as our brains use categorization to offer some sense of coherence and control over a chaotic world, our brains use selective attention as well. We cannot possibly take in all of the stimuli with which we are constantly bombarded. Based on our goals and our expectations, we make choices—often unconsciously—about what we attend to and what we do not.

Perhaps the most famous demonstration of selective attention was developed by two cognitive psychologists named Daniel Simons and Christopher Chabris. The demo involves asking people to watch a silent, thirty-second video clip of two teams of people (one in light-colored shirts, the other in dark-colored shirts) passing around a basketball. Unsuspecting viewers are asked to count the exact number of passes made by the team in the light-colored shirts. People are so focused on accurately counting the number of passes that more than half of them completely miss the gorilla in the room: someone in a gorilla suit enters the scene on the right, pauses in the middle for a chest pound, and then exits the scene on the left. Their attention is so focused on the task at hand that their brain records the gorilla as irrelevant. The effect is so strong that those who miss the gorilla are shocked later by the realization that they never saw the giant animal enter the scene.

The "invisible gorilla" reminds us of how selective our social

perception may be. Many officers who patrol diverse, high-crime communities come to view the racial disparities in policing as the sole result of who commits the crimes. People who live in those communities view those disparities as a result of police bias, because they know that the majority of their neighbors are not criminals.

In procedural justice training, officers are taught to reorient their view—to think about every interaction with the public as they would a bank transaction. They can use that interaction to make a deposit that will increase trust and improve police-community relations, or they can allow it to become a withdrawal, decreasing trust and increasing police-community tension. Each interaction has the capacity to influence people well beyond the individual officer and resident directly involved, and has the potential to strain relations between police departments and entire communities in ways that harden over time and are tough to rectify.

AN IMPERFECT SHIELD

LeRonne Armstrong grew up in the 1980s in West Oakland, in an all-black neighborhood known mostly to outsiders for its high crime and housing projects. The only white people he saw regularly were teachers and police officers, and neither seemed to care very much about boys like him. In fact, young LeRonne feared the police more than he feared the criminals. You could avoid gang members' wrath by knowing what colors not to wear, what streets you shouldn't cross, which blocks to avoid. But the police were unpredictable and often seemed intent on inflicting misery. The only rule that made sense to him was what the old folks used to say: if you see the cops, you run as fast as you can and hope you don't get caught.

"Growing up there, some of the most violent people I've seen were actually police officers," Armstrong told me. "The way they used to jump out on people and just beat people up. You were scared of what could happen to you. . . . You would live your life fearing law enforcement. 'Don't talk to them. Don't look at them.' That's what you were told."

By the time he was ten, he was primed to panic at the sight of a patrol car. Whenever he and his buddies saw a cop car slow down, they would take off. "We were young boys not engaged in criminal activity, and we just made a decision that we were going to run. Because we were afraid they'd get out and maybe grab us and slam us on the car."

By the time he was thirteen, the crack cocaine epidemic had upped the ante. Drug sales, turf wars, raging addicts, and thieves made the neighborhood more dangerous and a bigger target for police. Residents were faced with a sort of Hobson's choice: endure the daily dangers of the violent drug trade or seek help from brutal and indifferent officers. Even as a kid, Armstrong remembers feeling trapped: "Who wants to live like that?"

He and his brother, then sixteen, were solicited to join the ranks of dealers. "Nearly every boy between fourteen and twenty-five was selling crack," Armstrong recalled. "They'd seen the money and the ability to get that money in the fastest way they'd ever seen. Just about every boy was trying to be part of these drug-selling rings." The gangs became more violent and territorial. Between their clashes and the heat from police, his neighborhood began to feel like a war zone.

His family felt the impact of the change firsthand. His mother had five brothers, all of whom wound up spending time behind bars. So she tried to inoculate LeRonne and his brother against a life of crime.

Even when he was only nine years old, his mother would haul LeRonne and his brother to visit her brothers at the county jail in Oakland. The cramped visiting room smelled like bleach and was lined with tinted windows so tiny and dark they had to squint to see the shadowy shapes of prisoners on the other side. LeRonne was so small he had to stand on a stool to peer through the glass at the blurry image of whatever uncle he was talking to on the jail phone. He dreaded the twice-weekly trips, but "she would just keep dragging us and dragging us." After months of visits, he finally complained to his mother one night on the way home: "Ma, why you keep making us come to this place? I hate going here. I hate talking to them. I hate getting on that phone." She stopped the car and addressed that head-on: "I just want you to hate it so much that you never, ever find yourself behind that glass." That moment would stick with him for the rest of his life. His mother never took him to that visiting room again.

Still, a mother can do only so much to shield her sons from trouble. When LeRonne's older brother was sixteen, she arranged his transfer to a better high school in a different neighborhood. But barely a week into the new school year, he got into a fight with a local kid in his first-period class. The authorities broke it up. Armstrong's brother headed back to class, but the other boy went home and got a gun.

Armstrong describes what happened next in a voice flattened by layers of sorrow and pain: "My brother's on his way down the hallway to the third-period class. The same kid he had a fight with comes from behind, shoots him in the back three times, and kills him in the hallway of Oakland Tech High School."

The loss of her older child destroyed his mother, he said. His family unraveled as she shrank into a depression so deep she could barely function. "I could just see the grief all over her," he said. "It was so difficult to see her like that, because she had tried so hard to make a better life for us."

Her brothers demanded that a price be paid. Local gangs pressured young LeRonne to retaliate. One of his uncles handed the thirteen-year-old a gun, offered him a ride to where the killer hung out, and issued a command: "You have got to do this."

LeRonne realized that his uncle was trying to school him in the ethos of street survival. "But I'm looking at my mom and I'm just, 'Man, I can't do it.' I just couldn't," he said. "She was in such a bad place that if she lost both of us because I went to jail for doing something like that, she would be devastated . . . she wouldn't survive that." He couldn't bear the idea of his mother visiting him behind bars.

Still, he knew that not going after his brother's killer would have its own cost. He would be punished by a community that tied respect to retribution.

It was the most difficult decision of his life, he says now, at forty-four years old. "Normally, people would say that not killing somebody is like a pretty simple decision. . . . But, where I grew up, it wasn't at all."

His choice took him from being a popular kid, comfortable with everyone, "to this kid that was shunned and ostracized. They called me a punk and called me scared. . . . I had let the neighborhood down." But he made peace with his outlier status. His mother had tried to protect her boys the only way she knew how, and he'd done what he needed to do to protect her.

The teenager turned his focus toward studying and sports. He carried his basketball everywhere to send a signal to neighborhood toughs that he was, symbolically at least, in another category: outside the bounds of their influence and hectoring.

Basketball became his ticket to college. After graduation, when his plans to play professionally didn't work out, a friend got him a job with the probation department in Oakland in 1995. That brought Armstrong face-to-face with kids not much different from the boy he had once been. He knew how easy it was for good kids to be drawn off track. He wanted to steer them in the right direction before they needed punishment or rehabilitation. That meant setting a different tone in his community, so he decided to join the Oakland Police Department.

As a product of West Oakland, Armstrong understood forces that other officers did not see. And once he began patrolling the streets, he was able to recognize patterns that residents didn't perceive.

The day after he graduated from the academy, Armstrong wound up in the locker room next to an officer who'd been so notorious in his neighborhood that he'd been given a nickname by residents: the Slapper. The officer would roam the streets, intimidating everyone in sight, leading even little kids in the neighborhood to scatter. "He was known for talking mess," Armstrong recalled. "Then, if you talked back, he would slap you."

Now, decades later, there they were: Armstrong and the Slapper sitting side by side, serving on the same team. The Slapper had no idea that Armstrong had grown up in the neighborhood he had once brutally policed. He greeted the rookie with a smile and a nod: "Hey, youngster, how you doing?" Armstrong stared back at him in disbelief.

This man who'd routinely disrupted their lives for years, unleashing widespread panic, who'd dictated whether they would walk or run or be knocked to the ground, suddenly seemed so ordinary: "like an old, nice uncle or somebody," Armstrong recalled.

It was hard for Armstrong to reconcile the conflicting images: how the good guy in the locker room could be a merchant of terror on the streets. And now Armstrong was no longer a random black man with a target on his back but a member of the force. There were layers of complexity that he simply hadn't expected. In myriad ways, he would have to learn to manage the tension between his racial identity and his identity as a cop.

He remembered officers clapping at roll call when the death of a hard-core criminal was announced. He felt conflicted by that. "If a person's breaking the law, you want to hold them accountable for that, but I wouldn't want to celebrate their death," he said. "I think in the minds of these officers, they thought the community is safer because that person is no longer there."

He realized that the sense of "protecting the community" was strong among even the most hard-nosed cops. But too often they couldn't tell bad from good, so everyone was treated like a suspect. That, in turn, fueled resentment and eroded residents' trust in the department. Then, when community members balked at cooperating with the police—eyewitnesses wouldn't talk, victims wouldn't ID their assailants—some officers took that to mean "we're the only ones that actually care," Armstrong said. "They felt that 'it's just us; we're the only ones trying to figure out who killed these people.' And that really reinforces that 'us against them' mentality."

With a foot in both worlds, Armstrong, now an Oakland deputy chief, understands both the roots and the results of that "don't snitch" mentality. "It's always disappointing for me," he said. "If nobody says anything, then we're accepting that this is okay. We're saying, 'We're fine with this.' . . . Because of my own personal experience of having a brother killed, I know that you don't want people to get away with it. You don't want to feel like the person who was responsible is not going to be held accountable. But this is a community that feels like they don't trust law enforcement enough to share information." They're afraid to talk because they fear police can't or won't protect them.

The fallout from that reluctance cuts both ways: It makes it harder for police to solve crimes and keeps a vast majority of law-abiding residents at the mercy of a small minority of criminals.

"Do you condone the violence? No, you don't, but what can you do, particularly when you don't have a relationship with law enforcement?" Armstrong said. "So you are literally forced to stay in your home and keep to yourself and not be able to actually be a part of the community, because of what's going on. . . . I think even law enforcement doesn't recognize the people behind the walls."

As a newly minted police officer, Armstrong gradually came to understand how things operated outside the small sphere of his own neighborhood. He saw crime trends throughout the entire city and realized that patterns he thought were specific to his neighborhood were occurring in other places as well. And he saw stark evidence of the racial dynamics in play during even routine policing.

When Armstrong stopped a black man for a traffic violation, the driver would get noticeably nervous. He'd fumble around, trying to collect his license and insurance papers. Even when the men's paper-work was in order, Armstrong could see the fear in their eyes and hear it in their voices.

When he stopped white men, there was a completely different pattern, he said. Often, they would be defiant and challenge him: "What did you stop me for?" Armstrong had no idea you could talk to a policeman that way. He'd been so conditioned to fear police that if he was out of uniform and pulled over by a cop, he would have felt just as nervous as those other black drivers.

Seeing grown men in their fifties and sixties cower before cops made him think. He wanted to police in a way where community members felt respected. "I had this utopian belief that I could im-mediately change things," he said. But the problem was bigger than any one officer or any individual decision or even any one police department. The problem was rooted in a mind-set, a carryover from years past, that promotes instinct and aggression as the foundational elements of good policing.

"They used to train us on this when I came on a long time ago," Armstrong recalled. "They'd always say, 'Trust the hairs rising on the back of your neck.' If the hair is rising on the back of your neck, there is probably something wrong with this person.

"I'd think, 'Dang, that's really subjective.' That has everything to do with me and nothing to do with the other person. I never un-derstood that. . . . And just last week, when I was at a training, I still heard people saying that."

INNOCENCE IN THE PARK

I'd just spoken at a conference on the death penalty in Monterey, California, and my husband, Rick, and our three boys had come down from Palo Alto to join me so we could visit Fisherman's Wharf, a popular tourist attraction. It was a sunny day in February 2008.

We were walking back to the hotel after a wonderful time at the Monterey Bay Aquarium when we stopped to rest at a quiet local park. Rick was carrying Harlan, our youngest, who was four years old and sound asleep on his dad's shoulder. Ebbie, then ten, and Everett, six, were running around, burning some of the boundless energy that boys that age always seem to have stored up.

Once I caught my breath, I noticed a police officer walking up to a young black couple seated at a picnic table next to ours. The officer approached and homed in on the boy, who looked to be about sixteen. I could see the teenager tense up. Even though this was ten years ago, I'd already worked with the police enough to know that you're not supposed to interfere. At the same time, I didn't feel comfortable leaving the scene.

The police officer began directing his attention to the teenage boy. The girlfriend drifted toward the outskirts of their conversation, circling nervously and studying the pair with a worried expression. I was stunned by how suddenly the atmosphere in that tiny space had changed. Just a few yards away, my own kids were still laughing and playing on the grass—a counterpoint to what felt to me like a vaguely sinister drama unfolding on what had been, until then, a pleasant day.

The officer began checking their IDs and calling the information in on his radio. Another officer showed up in a cruiser. The girl flipped open her cell phone and made a call. "I don't know what to do," she said, in a voice that seemed to tremble just a bit. "We were just out here sitting in the park. I don't know why they're stopping him. What should I say? What should I do?" I could hear a woman's voice on the other end of the line, but I couldn't make out her words. I imagined a mother, about to be worried sick.

It turned out that a crime had been committed nearby and the boyfriend matched a description of the suspect. *MALE BLACK*. The officers asked him to stand; one pulled out a camera and began photographing him—right there in the grassy picnic area next to Fisherman's Wharf.

I looked over at my boys and could tell they were completely oblivious to what was shaping up to be a rather emotional encounter. They were playing with a ball, running and laughing, comfortable and secure. I studied them for a while, and it struck me how perfect the picture was from my vantage point.

I turned away from them to watch the teenager standing stiffly as the officer's camera clicked and families around us impassively looked on. I wondered what I would say over the phone the day my own son called with fear in his voice, because he or a friend was inexplicably stopped and questioned by police. I felt suddenly frozen, unbearably aware of all the ways their lives would change as they moved beyond the bubble that boyhood in suburbia provided.

My boys were going to grow older and they were going to be fearful and the cops were going to be fearful—unless we all could find a way to free ourselves from the tight grip of history.

CHAPTER 5

How Free People Think

I t was the spring of 1993, the day before I was to graduate from Harvard with a PhD in psychology. My six years at the university had not been easy. I was a first-generation college student and never felt comfortable in a place where your entire worth as a human being is based on how intelligent people thought you were. My father had been my role model—a man who dropped out of school in the eighth grade to help support his family. They needed him, and he answered the call.

I had done well as an undergraduate at the University of Cincinnati. Then I landed in the Ivy League, surrounded by privilege and a little disoriented as I tried to figure out how graduate school worked. Life there sometimes seemed like an endless series of embarrassments: There was always some word I didn't know, some fancy place I'd never been, some obscure reference in a professor's lecture that only I had failed to understand. On the other hand, there were incredible resources, including a constant stream of engaging presentations by scholars from across the university and around the world. Harvard was a mecca for knowledge creation, and I soaked it up. And as my graduation neared, I got word that I'd been selected to be one of two PhD candidates awarded the signature honor of carrying the flag for the Graduate School of Arts and Sciences during Harvard's commencement procession. I would lead hundreds of graduates from dozens of fields of study into Harvard Yard, where we would take our seats among thousands waiting to hear parting words from university officials and global leaders.

But on the day before commencement, I wasn't thinking of any of that. I was bone tired and simply trying to make my way to my friend April's Boston apartment. April and I had been up all night cooking and spent all morning serving faculty and administrators at a brunch on campus. We'd started a makeshift catering service to earn the money that helped pay the rent and keep the lights on while we were in graduate school together. April was a great cook, and I was good at working hard, arranging platters, and doing food prep. We catered for private parties many evenings and weekends, serving academics and organizations on campus. Our specialties were seasoned collard greens, candied yams, smothered turkey breasts with cornbread stuffing, and pecan pies with dollops of fresh whipped cream. People loved our authentic southern meals, and we made everything from scratch.

On that day in June, we'd cleaned up the venue, loaded our cookware and serving dishes into the trunk of my car, and headed for April's apartment, located in a Boston housing project about twenty minutes from campus. As April drove, I noticed a police cruiser behind us. His flashing lights came on as we neared the entrance to the complex, and we pulled over to the curb. We hadn't been speeding. In fact, we'd obeyed all the rules of the road, which is saying a lot for driving in Boston. We had no idea why we were being stopped, and the officer had no intention of clearing that up.

He approached the car with an order: "I need your license, registration, and proof of insurance." We both handed over our driver's licenses, and I fished in the glove compartment for my insurance and registration information, which I gave to him as well. My nine-year-old Nissan Sentra—a gift from my parents soon after I left home for college—still bore Ohio plates and was in my mother's name. We asked the officer why he was stopping us, but he ignored the question and headed back to his patrol car. We could not imagine what was going on or why we'd been stopped.

Several minutes passed before he came back. "Does this vehicle belong to you?" he barked. I tried to explain that the car was registered in my mother's name, but the registration was six weeks out of date. "What's your mother's name? What year was she born? What is her Social Security number?" Jeez. How would I know my mother's Social Security number?

"I'm not sure . . . ," I started to say, but before I could finish the sentence, he turned on his heels and headed back to his patrol car. We sat and waited, quietly speculating about what he might be suspecting us of. Did he think the car was stolen? We were just a few steps from April's giant apartment complex, which was home to a high concentration of low-income black tenants.

After a long wait, we watched as a tow truck appeared and pulled to the curb right in front of our car. As the driver began lowering his tow apparatus to the ground, the police officer suddenly materialized right outside my door. "Exit the vehicle," he said. I didn't budge. "Exit the vehicle," he ordered again, a bit louder this time. It became clear that he had decided to have my car towed. "Exit the vehicle!" All this for expired tags?

I looked at him, exhausted and bewildered, trying to wrap my mind around this sudden turn of events. April and I had worked day and night and just wanted to be left alone. But this officer came along and decided he wanted to take our car. He didn't let us know why or explain anything. He didn't want to listen to anything we had to say. He'd decided we were not worthy of his respect. So I made my own decision: "No, I am not getting out of the car." I had a right to protest.

The officer called for backup. One cruiser came, then another, then another and another. That's when I began to feel afraid for the first time. As the officer's backup flooded the streets, our backup began to gather on the sidewalk. At least a dozen people, mostly young black men from the apartment complex, began to mill around, waiting to see whatever would go down.

Until then, I was attempting to stand up for my rights. But when five cruisers circled us and a crowd began to gather, I realized what a volatile situation we were in the midst of. At that point, it wasn't defiance but fear that kept me inside the car. Outside, I didn't know what might happen to us with all those officers poised for action. I heard a female officer yell, "They won't get out. Just cut 'em outta there." I imagined a cop slicing through our seat belts with a knife.

Instead, the officer who had stopped us reached in, unbuckled my seat belt, and yanked me out of the car. I remember April yelling out to me, "Don't resist! Don't react!" Listening to her voice, I stood on the sidewalk and placed my hands behind my back, ready to be cuffed. The officer pulled and folded my arms high behind my back. Then he lifted my 105-pound frame off the ground and body slammed me, hard, on top of the roof of my car. The blow made a loud noise and knocked the wind out of me. I began to panic. I could no longer breathe. My eyes stretched open as I gasped for air. One of our bystanders yelled out to me, "Are you okay?" But I could no longer speak.

I went limp and my body slowly slid down from the roof of the car and onto the ground. As the officer slapped the handcuffs on me, I heard someone in the crowd shout the plaintive line made famous by Rodney King, whose beating by Los Angeles police had led to riots the previous year when the officers accused of using excessive force were acquitted: "Can we all get along?" As the officer walked me to his patrol car, I made eye contact with his supervisor. "Did you see what just happened? Did you see what he did to me?" I pleaded. I heard him respond, "I didn't see a thing," as the officer shoved me, handcuffed, into the backseat of his patrol car.

I began yelling over and over: "I'm going to file a complaint! I'm going to file a complaint!" They drove April and me to the police precinct in separate cruisers, then handcuffed us both to the wall once we were inside.

· · ·

Then and now, in cities across the country, stopping drivers for equipment-related issues—a broken light, an expired tag, a faulty turn signal, an unfastened safety belt—is a time-honored way to investigate who these drivers are, what they are doing, where they are going and why. Those discretionary stops give officers wide latitude to follow up on their slightest suspicions. Many departments consider such stops valid crime-fighting tools. But their hunch-based foundation can both reflect and activate biases in ways that deepen racial disparities in treatment.

In fact, when black drivers are pulled over, they are more than twice as likely as white drivers to have been stopped for a high-discretion equipment violation as opposed to a moving violation. That's according to a meta-analysis of 18.5 million traffic stops across the country between 2010 and 2016, conducted by my graduate student Nicholas Camp. That scrutiny of black drivers has consequences beyond the ire of inconvenience they endure. It can seed the kind of lingering resentment that tilts even law-abiding people against the police.

In some jurisdictions, equipment-stop violations amount to a sort of sub-rosa tax on blacks and low-income people, who are pulled over and fined to generate municipal revenue. A federal probe of the Ferguson Police Department released in 2015—after the fatal police shooting of Michael Brown led to nationwide protests—concluded that officers were instructed to fill city coffers through informal ticket-writing quotas. That led them to "see some residents, especially those who live in Ferguson's predominantly African American neighborhoods, less as constituents to be protected than as potential offenders and sources of revenue," the Department of Justice report stated.

While blacks made up 67 percent of Ferguson's population, they accounted for 85 percent of vehicle stops and 90 percent of citations. And though black drivers were twice as likely to be searched by police, they were 26 percent less likely than whites to be found in possession of contraband.

The federal investigation concluded that "this disproportionate burden on African Americans cannot be explained by any difference in the rate at which people of different races violate the law. Rather . . . these disparities occur, at least in part, because of unlawful bias against and stereotypes about African Americans."

The fallout from that sort of disproportionate treatment magnifies the tensions that can accompany even benign traffic stops. Many black people—whether they have clean records or criminal ones—worry about what might happen when they see the flashing red lights of a police car in their rearview mirror. They worry about being placed under suspicion. They worry about being disrespected. They worry about how the police will treat them, and how they might react.

Those concerns are not unfounded. Of the thousand or so people who are shot to death by police officers in the United States each year, 11 percent of those fatal encounters begin with a traffic stop for something as innocuous as a loud muffler or a broken taillight.

My research at Stanford has shown that what dictates whether a routine stop escalates can be something as basic as the way police officers talk to the drivers they stop.

Traffic stops are the most common form of police contact with the public; more than one U.S. driver in ten is stopped by officers each year. But until recently, no one has been able to dissect the masses of individual encounters to see where the triggers might lie. Now body cameras worn by police officers are giving us access to how these stops unfold in real time. From the moment the cruiser lights come on, we can examine how trust is built or eroded one interaction at a time, and we can look for broad patterns across thousands of interactions.

With a team of linguists, social psychologists, and computer scientists at Stanford, I've been able to evaluate the language that officers use during routine traffic stops so that we can rigorously test whether there are racial differences in the way officers communicate with black drivers and white drivers.

In our study, conducted from 2015 to 2017, we analyzed footage from nearly a thousand traffic stops made by 245 officers in Oakland. From the transcripts of those stops, we isolated more than 36,000 utterances—greetings, comments, words, statements, and observations—that officers directed toward those whom they stopped.

We wanted to know if people might perceive differences in the respect communicated by the officers, depending on the language used. To measure that, we asked a group of college students to rate a sample of 414 utterances, using a four-point scale to measure the degree of respect, politeness, friendliness, formality, and impartiality the officer conveyed. They were not given any information about the race or gender of the officers or of the drivers.

That evaluation found that the officers were professional overall. But when officers were speaking to black drivers, they were rated as less respectful, less polite, less friendly, less formal, and less impartial than when they spoke to white drivers. These variables were all conceptually overlapping, so we collapsed them into one variable that we labeled "respect."

Once we understood what people perceived as more or less respectful, we used machine-learning techniques to automatically comb through nearly 500,000 words from transcripts of stops, tally the words that signified respect, and assign each utterance a respect score. Again, we found that Oakland officers were generally respectful. However, when we sorted those respect scores by the race of the drivers, we found dramatic differences.

Officers were significantly more respectful to white drivers than they were to black drivers: more likely to use formal titles with white drivers (for example, "sir" or "ma'am"); more likely to express concern for the safety of white drivers (with "Have a safe night" or "Drive safely"); more likely to offer reassurance to white drivers (as in "Don't worry" or "No problem").

That "respect deficit" with black drivers emerged early—during the first five seconds of a stop, before the driver even had a chance to speak—and persisted throughout the course of the interaction. That's in line with what happened during my traffic stop in Boston well over two decades ago.

And our research showed that black police officers were just as likely as white officers to exhibit less respect to black drivers. The drivers' race trumped the officers' race. In fact, the officer who pulled me over and arrested me in Boston was black.

Much of what happened to me that day was part of a pattern that I could see only decades later with the advent of body-worn cameras. From the footage of those cameras, for example, our research team has learned that the respect deficit black drivers experience is present regardless of the severity of the offense—whether they were dangerously speeding or, as in my case, driving with recently expired tags. And when the officer uses less respect at the beginning of the stop, the driver tends to express more negative emotions later in the stop. I still remember how I fumed that day from the feeling that I'd been denied even a modicum of respect.

It turns out that based on the officers' words alone, our researchers could use a simple computational model to predict whether the person an officer had stopped was black or white.

We tried controlling for other factors, but those differences in police language could not be explained away. We found clear racial disparities even when we took into account the driver's age, gender, and criminal history; the location of the stop; and the severity of the driving offense.

The study didn't allow us to pinpoint precisely what led to the racial differences in language use. The differences could be driven by bias, but they could also reflect a host of variables that we didn't test for directly, including ingrained cynicism about police-community relations, officers' habitual enactment of institutional norms, or even their deliberate well-intentioned effort to relate or connect to the people they police by using language they think is most familiar to different racial groups.

But we do know that regardless of the source of the racial differences, the stakes are higher than hurt feelings or raised voices. An officer's language and the attitude it conveys could decrease a black driver's inclination to cooperate. That increases the likelihood that the interaction might escalate and lead to an altercation and an arrest—or worse—that could have been avoided.

"You're riding down the street. You get stopped. You protest. You wind up with a conviction on a minor event," explained Oakland civil rights attorney John Burris, who has worked as both a prosecutor and a public defender. "That's how a minor traffic offense turns into a criminal case."

That "minor traffic offense" became a conduit to a criminal justice system that had its hooks in me.

NOT QUITE FREE

When I was handcuffed and arrested in Boston, I knew from watching TV that I could get one telephone call to contact my lawyer. Of course, I didn't have a lawyer. The only thing I had was a piece of paper where I had written the telephone number of Margot Gill, a dean of Harvard's Graduate School of Arts and Sciences. Just days before she'd been walking me through the details of my role as commencement marshal: how high to hold the flag, which pathway to take, where in the front row I would sit when the procession ended. When she'd told me to contact her if I had any problems, I don't think a call from jail was what she had imagined.

"Well, I ran into a problem," I told her on the phone. "I'm here at the police precinct, handcuffed to a wall." She asked to speak to someone in authority. I handed the phone to the one officer at the station who'd actually taken the time to listen to us. After she finished speaking to both him and the arresting officer, we were free to go. I don't know what she told them. But they hung up the phone and unlocked us from that wall. And we walked out of there.

Unlike most arrestees, we did not have to post bail to leave. We were released on our own recognizance because someone important was able to vouch for us.

Each year, more than eleven million people are locked up in local jails across the country. Almost three-quarters are being held for non-violent offenses (like traffic, minor drug, or public-order violations) for which they have been arrested and charged but not convicted. They're behind bars because they can't afford to post the bail that's required for pretrial release. Under the centuries-old cash bail system, defendants have to post an amount assessed by the court to guarantee they will show up for trial. That means those with the money or resources to bail themselves out get to go home while people who can't afford the bail are stuck behind bars.

The pretrial detention rate for blacks is four times greater than that for whites charged with similar offenses. That is, in part, because the formulas used to calculate bail often rely on factors—job stability, arrest history, family resources—that circumstantially disadvantage young black men. Analysts estimate that the bail premium charged to black male defendants is 35 percent more than what white defendants pay.

The inherent unfairness of the bail system has led to calls for reform. Several states are moving away from rigid bail schedules that set amounts commensurate with the gravity of the criminal charge and adopting instead computerized risk assessment tools that predict whether the accused is likely to show up for trial. In August 2018, California became the first state in the nation to outlaw cash bail and give more discretion to judges, armed with computerized risk assessment scores, to allow pretrial alternatives to jail.

That may indeed narrow the gap between rich and poor, but it might also ultimately enhance and institutionalize existing disparities between blacks and whites. Judges are not immune to the pull of their own unconscious biases, and the algorithms that risk scores rely on have already been shown to tilt against blacks. A 2016 investigation by ProPublica of a risk assessment system used in Florida found that even after controlling for criminal history, recidivism, age, and gender, black defendants were 45 percent more likely to be assigned higher risk scores than whites.

Being behind bars for months awaiting trial can unravel a life: the accused can be fired from a job, be subject to eviction, incur debt from being unable to pay bills, lose custody of children. Many defendants are so desperate to be free that they bargain for a short sentence or immediate release by pleading guilty to whatever lesser charge the prosecutor presents. That can saddle them with a criminal conviction that has lifelong consequences, limiting where they can live, what jobs they can perform, their ability to vote, and their eligibility for college student loans. The effects can cascade before they even realize they are trapped inside a vortex that just keeps spinning out of control.

"People plead guilty because they don't want to be in custody," said Burris. "You get a public defender and the public defender is overwhelmed and they're trying to reduce their caseload. They look at the case in front of them and—in the absence of proof of innocence— suggest a plea deal." With the promise of freedom or a brief stint in custody, "people plead guilty to crimes they didn't commit. . . . That swallows them into a system where they don't deserve to be," Burris explained.

The isolated decisions that individual black defendants make to accept a plea deal are understandable. Terrible things can happen to even the most innocent person once he's on the other side of a prison door. However, in the eyes of the public, each criminal record, regardless of its origin, becomes another thread that ties blacks, as a group, to crime.

The plea-bargaining system is a clear example of how institutional practices can directly affect the mental connections we make. The system puts pressure on blacks to accept the criminal label, conditioning the public to associate blacks with crime. That can strand black people on the wrong side of the social divide, beyond our moral concerns.

Yet plea bargaining is a potent force in the criminal justice system, because the process would disintegrate under the burden of a trial in every case. In fact, 94 percent of cases involving criminal charges never go to trial; they are settled when the defendant agrees to plead guilty in exchange for leniency in sentencing.

The pressure to plea-bargain comes from all sides and is applied to prosecutors as well as to defendants. Because bargaining saves the court system time and money and improves conviction rates, there is a general push toward it. And American-style plea bargaining has been spreading around the world. A study by Fair Trials found that in 1990 just nineteen countries used some form of plea bargaining; by 2017, sixty-six nations had adopted the practice. In England, Australia, and Russia, more than 60 percent of criminal cases are now settled by plea deals.

In the United States, racial disparities intrude on the process. Black defendants are more likely than whites, Asians, or Latinos to be offered plea deals that require prison time, particularly for drug-related crimes. Blacks are also more likely to rely on the free public defender system, which puts them at a distinct disadvantage. Black defendants who hire private attorneys are almost twice as likely to have the primary charge against them reduced than are the black clients of public defenders.

"You always felt like you were fighting uphill," said Burris. "That we're all just on this treadmill, working through the system. There's no real end in sight. Guys come in and you're slow walking them to state prison."

THE AFTERMATH

The day after my arrest, my wrists were still sore from the tight handcuffs. Three different areas around my sternum were bruised and swollen. My chest hurt with every breath. But I was determined to carry that flag at commencement.

Dean Gill had warned me days before that the flag was going to be heavy. It sat on top of a thick wooden pole, and I had to hold it up high as I walked so that the hundreds of folks in the procession could follow it from behind.

When I hoisted the flag, my body ached under my bright crimson graduation robe; the pain kept my mind tethered to all that had transpired the day before. It was unsettling to realize how close I had come to being shut out of all the pomp and circumstance on this glorious sunny day in Cambridge. Music and good cheer accompanied our march along the route. I led the graduates to Harvard Yard, where row upon row of white wooden chairs faced a stage built just for this purpose.

The PhD students were seated near the front. When I took my seat, I felt a flush of relief—that I had carried the flag the entire way, that I had made it through six years of struggle, that I was no longer handcuffed to a wall. When my name was called and I walked across the stage to receive my diploma, the shadow of the previous day was close behind me.

I'd felt so proud in the run-up to this moment. In fact, I had just picked up my dissertation from the bindery the same day that the officer waylaid me. It was bound in black leather, with my name and its title—"Where the Invisible Meets the Obvious"—embossed in gold letters along the spine.

My dissertation focused on the role that race can play in the judgments we make about others' behavior. I'd spent years studying racial stereotypes and sociolinguistics at Harvard. Yet all the laboratory research I'd done had not prepared me for the real-life prospect that one surly policeman, hell-bent on punishing me, could hijack my future and its possibilities. That encounter cost me more than a brief forfeiture of liberty: I lost my sense of security. I felt newly vulnerable. I felt defeated. I'd been so focused on understanding how we judge others; now I had to confront what it means to be judged.

And my ordeal still wasn't over. The day after I led the commencement march, I was due in court to face a judge who would decide where I would walk next.

Dean Gill accompanied April and me to the courthouse. We all arrived in suits, prepared to face the judge and the news to come. The judge called my name, and the three of us stepped forward as the charge was read: assault and battery on a police officer.

All three of us gasped. How could I be charged with assault when I was the one who got roughed up?

The assault charge was based on a single claim in the police report: I'd placed my finger on the officer's hand as he unbuckled my seat belt so he could drag me out of the car.

The judge found the charge as perplexing as I had. She was seated so high up that I had to strain to see her face, but even at a distance I could tell she looked confused. She began flipping through the pages of the police report. Then she looked up and asked, "Was there a language barrier here?" The dean handled that one: "No,

Your Honor. Not on this side." April and I just stood there, open-mouthed and wide-eyed.

The judge's expression turned from confusion to disgust. "It's not against the law to sit in the car," she announced to the court. "I don't understand this. . . . I'm dismissing all of these charges!" She picked up her gavel and banged it, signaling the hearing was done. "Dr. Eberhardt," she said, "you are free to go."

Dr. Eberhardt. That was the first time that anyone had addressed me by that title. At that moment, in that setting, it took my breath away to hear it and to consider everything that it represented. After all, during commencement day when that honorific was bestowed upon me, I was preoccupied not with celebration but with whether I'd leave Cambridge with a criminal record.

STILL NOT QUITE FREE

When I left Harvard, I filed my story away in the back of my mind. It was painful to think about or to discuss—just one more thing that separated me from my Ivy League colleagues. But it did influence my scholarship, by broadening the scope of my work to include the influence of power dynamics and the role of race in the criminal justice process.

The United States has the highest incarceration rate of any industrialized nation in the world. We account for only 4.4 percent of the world's population but house 22 percent of the world's prisoners. More than 2.1 million Americans were behind bars in 2017, and almost 95 percent of those prison inmates will reenter society after their terms are done.

More than 700,000 people are released from American prisons

every year. Many leave with little more than a bus ticket and a bit of pocket money—from $5 to $200, depending on the state. Two out of three will be rearrested within a few years of their release.

Most of those arrests are not for new crimes but for breaking the rules of parole that govern newly released inmates. That mandatory supervision subjects them to years of routine surveillance and reimprisonment for mundane offenses, including failure to secure employment, inability to pay court fines and fees, and missing appointments or curfews. Their status alone dictates their standing in society. Parolees can be stopped and searched by police at any time, even absent probable cause or reasonable suspicion.

In fact, the web of restrictions that parolees live under can imperil the freedom of anybody who looks like them or lives near them. In many heavily black urban neighborhoods, people complain that "Are you on probation or parole?" is often the first question a police officer asks on a routine traffic stop. That presumption is applied to the law-abiding and the convicted criminal alike, because the public presence of ex-inmates blurs the line between the incarcerated and the free.

Because blackness is both statistically and stereotypically intertwined with crime, race can be reflexively treated as a visible marker of criminality.

In Oakland, for example, although blacks make up less than 28 percent of the population, 70 percent of those on probation and 61 percent of those arrested are black. Those racial disparities essentially criminalize entire neighborhoods, encouraging indiscriminate law enforcement stops and keeping in motion the revolving door between freedom and prison.

The prison experience has been shown to dramatically deepen social inequality, marginalizing former inmates in almost every significant sphere of life and stigmatizing their families and communities.

A prison record can stifle earning potential, limit housing options, and derail educational aspirations. Many ex-inmates are barred from living in public housing, screened out of low-income housing-assistance programs, and deemed ineligible for food stamps. In some states, former inmates are banned from certain professions—dental hygienist, barber, nursing-home aide. And even absent formal prohibitions, potential employers are often wary of prospects burdened with criminal records.

Pinpointing the precise role that past incarceration plays in future employment can be tricky. People with criminal records often don't have the same skills, job histories, or work ethic as those without criminal records. But research shows that both race and criminal history can influence hiring decisions in ways that terminally handicap those emerging from prison.

In a now-classic study from 2003, sociologist Devah Pager constructed résumés that were carefully matched on every dimension except for whether the job seeker had a criminal record or a "clean" record. She then trained pairs of black men and white men (of the same age and presentation styles) to use those résumés and pose as applicants for 350 entry-level positions advertised in the Milwaukee area.

She found that those with criminal records received fewer callbacks from prospective employers than those with clean records. Black applicants received fewer callbacks than white applicants. In fact, even blacks with clean records received no more callbacks than white applicants with criminal records.

Years later, in a follow-up study using the same methodology and involving 250 entry-level jobs in New York City, Pager and her colleagues found that the disadvantage of a criminal record was particularly pronounced for blacks.

White applicants with criminal histories were much more likely to be interviewed by employers than blacks with similar records. The rapport-building opportunities that a personal interview offers yielded dividends: whites were better able to persuade someone to take a chance on them. White job seekers with criminal records were 30 percent less likely to be hired than whites with no criminal record, whereas blacks with criminal records were 60 percent less likely to be hired than blacks with no such record.

Racial disparities are woven through almost every layer of life on the outside after a prison term. Even the decline in the marriage rate among African Americans can be attributed in part to racial disparities in the era of mass incarceration. As Stanford legal scholar Ralph Richard Banks pointed out in his book *Is Marriage for White People?*, blacks and whites in the United States married at the same rate in the 1950s, but the black marriage rate has dropped dramatically over the last forty years as more black men were sent to prison and sentences increased.

The disappearance of those men and the burden on their families have destabilized entire black communities. The ripple effects of mass incarceration on children are particularly unforgiving. Some five million children—roughly 7 percent of all children living in the United States—have a parent who is currently or was previously incarcerated, according to data from the National Survey of Children's Health.

Those children tend to grow up with limited social and economic resources. They might be handed off to relatives or wind up in foster care. They are likely to have poor grades and display behavioral problems at school and to experience mental and physical health issues like anxiety, depression, and asthma. And they are significantly more likely than other children to wind up behind bars themselves.

THE INCARCERATED

There are real people, real lives, behind all the statistics. I wanted to learn more about what happened to those shadowy figures who churned through the system—the millions of men and women who'd been arrested, convicted, and sentenced by a criminal justice process that both accommodates and produces dramatic racial disparities.

San Quentin is the oldest and most notorious penitentiary in the California prison system. Its death row holds more than seven hundred inmates awaiting execution. The state has executed only about a dozen people in the past forty years, because of legal challenges to its lethal injection procedure and a backlog in the state's lengthy mandatory case reviews. As a result, its death row keeps growing. San Quentin is now home to more than one-quarter of the entire nation's death row population.

Yet San Quentin also hosts one of the most successful prison education programs in the country. The Prison University Project offers twenty liberal arts courses each year, taught by college professors. To date, 162 prisoners have amassed enough credits to earn their associate of arts degrees.

Research shows that inmates who participate in vocational training or academic remediation behind bars are up to 43 percent less likely to re-offend and return to prison. Yet only about one-third of American prisons offer education or job-training programs. On the whole, little is done in prison to prepare inmates for reentry, despite the obvious financial payoff for the investment; it costs less to help with reentry than it does to fund another prison term.

In 2010, I volunteered to teach an introductory social psychology course to thirty San Quentin inmates. I wanted to understand what life was like for them and to share the work I was doing. I was taking a chance that they would find it useful rather than discouraging. I also hoped that their insights would enrich my research.

The prison sits on a picturesque hillside overlooking the San Francisco Bay. But once you cross its threshold, the institution itself feels severe and regimented. To make my way inside, I had to be checked in by armed guards at two gates, raise my arms to be searched with a metal detector, and present my wrists for the invisible stamp that would allow me to pass into a sally port flanked by heavy iron doors. The doors clanged shut, trapping me there until another guard, perched behind bulletproof glass, released me into the inner courtyard.

I headed toward the education center, past the building that houses men condemned to death and a structure with "Adjustment Center" written in large letters on an outside wall. As I made my way down a hill toward the classroom, I saw dozens and dozens of inmates congregating in small groups in a vast open field. The image unexpectedly flustered me. I realized that I hadn't seen so many black faces in one place in Northern California. There were black men milling around everywhere; inmates who nodded and smiled as I passed, calling to mind the manner of hometown neighbors, uncles, and cousins.

I should not have been surprised by the huge number of black faces I saw. Although blacks make up just 12 percent of the U.S. population, nearly 40 percent of the nation's prison inmates are black. And while the U.S. incarceration rate has been climbing for every racial group over the past forty years—increasing by 500 percent—the rise for those who are poor and black has been especially steep.

According to research by sociology professor Bruce Western, black men born in the late 1940s who dropped out of high school had a 17 percent chance of going to prison by the time they were in their thirties, compared with a 4 percent chance for white male dropouts. However, for black men of my generation, the odds are crushingly worse. Nearly 60 percent of black male dropouts born in the late 1960s wound up in prison, compared with 11 percent of similarly situated whites.

Rising crime can't fully explain the disparities or the massive prison boom. In fact, crime rates across the country fell dramatically over the past twenty years, but incarceration rates continued to climb. That's due largely to a change in how we approached crime: The "war on drugs" imposed harsh penalties on hapless crack addicts. Then came "three strikes" sentencing schemes, which stiffened punishments for habitual criminals and required prison terms for a broader range of crimes. The sentencing enhancements—adopted by dozens of states during the 1990s, when gang violence and drug-related crime peaked—were particularly rough on young black men.

California's three-strikes sentencing law, approved in 1994 by 72 percent of voters, was considered the nation's toughest and most sweeping law of this kind. Over the next two decades, data would suggest that strict laws like California's—where a "third strike" could be something as minor as stealing a dollar in loose change from a parked car—did little to reduce violent crime. But the law did increase the prison population dramatically as more people served longer sentences for relatively petty crimes. And those new three-strikes inmates were disproportionately black.

Against that backdrop in California, a team of Stanford legal scholars, led by David Mills, mounted an initiative in 2012 to revise the law so that a life sentence could be imposed only when the third-strike conviction was a "serious or violent" felony. My colleague Rebecca Hetey and I wondered then how beliefs about the racial makeup of prisons might influence people's support for relaxing the law.

We devised a study that queried California voters on whether they believed the law was too harsh and showed them mug shots of prisoners that varied only in how many of the inmates in the photographs were black. When we tallied the responses, we found that the "more black" we made the prison by manipulating inmate images, the *less likely* these voters were to support scaling back the law.

More than half of those who saw the prison system as it actually was, at 25 percent black, were willing to sign a petition to rein in the harsh three-strikes provisions. But only about one-quarter of the group who saw images depicting the system as 45 percent black were willing to support the less severe sentencing scheme. The blacker the prisons, the more punitive the public was willing to be.

In the end, enough signatures were gathered to place the amendment on the November 2012 ballot. Rather than emphasizing the race issue, the policy change was framed in terms of saving taxpayers money and being smart on crime. The proposed amendment to the policy passed overwhelmingly.

• • •

By the time I arrived at the education building on my first day of class at San Quentin, a line of inmates had begun filing into the room where I was to teach. As the space filled, I caught the faint but unmistakable scent of Ivory soap, a fragrance ever present in my home as I was growing up. That fresh smell seemed to put a fine point on the balancing act I was about to undertake: teaching in a place that was clean but dirty—utterly foreign yet deeply familiar.

I began the way I begin every new quarter at Stanford: I asked the students to state their names and why they enrolled in the course.

One by one, the men introduced themselves. Some were there for reasons I'd expected: They thought the subject would be interesting. They needed the units to complete their college degrees.

But I also got responses that I'd never heard before: Several wanted to take the class to have something to talk about with their families; it was a way of staying connected. One inmate, a tall black man in his early fifties, was worried that his daughter was depressed; he hoped to learn something that he could use to help her through difficult times.

And then there was the Filipino man whom I guessed to be about forty years old. He had been locked up since he was fourteen. "I already know a lot about how things work here, inside San Quentin," he said. "I'm taking this class because I want to know how free people think."

He had spent his entire adult life behind bars and was desperate to understand precisely how imprisonment had warped his view of the world. And I was standing before him unwittingly shackled by the perceptions of a society that dehumanizes and discards men like him. It struck me then that we both were there to move a little closer to freedom.

It wasn't easy, as a professor, to make the adjustment. I had to prepare to lecture without the tools I'd become accustomed to: no computer, no internet access, no PowerPoint slides. With only an ancient overhead projector and a limited number of transparencies at my disposal, I was forced to rethink my approach. I quickly realized that I'd need to hold the inmates' attention with my voice alone. Suddenly the classroom seemed very quiet and I felt very small.

The men stared at me expectantly as I tried to get my bearings. I'd taught this subject many times and knew the spiel by heart, but this was so disorienting that I fumbled through my start.

I broke out in a sweat. But I couldn't tell if that was because I was nervous about teaching in an unfamiliar place or nervous about whom I was teaching. Maybe it was just that the room was hot and I was standing right next to the overhead projector, which was giving off additional heat. There was one thing I knew for sure: that crowded classroom felt like an alternate universe to me, and I had no guide available to interpret the most basic things.

I found myself acutely aware of body movement as I tried to find my comfort zone. I would notice even a small shift in how an inmate was sitting at his desk. My heart raced when I saw a hand rise. I'd remind myself that this was just a student asking a question. No need for alarm. But when one inmate abruptly stood and began walking toward me, I felt panic. *What is he doing? Are they allowed to just move freely around the room? What is going to happen next? Surely the guard outside our door will intervene if something is wrong.*

I peered out the window at the back of the class to see if the guard was reacting as the inmate passed me, headed for the door, and walked out of the classroom. I didn't know what to do or whether I should alert someone.

It turned out that my student was taking a restroom break—a basic thing I'd seen in academic settings thousands of times before. But I felt so off balance behind prison walls I couldn't trust myself to interpret even the simplest acts. I felt fear. I felt taxed. I found myself in a state where bias is most likely to get triggered.

At the time, I was immersed in research showing that the body movements of African American men are deemed more aggressive and threatening than those of other groups. Suddenly I felt like a subject in one of my own studies. I had experienced, in a strong and visceral way, a physiological response to the sight of that black man rising from his seat and moving toward the door. Unbidden, my own bias had exerted itself.

My apprehension eased as the course got rolling. It took only a class or two to feel comfortable with my students and to begin to appreciate what they had to offer. I went from looking for the prison guard to hoping he'd stay away, because his presence tended to stifle our classroom discussion. Whenever he came near the room, the students froze and the conversation went cold.

In time, our classroom became a sheltered space where the cultural practices at San Quentin could be suspended. It was the rare place in an institution divided by racial and ethnic ties where men of different races could mix and be together. I hadn't realized the extent of the racial separation until the day that a third of my class failed to show up. I was waiting for the missing students when a black classmate announced, "The white students won't be here today." In all my years of teaching, that was a phrase I had never heard uttered in an academic setting.

It turns out that there had been a problem in the unit where my white students were housed, and every inmate there was confined to his cell. Nobody could predict how long the lockdown would last. It would be two weeks before I'd see the white students in class again.

Typically, inmates did their time segregated by race. Although official segregation behind the walls was outlawed in 2005, prison officials in California—where institutions are overcrowded and inmates are aligned with gangs—have long relied on racial separation to manage divisions, reduce tensions, and curb gang violence. Inmates lived, ate, and socialized under a system that seemed to me a throwback to the racially restrictive ethos of the Jim Crow–era South. I felt as if I'd walked into a living history book.

The prison's practice both shaped and reflected the prisoners' lives. Segregation wasn't a rule but a culture that was self-imposed and reinforced by the institution—creating the perfect laboratory for the production of bias. Affiliating only with inmates of your race was a way of staying safe. Crossing the race line could get you abandoned, ostracized, or hurt, or worse.

Yet inside my classroom, inmates talked freely across race lines. Black, white, Latino, and Asian faces were transformed into individuals—classmates who had interesting thoughts and perspectives on the world.

Every class reminded me of the power of education to move us beyond our biases and reminded my students of the power of bias to shape their lives.

That first year, I adapted my typical introductory social psychology course to focus on race and crime. I chose discussion topics I thought incarcerated students would find particularly relevant to the circumstances of their lives: racial profiling, police use of force, the science behind false confessions, jury selection, eyewitness testimony, racial disparities in the criminal justice system. I worked hard to winnow big social psychological concepts into concrete topics that I felt would be of interest to students in a prison setting.

It took me a while to recognize that I'd underestimated them in ways that reflected my own one-dimensional thinking about men who were, in real life, more than their prison sentences.

Their interests, it turned out, were not much different from those of the college students I taught at Stanford. They wanted to understand the basic principles of psychology—the value of self, the role of culture, the need to belong, the fundamental desire for affiliation.

I'd been limiting them to their inmate selves, to this one aspect of their being. They were eager to move past the limits that incarceration

imposes and to explore the general ideas and theories that guide people as social beings.

I was surprised to find that I liked that approach much better too.
I could feel the men's intensity as they pondered the material, trying
to relate it to their lives. I could see how the science we studied helped
them understand themselves. Our class discussions provided a break
from the isolation that being locked up enforces and conveyed the
sense that they were part of some larger universal humanity.

Over the course of our months together, my lens broadened as
well. My students' perspectives helped me see in new and intriguing
ways topics I'd been teaching for years. Their intellectual exchange
during class discussions was energizing. But their struggle with basic
academic tasks exposed crippling educational gaps.

Our final class assignment was a term paper on a subject of their
choice. We talked about the format, the research, the content. I thought
I'd prepared them well—until the first drafts of their work flowed in.

I had never seen writing that bad. Many of these men who seemed
so wise and thoughtful in class wrote like elementary school students.

I didn't want to crush their enthusiasm, but I was determined to
do my job. I couldn't pretend that what they had written was ade-
quate. I got out my red pen and marked up their handwritten pages:
*What are you talking about here? . . . I don't understand what your thesis
is. . . . How does this relate to your subject?*

When we returned to class, I could tell they were excited to get
my feedback. I cringed as I thought about giving them papers nearly
obliterated by a cover of red ink. Why had I been so harsh? I tried to
soften the blow with a rambling explanation about how all my comments were offered in the spirit of making their papers better.

They were confused by their professor's unease. *Did my Stanford
students have a problem with harsh feedback?* they asked. "Sometimes," I

said. "When you have people who are used to getting positive feedback their whole lives and you tell them something different . . ." I caught vague expressions of amusement on their faces and cut my answer short.

I was trying to brace them for something—negative feedback—that had been a fixture in their lives. Criticism was a way of life for them. They couldn't understand why I felt compelled to shield them from harsh honesty.

"Some of us are doing life," one student reminded me. "I think we can handle a little red-pen criticism."

I handed back the papers. Their heads went down to study my comments. After some time, their heads lifted, and some seemed moved to near tears. "I just can't even believe it," one man said. "Somebody sat down and spent all this time on my paper, thinking of what would make it better and how I can improve. That's never happened to me before."

I offered them the chance to turn in a second draft for feedback, before the final version was due. And every student in the class took me up on that—even though incorporating my suggestions meant rewriting fifteen-page papers by hand, starting from scratch with a pencil and a sheaf of notebook paper. I critiqued those, and they re-wrote them a third time. They were hungry for rare validation and driven to be heard.

My students knew enough to recognize the bad choices and bad breaks that landed them in prison. But that didn't mean they had abandoned any hopes for their own rescue or achievement or education.

At the same time, with a course like mine, they were getting a better sense of how they as prisoners fit into a larger scheme. That was brought into sharp focus the day I used our overhead projector to display a graph that highlighted rising incarceration rates and the high concentration of black inmates. As I walked them through the numbers, the students sat transfixed. When I reached out to remove the graph, a hand went up with a request: "Can you show that graph again?" Others chimed in with the same request. They stared at the image as though it contained revelations they'd never had access to before.

To me, the graph simply described the environment they were surrounded by on a daily basis. To them, it offered a new way to see that world. Their own solitary, misbegotten lives were veritable data points in a broad public discussion about societal inequality.

In the same way that I realized, after decades of research and analysis, that my arrest in Boston was part of a larger picture of urban policing, the students were learning that they were part of something much bigger than themselves. They weren't merely individuals stuck behind the walls of a particular penitentiary; they were part of a larger pattern playing out in police stations and courtrooms and prisons across the United States—the fallout of our nation's fixation on mass incarceration. During the semester, we would discuss that graph again and again. The racial implications it raised came up in ways that surprised me, infusing my own perceptions with new sensibilities.

Near the end of the course, I introduced my students to a classic social psychology study that measured how the presence of other people influences a person's perceptions of danger.

In that 1968 experiment, researchers Bibb Latane and John Darley had participants sit in a room and complete a survey. Some were in the room alone, and some were there with other students who— unbeknownst to the student being studied—were actually part of the research team.

In both situations, a steady stream of white smoke was directed into the room through a gap at the bottom of a closed door as the surveys were being filled out. Researchers then tracked how long it would take the participant being studied to get up and leave the room.

About three-quarters of the students who were in the room alone assumed the smoke signaled an emergency and left to get out of harm's way.

But the students who were surrounded by others made a different calculation. Those others, who were in on the ruse, had been instructed to ignore the smoke and keep working on their surveys. And 90 percent of those being studied followed their lead and remained, even as smoke filled the room. Only 10 percent responded to the emergency by walking out.

The study had no racial component—or so I thought. I delivered the standard findings to my class just as I'd been trained to do: This study shows that we look to others to determine how to read a situation. An emergency is only an emergency when others around us perceive it to be so.

But my students saw the findings through a different lens. "It's not that you look to *anybody* to tell you how to recognize a crisis. Only certain people matter," one student opined.

Other students were similarly inclined. For years, they'd been complaining—in venues from jailhouse conversations to formal legal briefs—that racial bias is poisoning the criminal justice system. But no one ever seemed to be influenced by them.

"More and more black people are getting trapped in the system, but nobody sees a problem with that," one student said as his classmates nodded. "When we see smoke and yell 'fire,' no one hears. No one listens. No one moves."

THE DEATHWORTHY

Just as prison is reserved for those considered too dangerous to walk the streets, the death penalty—the ultimate sentence—is reserved for those deemed too evil to live.

The United States is one of only four industrialized nations in the world—along with Japan, Singapore, and Taiwan—that still executes criminals. The death penalty is legal in thirty-one of fifty American states, as of 2018. And in almost all of those states, the trial jury decides who lives and who is slated to die.

When jurors are deciding whether to punish someone with death, their calculations invariably involve the concept of retribution: *How far do we need to go to right the wrong that has been committed? What kind of penance would be just?*

That approach assigns a value to the lives of both the murderer and the victim. In the United States, racial disparities in death sentencing are in line with America's history of valuing whites and devaluing blacks.

In death penalty cases, where the stakes are irrevocably high, race can act as the thumb on the scale of justice. Decades of research have shown that murderers of white victims are significantly more likely to be sentenced to death than murderers of black people—even when controlling for nonracial factors that could influence sentencing.

In a landmark study, one of the most comprehensive to date, criminologist David Baldus found not only that those who killed whites were more likely to be sentenced to death than those convicted of murdering blacks, but also that black defendants were more likely to receive a death sentence than white defendants.

The underpinnings of the death penalty as "just deserts" for depravity are reflected in the eighteenth-century work of philosopher Immanuel Kant, who famously asserted that "punishment should be pronounced over all criminals proportionate to their internal wickedness."

What becomes the external proxy for internal wickedness? My research has shown that the mere physical features of black defendants can tip the scale toward execution. In cases involving white victims, the more stereotypically black the defendant is perceived to be, the more likely it is that he will receive the death penalty. Just as the blackness of a penal institution can increase support for punitive criminal justice policies, the blackness of an individual defendant can incline a jury to impose the most severe sentence.

To determine the impact of appearance on jurors' decisions, my team used photographs from Baldus's database of death-eligible defendants—black men convicted of capital crimes committed in Philadelphia between 1979 and 1999. We assembled groups of people who had no idea what our study was about and asked them to rate each photograph on how "stereotypically black" the face appeared. We let the raters know that they could use any number of factors to make their determinations, including skin color, facial features, and hair texture.

We applied their ratings to the photographs and examined the sentences those defendants had received. For black men convicted of killing black victims, there was absolutely no stereotypicality effect. The men whose faces were rated "highly stereotypical" were sentenced to death at exactly the same rate as those who were rated low in stereotypicality.

However, when we looked at black defendants who were convicted of killing white victims, we found a huge stereotypicality effect. Of the men rated low in stereotypical features, only 24 percent were sentenced to death. But more than 57 percent of the "highly stereo-typical" black defendants were sentenced to die for their crimes.

Looking "more black" more than doubled their chances of being sentenced to death, even though we controlled for factors like the severity of the crime, aggravating circumstances, mitigating circumstances, the defendant's socioeconomic class, and the defendant's perceived attractiveness.

That takes implicit racial bias to a whole other level. It's not just group membership that influences perceptions; it's whether an individual's physical appearance triggers the sort of pernicious stereotypes that suggest that blacks are inherently so dangerous they deserve extermination. That's a sign that our perspectives, our criminal justice process, and our institutions are still influenced by primitive racial narratives and imagery.

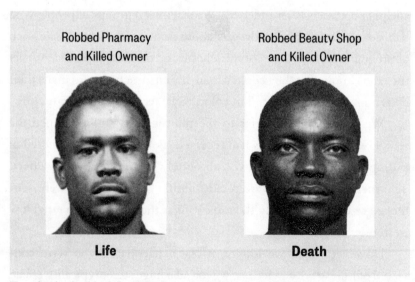

Two death-eligible defendants from the Baldus database. Although the defendants committed similar crimes, the defendant on the left received a life sentence, whereas the defendant on the right received a death sentence.

Indeed, concessions to implicit bias and bigotry have been incorporated over the years into our national perspective on fairness and liberty.

In a 1987 Supreme Court ruling upholding the death penalty for Warren McCleskey, a black Georgia man who killed a white police officer, the court considered a Baldus study of twenty-five hundred Georgia cases, which documented dramatic racial disparities in death penalty sentencing.

Justice Lewis Powell, writing for the five-member majority, acknowledged "a discrepancy that appears to correlate with race." But he dismissed the statistical evidence because "disparities in sentencing are an inevitable part of our criminal justice system."

The ruling came under heavy criticism from legal scholars and civil rights activists; it was even called "the Dred Scott decision of our time." The concern was that it made institutional racial bias simply part of the status quo. And its impact persists today, making it difficult to challenge racial bias in any phase of the justice system without proof of deliberate discriminatory intention.

Powell worried that ruling otherwise would have opened the door to discrimination claims related to all manner of "arbitrary" variables, "even to gender," he wrote. Or to "the defendant's facial characteristics."

Two months later, Justice Powell retired from the Supreme Court. He would later say that his decision in this case—which allowed McCleskey's execution—was the only Court ruling that he ever regretted.

CHAPTER 6

The Scary Monster

The question seemed innocuous enough. My oldest son had just started elementary school and wanted to know what his mother does at work.

"I know you are a social psychologist, but what does that mean?" he asked. "Nobody knows what that is when they ask me, 'What does your mom do?' And I don't know what else to tell them."

I explained that I study human behavior. I try to understand why people think and act the way they do. I walked him through a research scenario: "I bring strangers into a laboratory and keep track of how they react in different situations. I might show them faces on a computer screen, and then look to see whether they like some faces more than others. Is it hard for them to remember the faces when they're tired or in a bad mood? Does having other people in the room lead them to react in a different kind of way?"

I could see him taking in the image of Mom at work in the lab. I was feeling pretty pleased about how our conversation was progressing. Then he hit me with a question that sounded like something out of a horror movie.

"Have you ever asked someone to come into your laboratory and you put them in one of those *situations* and then, right in the middle of your situation, a scary monster jumps out from behind the computer screen and yells, *'Raaaah!!!?'*" He put his hands up high above his head, curled his fingers to mimic a scary monster's claws, and leaned in toward me, as if he were ready to do some damage.

We both laughed at the prospect of some imaginary monster infiltrating my research lab. Then I slowly came to realize that the idea was not as funny as it seemed: I was confronting a scary monster at work all the time.

THE SCIENCE OF THE SCARY MONSTER

When my son was a kindergartner, I was conducting neuroimaging studies on face perception. And I had just begun a project on the history of race and neuroscience. My plan was to write a paper that examined how scientists studied race using neuroscientific methods—from centuries past to the modern day. What I found on that trip back through time both intrigued and sickened me.

I wound up wading through reams of nineteenth-century essays and reports by prominent scholars, attempting to explain the inherent inferiority of blacks. It was at this point, near the beginning of my journey, when I first came upon that scary monster: racial bias of the most vicious kind.

As the slave trade to Europe and the Americas became a flourishing economic system, the subjugation and brutalization of millions of Africans was rationalized by science with theories that decreed the dark-skinned captives less than fully human.

The eminent British surgeon Charles White offered in 1799 what he considered empirical support for the theory that humans originated from multiple sources, asserting a natural hierarchy decreed by racial characteristics. In a volume of essays and engravings, *An Account of the Regular Gradation in Man,* White assessed physical features of different races—depth of jaw, size of skull, length of arms, angle of occipital bones—and declared that each race was a separate species, divinely created with specific immutable traits.

Europeans were the "farthest removed from the brute creation," he wrote. Africans occupied the lowest rungs, a bare step above monkeys and apes. Their darker pigmentation was considered proof that they were more primitive.

Based on the fifty black bodies White examined, "the African seems to approach nearer to the brute creation than any of the other human species," he wrote. What few advantages he allowed the Negroes— strong sense of smell, sound memory, superb mastication skills—were more aligned with dogs and horses than with human beings.

White's findings corresponded to contemporary views of the natural world: "Nature exhibits to our view an immense chain of beings, endued with various degrees of intelligence and active powers suited to the stations in the general system," he contended. Blacks were simply closer to the animal kingdom.

The same year that White's book was published, Samuel George Morton was born to a Quaker family in Philadelphia. He became an internationally admired scientist. He was a physician and Harvard professor. And he founded the field of physical anthropology, which relied on detailed anatomical assessments of once-living creatures.

Morton was obsessed with collecting and studying human skulls; in the 1820s and 1830s, he amassed more than one thousand from around the world and categorized them by race. He believed he could divine the intellectual ability of a race by measuring skull capacity. He poured lead pellets into skull cavities to estimate their capacities. He deduced that the biggest brains belonged to Europeans—with the English at the top of the heap.

Caucasians were distinguished by the "highest intellectual endowments," he wrote. Native Americans were "slow in acquiring knowledge, restless, revengeful, and fond of war." And Africans, "joyous, flexible, and indolent," were representatives of "the lowest grade of humanity."

Morton contended, as had White, that Europeans, Asians, and Africans were separate species, and Europeans were clearly the superior beings. That characterization was embraced by those in antebellum America who were invested in enslaving kidnapped Africans and in "civilizing" or exterminating Native American tribes.

If those groups were not actually human, or at least not as human as whites, there was no need to feel guilty about the atrocities visited on them and no moral threat to an American economy built on the slave labor of black people, who were bought and sold like property for almost 250 years.

Morton died in 1851. But his work was elevated to international prominence by a slew of scientists who also promoted the view that polygenism—separate biological beginnings for each racial group—naturally explained social inequalities.

That theory took a leap forward, enlisting the authority of religion, when Josiah Nott and George Gliddon popularized the science of racial inferiority in 1854 with their widely read book *Types of Mankind*. Their essays reframed the biblical story of creation: Adam and Eve were white; the other races were separate, lowly derivatives, placed by God in separate provinces.

To make their point, Nott and Gliddon displayed the skulls of whites, Asians, and blacks side by side—highlighting differences that they suggest even an untrained eye could see:

> The "Caucasian," *Mongol,* and *Negro,* constitute three of the most prominent groups of mankind; and the vertical views of the following crania . . . display, at a glance, how widely separated they are in conformation. . . . [S]uch types speak for themselves; and the anatomist has no more need of protracted comparisons to seize their diversities, than the school-boy to distinguish turkeys from peacocks, or pecaries [*sic*] from Guinea-pigs.

Nott—the owner of nine slaves—believed that slavery was the natural condition of servile blacks and pledged "in common with the Southern people [to] resist all encroachment on our constitutional and natural rights" to slave ownership.

That theory—known today as scientific racism—was given the imprimatur of irrefutable fact when it was embraced by one of the

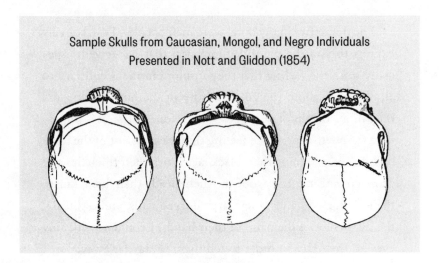

Sample Skulls from Caucasian, Mongol, and Negro Individuals
Presented in Nott and Gliddon (1854)

world's most revered nineteenth-century scientists, Louis Agassiz, known for groundbreaking research on how the physical contours of the world were formed. Agassiz was a prodigious scholar of natural history. In 1837, he was the first to suggest that Earth had been subject to a great ice age that led to mass extinction. In 1846, he emigrated from Switzerland to the United States and joined the Harvard faculty. By 1850, he was the most famous scientist in America. Several parks, mountains, lakes, and animal species are named after him.

But Agassiz also became a tireless champion of polygenism, situating its roots—as did White, Morton, Nott, and Gliddon—in biblical accounts of the creation of life. Agassiz claimed to be an abolitionist but considered black people personally repugnant and had no qualms about campaigning for separation of the races.

He was fascinated by Morton's collection of skulls and found confirmation for Morton's theories about blacks' inherent inferiority in his first encounter with actual Negroes. He described his shock in a letter to his mother:

> The domestics in my hotel were men of color. I can scarcely express to you the painful impression that I received, especially since the feeling that they inspired in me is contrary to all our ideas about the confraternity of the human type and the unique origin of our species. . . . Nonetheless, it is impossible for me to repress the feeling that they are not of the same blood as us. In seeing their black faces with their thick lips and grimacing teeth, the wool on their head, their bent knees, their elongated hands, their large curved nails, and especially the livid color of the palm of their hands. I could not take my eyes off their face in order to tell them to stay far away.

Agassiz insisted that he held no personal animus toward black people, no political interest in propping up slavery. But that claim did not stop pro-slavery forces from capitalizing on his stature as a scientist and claiming an alliance.

For much of the nineteenth century, an accumulation of scholarship focused on racial inferiority provided scientific cover for slavery. Before the science, suspicions were tempered by the possibility of change: the notion that the inferior could rise up the ladder. But once

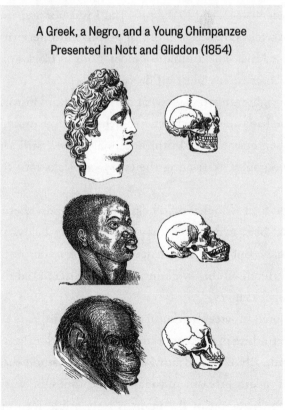

A Greek, a Negro, and a Young Chimpanzee
Presented in Nott and Gliddon (1854)

Here the Negro skull has been exaggerated by Nott and Gliddon to suggest its greater similarity to the chimpanzee than to the Greek god Apollo.

scientists decreed that the racial hierarchy was fixed, skin color and all the differences that implied became a permanent dividing line.

Black people were naturally positioned somewhere between chimpanzees and the highest order of humanity—a difference that could not be bridged by time or proximity.

I spent several years combing through the crumbling, yellowed pages of ancient history books, confronting crude science and garish illustrations of racial caricatures. None of the language I read was all that surprising. In my hunt through the dark ages, I expected to find the voices of scientists locked in the past. But I was not prepared for those primitive sketches, hailed as proof of permanent inferiority. The images repulsed me. The animalistic depictions of black anatomy bore no resemblance to any person I'd ever seen.

It was frightening to view what the late Stanford historian George Fredrickson had called "the black image in the white mind." I couldn't shake the sense that these loathsome images were still a part of our racial iconography, restricting the entry of blacks into the circle of humanity.

I hoped my research would help me explain how these racial narratives seed bias, even when they are operating below the level of consciousness. But first I had to accept that the underpinnings of my own scientific discipline were infused with discredited theories that relied on ape imagery.

Celebrated nineteenth-century French scientist Paul Broca is best known for finding proof that brain functioning is localized, a discovery that radically changed how scientists understood the brain and still guides medical treatment today. In the 1860s, he was the first to identify which region of the brain is responsible for our ability to produce speech. That small spot of cortex in the dominant frontal lobe is today known as Broca's area.

But Broca's interest in brain localization theories was tied to his belief in polygenism. Like many of his contemporaries, he believed that physical features predicted intelligence, and the features favored by European scientists were those they believed to be most common among Europeans. Broca argued that the frontal lobes responsible for higher reasoning were grossly underdeveloped in blacks while the occipital lobes that handle sensory processing were overdeveloped. He offered a scientific rationale for the presumed intellectual inferiority of blacks and used physical distinctions to explain social inequality:

> A prognathous [forward-jutting] face, more or less black color of the skin, woolly hair and intellectual and social inferiority are often associated, while more or less white skin, straight hair and an orthognathous [straight] face are the ordinary equipment of the highest groups in the human series. . . . A group with black skin, woolly hair and a prognathous face has never been able to raise itself spontaneously to civilization.

But Broca's belief in polygenism could not outlast Charles Darwin's theory of evolution. In *On the Origin of Species*, Darwin laid out an irrefutable argument for monogenism: different human races are all of one species. Darwin went on to locate the cradle of humanity in Africa (not Europe, as was commonly assumed) and to claim that we are not fixed but an evolving species responding to the demands of our physical environment.

Although Darwin's discoveries revolutionized science, the belief in black inferiority stood firm. Forced to view all races as members of the same species, scientists and public intellectuals could no longer consider blacks a lowly derivative of those white people whom God created first and in his likeness. Instead, whites became the latest, most complex, most intelligent, most evolved humans in this great chain of advancement. Darwin's radical ideas were quickly accommodated to a racial narrative about blacks that refused to die. And that is precisely what made that monstrous bias so scary to me: it never seemed to die.

Grotesque racial imagery and notions of white supremacy guided much of the scientific investigation of race throughout the nineteenth century, yet psychologists of that era conducted little research on prejudice. Instead, in keeping with scientists in other disciplines, they viewed black antipathies as natural responses to backward and inferior dark-skinned people.

After crude measurements of skull size fell out of favor as a way to certify intellectual inferiority, psychologists brought a new tool to the table—the intelligence quotient test. In the early years of the twentieth century, the IQ test became an instrument that institutionalized bias as it was widely applied to a range of disfavored groups.

By 1910, American scientists had begun administering tests they believed could quantify the mental shortcomings of blacks and natives, relative to whites. Ultimately, that tool was also unleashed on newly arriving immigrants from Europe in the form of a wooden jigsaw puzzle. Those who failed to assemble it quickly and correctly could be labeled "feebleminded." By 1915, federal law required that any immigrant who failed the test be turned away.

The puzzle was a categorization tool for "the sorting out of those immigrants who may, because of their mental makeup, become a burden to the state or who may produce offspring that will require care in prisons, asylums, or other institutions," explained Ellis Island physician Howard A. Knox, the puzzle's designer. He called it "our mental measuring scale." But it was also a symbol of the sweeping influence of the eugenics movement, which aimed to weed out newcomers from countries that might pollute the American gene pool.

Scores on the timed test were used to demonstrate the superiority of the Nordics and advance the case for selective immigration. Immigrants from southern and eastern Europe—Italians, Hungarians, Jews, Slavs—were considered undesirables, a drain on the system that could bring down the entire country. Their low scores, relative to the scores of people from Nordic nations, were used to demonstrate their inferiority. With the passage of the Immigration Act of 1924, the immigration of undesirable groups to the United States was drastically reduced.

For decades, IQ testing helped to map and tally supposedly inherent differences between ethnic groups—that is until Hitler's "Final Solution" exposed the ultimate evil of sanctioned racism.

THE NEW SCIENCE OF DEHUMANIZATION

I set out to explore old notions of racial inferiority so I could measure their residual influence on our minds today. I invited Phillip Goff—a former graduate student, now a professor at John Jay College of Criminal Justice—to join me. We started with some of the same methods we used to study race and crime. We'd learned that visual attention can be driven by stereotypic associations that we are not even aware are operating on us. We modified and re-created our earlier studies and found that subliminally exposing people to line drawings of apes led them to focus their attention on black faces in the same way that crime-related images had. In fact, the results suggested that the implicit association between blacks and apes was much stronger than the black–crime association.

Our brains are constantly being bombarded with stimuli. And just as we categorize to impose order and coherence on that chaos, we use selective attention to tune in to what seems most salient. Science has shown that people don't attend willy-nilly to things. We choose what to pay attention to based on the ideas that we already have in our heads.

That makes attention a mechanism for reaffirming what we already believe to be true about the world. As William James, widely considered the "founder of modern psychology," famously noted in 1890,

> Attention *creates* no idea; an idea must already be there before we can attend to it. Attention only fixes and retains what the ordinary laws of association bring "before the footlights" of consciousness.

The idea, even unacknowledged, that blacks are associated with apes leads us to focus our attention on black faces that, under ordinary circumstances, would remain in the shadows. That focused attention then serves to strengthen the association already in our heads. We see the world that we come prepared to see, even though those preparations are taking place unconsciously.

The black-ape association is sturdy enough to even skew the results of landmark findings in the behavioral sciences. I worked with Aneeta Rattan—a former graduate student, now a professor at the London School of Business—on a series of studies. We added a racial twist to the tried-and-true demonstration of selective attention, the well-known basketball game involving a gorilla. The demo involves a silent, thirty-second video clip of two teams passing around a basketball. When study participants are instructed to count the passes made by one team, roughly half of them are so focused on the task that they don't notice a gorilla mysteriously entering and exiting the scene.

In our twist on the experiment, we gave participants a list of names to sort through before they watched the video. Half the group was given stereotypically white names: Brad, Frank, Heather, Katie. The other group got stereotypically black names: Jamal, Tyrone, Nichelle, Shaniqua. When they watched the video, the group given the black names was much more likely to notice the gorilla. Simply bringing to mind African Americans, via the stereotypically black names, increased the chance that study participants would see the gorilla from 45 percent to 70 percent. And these were college students who, at the time, had no conscious awareness of the racial implications of ape imagery. It's as if the association had been quietly baked into their mental circuitry.

The black-ape association exists beyond the classroom or the laboratory. It's the focus of private jokes and the source of ugly social media memes. It even animates conversations in the law enforcement arena, where the risks and costs of bias are high and lives are on the line.

An investigation of the Los Angeles Police Department in the wake of the 1991 beating of Rodney King made public transcripts of LAPD officers' patrol-car computer chats, which likened blacks to jungle animals and mimicked stereotypical black dialect.

"Sounds like monkey slapping time," one message read. Another, from an officer who was ultimately convicted of beating King, described a domestic violence call involving a black family as "right out of *Gorillas in the Mist*." Officers had even coined a shorthand code for incidents involving black people: NHI. *No humans involved.*

And in San Francisco, as recently as 2016, a slew of text messages exchanged by police officers described blacks and other minorities as wild animals, cockroaches, savages, barbarians, and monkeys.

That kind of animal imagery is troubling, not only because of what it suggests about police attitudes and behavior, but because it can shape how the public evaluates the choices officers make.

In a study I published in 2008 with Phillip Goff and others, we showed people a video of officers surrounding and beating a suspect that our study participants could not clearly see. Some were led to believe the suspect was white, others that he was black. When we exposed the viewers subliminally to ape-relevant words before watching the film, they were more likely to view the brutal police treatment as justified, but only if they believed the suspect was black. Primed subliminally by words like "baboon," "gorilla," and "chimpanzee," they were more likely to believe that the black suspect's behavior made that kind of police violence necessary, that he deserved the beating he received. That's how strong the connection can be. Even when we don't feel or see it, it can operate on us.

• • •

When I set out to present our research on the black-ape association at scientific conferences, I knew I'd find the subject uncomfortable to talk about. But as it turned out, it was much more uncomfortable to hear the audience response. I had anticipated disbelief from scientists surprised by the strength and durability of primitive stereotypes from the nineteenth century. And my collaborators and I had one study after another at the ready to address their skepticism.

But it wasn't so difficult to convince them that blacks are linked—in the minds of ordinary people—to apes. Instead, it was disturbingly easy. The response we received from many of our colleagues, across a wide variety of disciplines, was a sign that the black-ape association registered more broadly than I could have imagined.

At almost every talk, I would take a question from a scientist— young, old, male, female—who would begin wondering out loud about whether our findings were simply due to the fact that blacks actually look more like apes than whites. "Couldn't all of these race effects you're showing simply be due to color matching?" someone would ask. Blacks and apes are similar in color, they'd note. When people see a dark-skinned person, they are more likely to attend to a dark hairy ape because they both look the same.

Those responses troubled me. They transported me back to the late nineteenth century, when psychologists did not question the inherent inferiority of blacks and thus felt no need to examine prejudice. Those reactions reminded me of the unease I felt as I thumbed through the weathered pages of books centuries old to find the most hideous images blaring out at me—black images in the minds of the most brilliant scholars of the day.

But we're now in the twenty-first century, and many scientists not only were unsurprised by our findings but did not believe that racial perceptions were the driving force that allowed the black-ape association to endure. They saw our results without the frame of stereotypes: what we were picking up on was a natural, rational association, not some lingering racial toxicity.

Before this moment in my career, it hadn't dawned on me that educated people would be comfortable enough, certain enough, to say such things in public at scientific conferences (much less think them in private). Even among my contemporary colleagues, this is how we are still seen.

The first few times it happened, it threw me. Then I came to expect it, and I would lay out the same response every time: We find no evidence for a black-squirrel association or a black-alligator association, even though squirrels and alligators are both dark. We only find evidence of a black-ape association. And we get the same results when we use line drawings of apes in our studies rather than dark photographs, so a strict color-matching hypothesis is not supported. In fact, we get the same results when we use words associated with apes rather than pictures. We get the same results when we use stereotypically black names instead of stereotypically black faces. And, by the way, we find no evidence for a South Asian–ape association, even though many South Asians have very dark skin.

The years spent presenting the work left me as disheartened and weary as the years I'd spent conducting the research studies. There is something destabilizing about having to accept that your tribe is seen as a permanent outlier in your country's collective consciousness. That, still, your dark skin is seen as a stain that no measure of progress can cleanly erase. And that many of my own colleagues—the tribe of my profession—harbored those same associations.

Even in my private life, that sadness followed me. On a regular basis, friends and acquaintances outside academia had always been interested to hear about what I was studying and what I had learned. And I had always been eager to talk about my work. But this research did not mix well with polite conversation. It became easier to keep the work private, to simply not talk about the scary monster that wouldn't die. My silence allowed me the escape I needed to try to separate myself from it.

In 2008, I headed to Poland to participate in a workshop on dehumanization. I wondered how the issue presented itself in other countries with other disfavored groups. I wondered whether the black-ape association was simply an American artifact.

I posed the question to conference participants from Poland, Portugal, Italy, Spain, Belgium, England, and Australia. They all knew the answer. With different accents, every single person at the table said the black-ape association was alive and well in their country too. There seemed to me to be no place in the world that was not polluted with the narrative of black inferiority.

Of course, on some level, I had already been primed for this. Contemporary news coverage of racial incidents on soccer fields across Europe and South America would occasionally jar me awake as athletes of African descent (or just dark skinned, no matter what their ethnicity) were jeered and taunted with monkey noises and forced to duck to avoid the bananas thrown at them from the stands. Sitting around that table in Poland, hearing one confirmation after another—hearing one story after another—forced me to accept that this was not just the province of sports hooligans but a broad sociological phenomenon. The more I learned, the more depressing it became.

I ended up collaborating on a project with researchers from the Poland workshop, as well as scientists from Canada, Costa Rica, Brazil, and India. In every one of those eleven countries and the United States, our data collection yielded strong evidence for a black-ape association.

Marginalized groups in countries all over the world are often discredited through animal imagery. Disfavored immigrant groups—Mexicans in the United States, Jews in Germany, the Roma in Italy, Muslims across the European continent—are frequently likened to insects, rodents, and other vermin known to invade spaces, spread disease, or breed rapidly. That has been a universal fixture of history.

When millions of Irish immigrated en masse to the United States in the mid-nineteenth century—on the same converted cargo ships that had carried enslaved Africans to American shores—they were greeted by blatant prejudice. Signs that proclaimed "No Irish Need Apply" were accompanied by simian images of Celtic ape-men with sloping foreheads and monstrous countenances.

But they were able, over time, to leave those ugly caricatures behind and become white. Blacks remain strapped to the ape association by a history of slavery, present-day disparities in almost every significant domain of life, and a collection of overlapping racial stereotypes that reinforce those inequities. In addition to being dark, blacks are seen as cognitively challenged, big, dangerous, aggressive, violent, unrestrained brutes—the very features that, unfortunately, many associate with apes.

Associations can lurk outside our consciousness even when we are not directly taught about them and even when we do not readily discuss them with others. Under the right conditions, however, those associations can be easily summoned. Certainly, the election of Barack Obama brought the black-ape association to the surface, resurrecting images and tropes that were presumed to have faded with (what we thought were) the last vestiges of the Confederacy.

In Orange County, California, a prominent Republican official sent an email to other party leaders with what was billed as a family photograph of Obama and his parents. It was two gorillas holding a baby superimposed with Obama's face. A government official in tiny Clay County, West Virginia, called Michelle Obama an "ape in heels" in a Facebook post celebrating Donald Trump's election. Even their daughter Malia was maligned. Fox News had to disable the comment feature on an article about her decision to attend Harvard after readers flooded the post with racist comments, calling the teenage girl an "ape" and a "monkey."

For many Americans, that forced a sober reckoning about something we thought was in the past. The ascent of a black man to the pinnacle of prestige and power had triggered a virulent backlash—one that aimed to delegitimize the black family in the White House by separating them from the human family.

The demeaning images sickened but didn't surprise me. By then, I'd spent five years poking around in the dustbins of science, trying to figure out what brought us to this point. I'd begun this particular journey with faith in the power of modern-day neuroscience to dismantle the vestiges of scientific racism. And I would end the journey in an unlikely place: a classroom at San Quentin State Prison.

I stood there presenting my findings before people who struggled for their humanity on a daily basis. They listened with rapt attention: leaning forward, taking notes, and asking the kinds of questions I'd expected to receive at scientific conferences. But more than that, my work on race and dehumanization felt deeply familiar to them, though they never had the words available to discuss the impact it had on their lives. Their identity as human was constantly under threat. They were society's caged animals. And they were the only audience I presented this work to that did not squirm. They received it with gratitude.

When I ended the presentation, the students rose spontaneously, formed a single line, and began moving forward toward me. One by one, each man reached out to shake my hand. "Thank you for sharing your work." "Thank you." Again and again. And when the last student reached me, his arm outstretched, he shook his head from side to side and paused for just a moment to gather his thoughts. "I appreciate what you do. I really do," he told me, looking straight into my eyes. "But I don't know how you do it. We need this work, but how are you able to carry those facts. That's some real heavy shit you just shared." These were the parting thoughts of a black man serving a life sentence.

Their reaction led me back to consider, once again, what drew me to study the mental associations that fuel bigotry and shape inequality. Sure, it was depressing work. But I'd come to realize that I wasn't bound to the misery, even though that misery had begun to occupy more and more space in my mind. I could reconfigure my thinking and reconnect with the hope that had propelled me from the start.

I could pick up the tools of neuroscience to demonstrate how humans are not static beings affixed to a predetermined hierarchy. Our brains, our minds, are molded and remolded by our experiences and our environments. We have the power to change our ways of thinking, to scrub away the residue of ancient demons.

As social threats rise, cultural norms shift, and group polarization turns extreme, we are being subjected to ever more brazen displays of dehumanization—magnifying our worse impulses. We can't afford to let them flourish.

Part III

THE WAY OUT

CHAPTER 7

The Comfort of Home

I was still getting attuned to the nuances of motherhood when I headed into the Target store near Palo Alto with my five-month-old son. I set his car carrier on the floor next to my feet. As I sorted through the racks of baby clothes, he was staring bright-eyed up at me.

Out of the corner of my eye, I saw a little girl skitter around the corner and head toward us. I wasn't good yet at pegging children's ages, but she looked to be about three. She was wearing a big smile, a cute little dress, and a bow in her wispy blond hair.

She stopped when she spotted Ebbie; her eyes got as wide as saucers. I heard her take a deep breath as she stared at him, then let it out in a whoosh. She squealed with what sounded to me like joy and began to bounce in place and wave her hands around, as if the excitement were too much for her small body to contain. Then she turned on her heels and ran off, calling for her mother.

I scooped Ebbie up and followed the sound of the little girl's voice: "*Mommy! Mommy! Mommy!*" I could hear her from an aisle away, once she spotted her mother. "Mommy, Mommy! Guess what?"

she said, her voice vibrating with the thrill of discovery. "Guess what I saw! A brown baby! A brown baby! There's a brown baby over there!"

She was so excited, her innocence so unbridled, I couldn't help but laugh. I looked down at Ebbie and he looked back at me with these really big brown eyes. And then I thought, "You know, he *is* a brown baby." His skin was the color of milk chocolate, his hair a mass of curls in different shades of coppery brown, and I'd dressed him for the day in a pair of brown overalls.

I made my way around the corner toward the girl and her mother. This is so cute and funny, I thought. I approached the pair with a smile on my face, ready to share a laugh.

But her mom looked mortified. Her white skin had flushed a bright shade of red; her face, her neck, her chest, all signaled to me the embarrassment she felt. So worried about how I would react to her daughter mentioning the unmentionable, perhaps she didn't notice my smile. I watched as she turned and rushed off with her child.

Just a few steps earlier, I'd imagined that we were about to have this moment of bonding; she was part of the in-group of motherhood that I'd just joined, and I was as wide-eyed as her daughter about the wonder of that. In one brief encounter, I had witnessed the power of skin color to both delight and divide and, with her embarrassed departure, didn't have the chance to reach across that divide.

Our family had just moved from New Haven, Connecticut, to Palo Alto, California, which was and still is only about 2 percent black. We lived in a condominium complex on the edge of Stanford's campus where, of the hundreds of faces surrounding us daily, the only other black person we'd seen was Condoleezza Rice, heading for her car or taking out her trash.

This de facto segregation is not a unique phenomenon of Silicon

Valley (though it's rampant there). Multiethnic communities are multiplying across the country as urban areas become more diverse, but black and white Americans are still likely to wind up in separate neighborhoods. That little girl's unbridled surprise reflects that residential divide—a separation rooted in history, grounded by economics, and perpetuated through the enduring force of bias.

SEGREGATED SPACE

The patterns of residential racial segregation that we live with today are a legacy of our nation's not-so-distant past, when public institutions and private social forces conspired to keep white neighborhoods white by restricting where black people could live.

The federal government played a direct and deliberate role in creating segregated spaces: refusing to back mortgage loans in racially mixed neighborhoods, subsidizing private development of all-white suburbs, and restricting GI Bill housing benefits so that black military veterans could buy homes only in minority communities.

Those government practices were supported and reinforced by local laws and customs that allowed segregation's reach to extend to schools, hospitals, hotels, restaurants, and parks.

Discrimination—not income or choice or convenience—dictated where black people could live. As far back as the early twentieth century, zoning regulations in many cities forbade blacks to move into white neighborhoods. Black families who tried to integrate were often met with mob violence. Civil rights groups turned to the courts for remedies, and racial-zoning ordinances were outlawed by the Supreme Court in 1917. But that ruling paved the way for a new segregation tool that was just as potent and harder to fight. Racially restrictive covenants were written agreements that obligated white homeowners to refuse to sell, rent, or transfer property to "any person not of the Caucasian race." Anyone who dared to violate the covenant could be sued or forced to move.

In states across the country—from California to Montana to Maryland to New York—courts upheld the eviction of blacks from homes they had purchased, ruling that unlike formal zoning restrictions these were voluntary private contracts. As a result, by the 1940s, 80 percent of the neighborhoods in cities like Chicago and Los Angeles were off-limits to blacks.

The covenants were invalidated by the Supreme Court in 1948. But the residential patterns and ethnic ghettos they created continue to exist—accelerated by actions and edicts of the federal government.

Federal money helped ensure that segregation flourished in the 1930s and 1940s. Depression-era public housing projects, built with taxpayer funds, were designated either black or white. Private builders could get federally backed loans only if they inserted racial restrictions in their subdivision deeds. The federal agency created to make home ownership accessible refused to approve bank loans to black people, or even to people who lived near black people.

It wasn't until 1962—with the civil rights movement well under way—that the principle of equal opportunity in housing became a national concern, and President John F. Kennedy ordered federal housing agencies to stop discriminating. Two years later, the Civil Rights Act of 1964 banned racial discrimination by any organization that received federal funds.

But neither remedy had much impact on a housing market that was driven by private brokers, bankers, and builders. It would take another four years—and a wave of urban riots—for Congress to pass the Fair Housing Act of 1968, with its wholesale ban on discrimination in building, marketing, financing, leasing, and selling residential property.

By then, the instruments of government-sanctioned bias—zoning restrictions, racial covenants, mortgage refusals, and a building boom in suburbs open only to whites—had already taken their toll, forcing black families to crowd into undesirable areas where amenities were few, the housing stock was often decrepit or cheaply built, and the streets were lined with factories spewing industrial pollution.

The residue of those discriminatory practices lingers today, fueling stereotypes that seed the stigma attached to black people and black places. Research has shown the power of those stereotypes to shape one of the most fundamental decisions of our lives: where we make our homes. African Americans are more likely than any other group to live in segregated neighborhoods. That residential isolation persists across the social and economic spectrums, in cities large and small. And it is reinforced by prejudicial associations that are shocking to document.

More than half of whites say they would not move to an area that is more than 30 percent black, because they believe that the housing stock would not be well maintained and crime would be high. In fact, according to studies by sociologists Lincoln Quillian and Devah Pager, the more blacks there are in a community, the higher people imagine the crime rate to be—regardless of whether statistics bear that out. That correlates with fear and with bias. The "blacker" they believe their neighborhood to be, the more likely whites are to expect that they will be victimized by crime. The sheer presence or absence of blacks in a space is taken as a true indicator of danger, distorting safety perceptions and biasing people's sense of risk.

Race affects people's judgment of physical conditions as well. Sociologists Robert Sampson and Stephen Raudenbush have found that the more blacks there are in a neighborhood, the more disorder people see, even when their perceptions don't correspond to measurable signs like graffiti, boarded-up houses, or garbage in the street. And black people are just as likely as whites to expect signs of disorder in heavily black neighborhoods.

That suggests a sort of implicit bias that has more to do with associations we've absorbed through history and culture than with explicit racial animus. But the outcome is tragic nonetheless. Decades of studies have shown that white avoidance of neighborhoods with more than a handful of blacks is a key driver of the kind of racial segregation that fosters inequality in every area of life, from school to employment to health care.

The relationship between race, space, and inequality was a theme of a paper I published with social psychologists Courtney Bonam and Hilary Bergsieker in 2016. Our research has shown how collective stereotypes shape individual housing choices, even when we think our actions are race neutral. Negative perceptions tied to race and physical space encourage social distance in ways that reinforce segregation and keep us from getting to know one another.

In one online study, we asked people to list the characteristics of spaces associated with black people. There was high agreement among people of every race on what those characteristics were: *impoverished, crime-ridden, run-down, dangerous, dirty.* Just as people share stereotypes about social groups, so too do they share stereotypes about the spaces those groups occupy.

In another study, we recruited people who were house hunting on Craigslist and asked them to evaluate a hypothetical home being sold by the hypothetical Thomas family. All participants saw the same pictures of a three-bedroom suburban home on a quarter-acre lot and read the same description of its features and improvements. We changed one variable only: the race of the homeowners. Some participants were shown a photograph of a clean-cut black family standing in an empty room in the house; others saw a similar white family in that same spot.

The house hunters we queried evaluated the house being sold by the black Thomas family more negatively than the identical house occupied by the white family and predicted that more would need to be done to spruce it up to attract buyers. In fact, simply imagining other black families in the neighborhood led them to set the value of the home at nearly $22,000 less. And even when we gave them no information at all about the surrounding community, they pictured a neighborhood with limited access to shopping, inferior city services, mediocre schools, and less well-maintained properties when the prospective seller was black.

In some ways, that reflects a rational perception, with roots in real estate history. Fifty years ago, it was common for lenders to summarily draw red lines on a map around black areas and refuse to loan money to people who wanted to buy homes there because financial investment was considered too risky, the substandard neighborhoods too unlikely to hold their value. That sort of redlining shaped both perception and reality. Exposing even open-minded buyers to a photograph of the black Thomas family tapped negative space-based associations, which left our participants feeling "less connected" to the neighborhood. Even when a black family is moving out, they leave behind a taint that renders their home less valuable simply because they have lived in it.

You don't even need a family picture to trigger that taint. In one study we conducted, participants were asked to take the perspective of an employee at a chemical company tasked with finding a site for a potentially dangerous chemical plant. Half of our study participants read that the neighborhood under consideration was predominantly black while the other half believed it was majority white. When participants thought they were considering a black neighborhood, they were more likely to assume that there were already industrial facilities there, to feel less connected to the neighborhood, and to express less opposition to building the chemical plant there. Stereotypic images of black spaces, buttressed by historical and current-day racial inequalities, led our study participants to imagine black space as polluted. And that image led them to be less protective of the space and more inclined to compound existing environmental threats.

POLLUTED PEOPLE

The same associations that lead us to judge spaces as dirty and polluted can transcend those spacial boundaries and cling to the people who have called those places home. Across history and around the world, immigrants have borne the burden of that sort of place-based prejudice that presumes that the stench of squalid places clings to human beings. The perceived taint of the countries they've fled follows them to new homes, influencing public discourse over their presence and limiting the choices they can make.

Research has shown that attitudes about immigration are largely shaped by concerns about the cultural impacts of a flood of newcomers, their differences from the dominant stock. And that has led to the creation of policies to contain them, both in the United States and in European countries.

In the United States, that's taking shape in travel bans, limits on refugees and asylum, proposals to end the practice of "chain migration" that allows legal immigrants to bring their families here, and harsh policies that separate children from parents caught trying to cross the country's border with Mexico.

In Europe, immigration is being framed as a security risk as waves of people from Africa and the Middle East pour into once largely homogeneous nations. Perspectives on immigrants are shifting across the European continent, and hate crimes aimed at Muslims are rising dramatically, fueled by the same concerns about social disruption and notions of inherent inferiority that have fed the separation of races in America.

Newly arriving immigrants are often described in terms that suggest pollution: "dirty," "filthy," "diseased." Those perceptions can spontaneously trigger a cascade of protective impulses—even among people who support immigration and welcome newcomers. Yale social psychologist John Bargh and his colleagues have studied the connection between immigration status and fear of disease. It is tighter than we realize.

In an online study measuring attitudes on immigration—conducted in the midst of the 2009 swine flu epidemic—study participants read about the threat of the flu virus just before they were surveyed on their feelings related to immigration. Afterward, they were asked if they'd been vaccinated against the flu. Bargh found that those who had not received flu shots expressed more negative views about immigration than those who had been inoculated against the virus. Their sense of vulnerability to disease was tied to unacknowledged fears about infected immigrants.

Immigrants aren't the only group viewed through the lens of bias as diseased outsiders. Homeless people are even lower on the sociological totem pole. Social psychologists Lasana Harris and Susan Fiske have found that homeless people are considered so tainted that their stigmatized status is reflected in the inner workings of our brains.

Typically, when you look at another person, an area of the brain called the left medial prefrontal cortex comes alive as neurons begin firing vigorously. Yet when Harris and Fiske showed pictures of homeless people to study participants inside a neuroimaging scanner, neurons that are typically highly responsive to the sight of others were significantly less active. Instead, the insula and amygdala—areas of the brain associated with disgust—were more active.

The circumstances of homeless people blunted the natural response to others whom we recognize as sharing our humanity. Living without the comfort of a home does more than reduce their status in society; their status as human beings begins to slip away as well.

Even when outlier groups are accepted by the dominant society, that acceptance can be provisional, tied to prevailing cultural, political, and economic winds. When fortunes turn, or a crime occurs, or social problems mount, they are easy targets for blame or persecution.

A student I met at Stanford, Mauricio Wulfovich, shared with me the story of his grandfather, a Holocaust survivor whose sister and parents died at the hands of a Nazi regime intent on exterminating Jews, a group that had been scapegoated, labeled "undesirable," and considered a threat to the Aryan concept of racial purity.

Mauricio's grandfather was fifteen, the youngest of six children in a family of shoemakers and tailors living in a Polish shtetl a hundred miles from Warsaw when the Nazis came. They gathered the Jews in a castle in the village, then crammed them into cattle cars like livestock and headed to Auschwitz, the largest of the German concentration camps. When they unloaded the captives, "there were two lines," Mauricio said. "One for the weaker people and one for the people who could work. My grandpa's father and his mom and his sister went with the people who went straight to be gassed. . . . That's the last point he saw anyone in his family ever again."

His grandfather credited his own survival to his obsession with appearing clean, healthy, and strong. "He thought appearance really mattered when the Nazis would choose who were the next people they were going to kill and who would get to continue working," Mauricio explained.

The prisoners could shower only outside in freezing weather, but he never missed a chance to bathe. He monitored his shoes for any grime he could wipe away. And he was always on the lookout to trade his daily rations—two pieces of bread—for nicer, better-fitting clothes. He figured he'd be considered more durable if he didn't look bedraggled. He couldn't escape his status as a Jew, but he could present himself as valuable, as worthy enough to live another day.

Mauricio heard bits and pieces of the story as he grew up. His grandfather died when he was nine. But he still remembers seeing two prisoner ID numbers tattooed on his grandpa's arm. One set of numbers had been crossed out and a second set added, he said, "because the Nazis were still figuring things out. They treated his arm like it was a piece of paper. . . . 'Oh it's the wrong number? Just cross it off and write another one.'"

Auschwitz was his "home" for two and a half years, until the camp was liberated when he was eighteen years old. He moved alone to Israel, then discovered he had a distant relative who'd settled in Mexico and made that his home. That's where Mauricio was born.

His grandfather's story highlights the potency of ancient stereotypes. The "dirty Jew" rhetoric that powered persecution of Jews since the Middle Ages had begun to penetrate the newspapers, pamphlets, and everyday conversations—every aspect—of twentieth-century German life. The ugly epithet had worked its way into the minds of the average citizen. Mauricio's grandfather understood that well enough, even as a boy, to marshal all his powers to repel it amid the filth, squalor, and deadly threat of the German concentration camp.

But sometimes the taint of stereotypes can't be cleared so efficiently. In the United States, European immigrants were able over generations to wash the dirt away and become absorbed into the American mainstream. Yet dark skin presents a different predicament, with its persistent visual connection to damaging tropes that have endured for centuries.

Thomas Jefferson understood this back in the late eighteenth century when he considered the plight of black slaves in the southern states. In *Notes on the State of Virginia*, he referenced the "immoveable veil of black" that would always signal African heritage. This "unfortunate difference of color," he wrote, "is a powerful obstacle to the emancipation of these people." The father of the Declaration of Independence suggested then that American blacks might be forever marked as outsiders by skin color. And two hundred years later, the renowned African American author Ralph Ellison wearily agreed. Blacks in America are like "flies in the milk," he wrote. "Negroes suffered discrimination and were penalized not because of their individual infractions of the rules which give order to American society." Rather, it is our dark skin.

ABSORBING SPACE

Part of the stigma of black skin has to do with cultural associations that mark white as a sign of purity and black as something else entirely. Indeed, research shows that people quickly and effortlessly associate the color black with immorality. Social psychologists Gary Sherman and Gerald Clore found evidence for this automatic association in a series of studies that involved a standard color-naming task. Study participants were shown a series of words on a computer screen. Each word appeared in white font or in black font. The researchers found that people were faster to name the color of words having to do with immorality (for example, "vulgar") when they appeared in black font than when the same words appeared in white font. Likewise, people were faster to name the color of words having to do with morality (for instance, "virtuous") when they appeared in white as opposed to black font. "Sin is not just dirty," the authors write, "it is black. And moral virtue is not just clean, but also white."

These associations allow implicit bias to turn skin color into a value judgment. But skin color is really just a marker for where on earth our ancestors have lived. Across tens of thousands of years, as humans have migrated around the globe, our skin color has changed to meet the demands of the new environments that became their homes.

As harmful ultraviolet radiation emitted by the sun beat down on early humans, the melanin pigment that our bodies produce came to the rescue. Melanin provides protection. And the more melanin our bodies produced, the darker our skin appeared. Melanin is produced by a variety of species—from frogs to dates—and like humans their color darkens in accordance with the environment of their habitat. "Skin color," anthropologist Nina Jablonski explains, "is one of the most obvious patterns of human biological variation." And melanin is highly responsive to the physical space we find ourselves in.

Just as physical space can change how we look, the particulars of a specific space can influence how our minds work and what judgments we make. I learned to appreciate that power the summer I traveled to Jamaica for a family vacation with my husband and our three teenage boys.

My husband, Rick, is the adventurous type. So when he decided he wanted to drive us through the noisy, congested city streets of Montego Bay and along winding country roads leading who knows where, I got a little worried. In Jamaica, they drive on the opposite side of the road, British style, with the steering wheel on what Americans would consider the passenger side. My husband had been driving on the right side of the road for thirty-five years. The scientist in me wondered if that long indoctrination had left its mark on the neural pathways of his brain. The mother in me just hoped our family would make it to our destination unscathed.

"We are American," I reminded Rick as we picked up the car and settled into our unfamiliar spots. Everything around us seemed to be on the wrong side, including the streetlights and signs. The boys got a kick out of seeing their dad maneuvering the steering wheel from the opposite side of the car. I sat in the front next to him, determined to be the sentry who would ensure that we stayed safe on unfamiliar roads in this unorthodox arrangement.

Right away, I could tell we were going to have problems. From my perch on the left side, where the driver should be, it took some time to shake the feeling that I was the one actually driving. I had to try hard to keep my arms from moving up to grab a steering wheel that was not there. I found my right foot pressing down to slow the car as we closed in on the traffic ahead.

The first time I saw a car heading toward us from the opposite direction, I was ambushed by panic. "Stay left! Stay left!" I warned. Yet even as I yelled out the correct advice, something inside me kept signaling that we should stay to the right. That mental tug-of-war set my heart to racing. *We are headed for disaster,* I thought, as yet another car zipped past us on what felt like the wrong side of the street. I knew in my mind where we were supposed to be, but my body was feeling something else. Everything inside me was spontaneously firing, signaling, "This is wrong. You are in danger! Get over to the right."

By the time we made it to the center of town, rush hour was upon us. I don't like being in rush hour traffic in California, let alone in a foreign country on the wrong side of the road. But I needed to stay calm as we navigated avenues crowded with cars, bikes, motorcycles, and people standing in the middle of the street peddling their wares.

We finally made it to a long stretch of highway that headed toward the countryside. We relaxed enough to enjoy the scenic vistas we passed and even made a brief stop at a local tourist spot. It wasn't until we headed back to town that our driver's mental gymnastics faltered.

As Rick began to merge onto the highway, the boys began screaming in the backseat. I turned my head to see what was wrong and got the scare of my life: Two giant eighteen-wheelers were speeding straight toward us, barreling down the highway, side by side, at breakneck speed. But Rick had not noticed them, because he was looking the other way—in the direction that traffic would be approaching if he was merging onto a road in California. I joined the yelling, but Rick was focused on the task at hand, steadily creeping onto the highway into the path of the trucks—still looking the other way, not comprehending what all our fuss was about.

The truck drivers never slowed, presuming we would stop. Who wouldn't stop? In a fury, I yelled as loud as I could, "Stop! Stop! Stop the car right now!" The panic in my voice led my husband to slam on the brakes, and we all watched as the trucks sped past, just inches away from the front of our car. I was sweating profusely, and my heart was pounding hard. We sat for a long few moments in stunned silence.

A lifetime of driving on the right side of the road in the United States had shaped my husband and me more than we realized. It shaped not only how we situated our vehicle on the road but also where we were inclined to look, how and when we turned our heads, and what captured our attention. It shaped a cascade of reflexive choices that every driver makes.

There was a complex, coordinated system within us, operating beneath our awareness and difficult to override. A whole host of actions are required to support the act of driving, but we had become oblivious to them over decades behind the wheel; we operated on "instinct," though it was wholly learned. I'd gotten in the car that day expecting to provide an extra set of eyes that could help protect our boys, yet it was precisely because our sons had no driving experience that they could see the trucks that Rick and I had missed. They had not been conditioned to look only in certain ways or expect to see specific things.

In many ways, this is how bias operates. It conditions how we look at the world and the people within it, despite our conscious motivations and desires, and even when such conditioning can put us in harm's way. Just as drivers are conditioned by how the roads are constructed in their native land, so too are we conditioned by racial narratives that narrow our vision and bias how we see the people around us.

MIGRATING

Spend enough time in any one place, and its default conditions can become your comfort zone. For white southerners in the early twentieth century, that default required African Americans to occupy a subservient role that had advantaged generations of whites—a role rooted in narratives of black inferiority that had persisted since slavery.

My father's great-grandfather and his two brothers were born into slavery in Georgia in the mid-nineteenth century. Each boy was sold to a different slave owner. One brother became the property of the Herd family, the other became the property of the Fittens, and my father's great-grandfather belonged to the Eberhardts. After slavery ended in 1865, all three took the surname of their owners and became sharecroppers, farming small patches of land near where they'd been enslaved.

The prospect of sharing power with blacks in the aftermath of slavery led southern whites to create a racial caste system that continued the repression of black people, by custom and by law. Relying on the sanction of Jim Crow restrictions, white southerners built a physical environment to support and reinforce black inferiority. Everyday routine interactions conditioned everyone to know and accept their place. A black man had to step off the sidewalk to let a white man pass. A black woman was never addressed with the honorific "ma'am." The narrative of inferiority was inscribed on everything they saw, did, and touched.

In 1910, almost fifty years after slavery officially ended, African Americans made up 10 percent of the U.S. population. But 90 percent of black people still lived in the South, where the promise of Reconstruction had been obliterated by the white backlash of terrorism and Jim Crow laws.

Over the next decade, blacks began leaving for the same reasons maligned peoples all over the world migrate: to exchange repression for opportunity. As the demands of World War I expanded the labor market, black southerners streamed into northern cities, lured by the prospect of better, freer lives. That migration would change the complexion of urban industrial hubs like Chicago, Pittsburgh, New York, Cleveland, and Detroit.

In 1921, my father's grandparents, York and Emma Eberhardt, left their home in Hartwell, Georgia, to join the first wave of black migrants who left the South. Along with a million others, they headed north, enticed by industries wooing southern blacks with advertisements in black newspapers, offering transport and well-paying jobs. They landed in Cleveland, where York found work as a laborer in a coal yard and later at the Cleveland Railway, laying track. They moved into an area that would become known as part of the Central Avenue ghetto; the neighborhood had been home to poor Jews and immigrant Italians, but the flood of southern newcomers turned it black. It was in Cleveland that their son Hoyt met and married his sister's best friend, a young woman named Bessie. They had six children. My father, Harlan, born in 1936, was their second child.

My mother's family was part of a second migration wave, which began in 1940 and drew five million more southern blacks to northern cities. My mother's parents were both raised in Anniston, Alabama. They left the South behind in 1948 and landed in Cleveland, where they lived until they died.

Many black families I knew with roots in the South went back to visit regularly. But we never did. I never saw Anniston or knew what made them leave so abruptly. It wasn't until I began writing this book that curiosity prodded me to search the leaves of my family tree for insight into their journey. I tracked down my grandfather's cousin in Chicago, and she helped fill in missing pieces of their history. At ninety-two, Jean still had incredibly sharp memories of growing up with my grandfather in Anniston.

My grandfather and his younger brother had moved in with Jean and her mother after their parents died when the boys were still in elementary school. Sidney was "quite sophisticated" even then, Jean recalled. He was active and sociable and "into everything." As the boys came of age, Sidney stayed on the go, until he fell in love with Mabel and married her in 1935. They bought a small house and had two children—a boy they called Sunny and a girl, my mother, whom they called Little Mary.

Sidney was working at the steel mill in Anniston, just up the street from Jean, when the trajectory of his life changed overnight. Jean remembers the day she saw him rushing toward home with his work clothes on, in such a hurry that it was clear to her that something must have happened on the job. Sidney had always been on the "jumpy side," she said, but never this anxious. "He came and asked me if I had any money because he was going to leave Anniston and he had to go right away," Jean recalled.

She handed over what money she had, and Sidney took off running down Cooper Avenue, toward downtown. He boarded a train and vanished, without even saying good-bye to his wife and children. He called home after he landed in Cleveland, where an older sister was already living. A few weeks later, Mabel, Sunny, and Little Mary boarded the "Colored Coach" on a train headed for Cleveland.

Jean never found out what happened at work to send him fleeing—and considered it "undignified" to ask—but she still remembers the fear on her cousin's face. "I gave him everything I had because he looked like he needed it. I didn't know what was wrong, but I knew something was wrong."

As Jean spoke, I imagined my mother at nine years old, suddenly deprived of a father she loved. I imagined her wrenched from the only home she'd known. What did her mother tell her about why they had to move? What could have happened to make her father leave so abruptly? How could she comprehend leaving the comfort of home for a mysterious place, far, far away in the North?

Whatever peril he faced that day in Anniston, Sidney could not rely on the police for help. The experiences of others had taught him that. It was safer to flee. "If he was in trouble, the last person he's gonna call is the police," Jean explained to me. "Oh no. You end up getting killed fooling around calling the police." Jean took a thoughtful pause before she offered a final underscore: "I just never heard—and this is the truth, Jennifer—I have never heard in Anniston in all the while I lived there of anybody that had called in the police."

Her stories made clear that what made the South so difficult for blacks was more than the constant reminders of second-class citizenship: the separate drinking fountains, schools, restaurants, restrooms, and areas for waiting, sitting, standing, and healing. It was the ever-present threat of violence, without protection or redress. Segregation was the rule, and the police, widely considered an extension of the Ku Klux Klan, were the enforcers. "Colored people, if you want to know about that, they took care of themselves," Jean explained to me.

The South was especially perilous for colored girls, who were often preyed upon by white men who knew there would be no consequences for raping and assaulting them. According to the city's historical records, it wasn't until 1965—long after my mother's family had left the South—that a white man was ever convicted of a crime committed against a black person in Anniston.

Jean still remembers the rules black girls had to memorize before puberty arrived: If they were by themselves and thought they were being followed, they should duck inside the nearest safe space and not leave until a friend or family member arrived. "They had certain places that were set up for you to go in and call to see if you can get somebody to come and help you," Jean recalled. Every girl had to know where those safe spaces were.

Anniston was segregated in every way imaginable then. Blacks had no choice but to steel themselves against the indignities. Jean still recalls the trips downtown that took her along a path through the park "right by the white kids in the pool that black kids couldn't go in." The lines were so rigid that whites who lived "too close" to blacks were tainted by proximity and labeled "poor white trash."

Every action, big or small, was evaluated on the basis of whether it upheld or challenged the social order, and any challenge could be met with violence. Jean was just a small child when that reality was seared into her psyche. She remembers a day in the early 1930s when masses of white people began congregating on a narrow two-lane road that led out of Anniston and toward Atlanta. Jean was too far away to see them clearly, but she could hear their footsteps and the sound of their voices as they moved through town. And she could sense the anger building in the air and feel the fear emanating from the black people surrounding her. That made her feel afraid too. She listened to the murmuring of her relatives and neighbors to figure out what was happening.

The commotion in the distance turned out to be the rallying of a lynch mob, gathering to hang a black man whose crime was being too prosperous. "His farm did better than all the others," Jean explained. That was too much for struggling white farmers to accept as their fortunes fell during the Depression. The mob was led by a minister who pastored the largest white Baptist church in Anniston. To this day, Jean is stung by the irony: "How can a minister of a church lead a lynch mob?"

For years after that, whenever her family took the highway toward Atlanta, Jean would look out the car window as they passed the church and revisit that day. Over and over again, she'd find herself bewildered by a question that had dogged her since she'd heard that high-spirited white crowd heading off to kill a black man: *"Why do they hate us so much?"*

She asked her mother often and got the same weary reply every time: "It's our color."

Could it really be that simple, that unsatisfying? What could make ordinary people so unwilling to look past skin color to character; so hateful they celebrate that hate with deadly transgressions?

More than eighty years later, Jean is still wrestling with that. "I just, I never can put it together. Jennifer, I have never been able to understand."

• • •

I arrived at the opening of the National Memorial for Peace and Justice in Montgomery, Alabama, on April 25, 2018, just a month after my conversations with Jean. Known as the Lynching Memorial, it was created by the Equal Justice Initiative under the leadership of Bryan Stevenson to honor those families who experienced the racial terror of lynching. And indeed, people traveled from near and far, seeking recognition, seeking accountability, seeking truth and reconciliation. The memorial was envisioned as a place of healing—much like the Holocaust Memorial Museum in Washington, D.C., or the Apartheid Museum in Johannesburg, South Africa. The Lynching Memorial has emerged as a powerful symbol of how we—as individuals and as a nation—can reckon with the legacy of racism and address bias, even bias of the worst kind.

Lynchings—unprosecuted murders by mobs of unidentified people—occurred all across the United States from the mid-nineteenth century to the mid-twentieth century but were concentrated in the South, particularly in Mississippi, Georgia, and Alabama. The Lynching Memorial sits on a hill overlooking downtown Montgomery, the original capital of the Confederacy. Its wide-open floor plan, stripped of exterior walls on most sides, exposes the building and visitors alike to harsh elements from outside. On display is a collection of eight hundred rectangular metal boxes, each standing six feet tall, one for every county in which a lynching has been documented. As the planks of the wooden floor begin to slope down, visitors to the memorial are forced to look up at the rusted metal boxes, each hung from a long pole affixed to a ceiling rafter—much as the dead bodies of lynching victims dangled from trees.

I found a series of small plaques with short phrases etched on them, telling the stories of everyday perils that black people in Alabama faced. The earliest lynching noted was of Jack Turner, who was killed in 1882 for organizing black voters. Seven black people were lynched in 1888 for drinking from a white man's well. Jack Brownlee was lynched in 1894 for having the man who assaulted his daughter arrested. The list was long—with 340 names of black people lynched in Alabama alone between 1877 and 1943—and it's growing as researchers unearth more documents and oral histories. The last account I read was from 1940: Jesse Thornton was lynched for addressing a white police officer without using the title "Mister."

Standing there, absorbing those accounts of wanton savagery, led me to wonder anew what might have caused my grandfather, frantic and frightened, to make such a hasty retreat. What terrible fate had he managed to outrun when he sought safety and solace in Cleveland?

FIGHTING BIAS IN NEW PLACES

My family's physical trek from subjugation to what they hoped was freedom mirrors journeys still being made by ethnic groups all across the country and all over the world. Their move was about more than family mobility. It reflects the way that space has been used to subjugate people, the way residential restrictions can be employed to diminish potential. Whether by rule or custom or circumstance, when you dictate where people live, where they can eat, where they can sit, where they can swim, space becomes a stigmatizing force that separates and isolates, keeping people in their place and enforcing social inequality.

Space can also liberate. When people leave an oppressive physical space, they are often driven by the rudiments of life: they want better schools, more jobs, safer streets. But the rewards can range beyond basic needs. Physical relocation can present a way to grab the rings of social mobility, to move beyond stereotypes and ultimately blunt the impact of bias.

Soon after Jean helped my grandfather escape, she too left Anniston and settled in Chicago. She arrived as a professional, having been educated at Tougaloo College—a black college just outside Jackson, Mississippi—and later at the Atlanta School of Social Work. Jean arrived hopeful about her prospects for a better life. Yet the North did not offer the refuge she had imagined. Her racial status still barred her from holding certain jobs, shopping in certain stores, and living in certain neighborhoods. In fact, the residential segregation in the North seemed more severe, if less explicit, than anything she'd encountered in the South.

She remembers how quickly whites fled that nice Chicago neighborhood just as she and her husband were settling into their new home. It was common for local real estate agents to stoke fears of rising crime and falling property values among white residents as blacks moved in. Whites, anxious to leave before their white space turned black, would sell their homes at a loss to get out fast. Jean met the nice white man whose family lived across the street from them— but only once. "He said the one thing about him and his wife, they were not going to move," she recalled. "Max, my husband, said to me, 'How long you think he'll be here?' I said, 'They're leaving this week.'" And sure enough, they did.

In the South, black people had long been a constant presence, accommodated if not ever fully accepted. But as blacks migrated by the millions to the North in the 1930s and 1940s, they were viewed as an ugly invading force, and northern cities had to be reshaped and fortified to weather the storm.

As historian Richard Rothstein describes in his book *The Color of Law,* private and government forces conspired to block integration and protect the reigning social order. White neighborhoods had to be protected from "the encroachment of the colored race," one prominent city planner explained. "Race zoning is essential in the interest of the public peace, order, and security."

Real estate agents were warned against selling to "certain racial types"—specifically blacks and foreigners—because their mere presence would "diminish the value" of every home in the neighborhood. The gleaming suburban subdivisions that sprang up after World War II were eminently affordable, but off-limits to blacks.

As black families would discover over decades in their new northern homes, the sense of fear, revulsion, and entitlement that racial advancement provokes can allow bias to migrate to new spaces.

The rings of social mobility were closer but still swinging out of reach.

. . .

Bias both propelled and shadowed the movements of twentieth-century migrants in ways that were simple to define and easy to see. Today, in the twenty-first century, bias has found a new accessory in technology that magnifies what we see but leaves us ill equipped to decipher its meaning.

Surveillance cameras have gone mainstream, guarding our front doors. Online social networks connect us to our neighbors. But the same tools that promise security and promote camaraderie can foster a sort of tunnel vision that distorts our sense of danger, heightens suspicion, and even puts the safety of others at risk. Residents can circulate photographs of "suspicious" strangers to neighbors and police with the touch of a button and without any evidence the person is doing anything wrong—a practice that can amplify and justify bias in the minds of locals primed by worries about the safety of their homes.

And the same technology that stigmatizes innocent targets is also being used to document and share disturbing displays of bias that might have been invisible before: black teens accosted and ejected by a white resident from a North Carolina community pool, Latino restaurant employees yelled at and threatened for speaking Spanish in New York City, an Asian American woman whose Airbnb reservation was canceled because of her ethnicity. As the host explained in a text message, "One word says it all. Asian."

We are building more advanced systems to screen some people out and welcome others in, but who gets put in which category? That's the ultimate choice, one we make over and over every day. And while we expect technology to make us less fearful, it also encourages us to act more quickly on the fears—acknowledged or not—that we harbor. Sometimes its mere existence seems to prime us to confront the bogeyman we think we need protection from.

A white homeowner in Michigan who took off with his shotgun after a black teenager who rang his doorbell hadn't even bothered to check his security camera, until after police were called. The boy had stopped to ask for directions to the local high school, but the white woman who opened the door was so shocked to find him there, she hollered for help. Her husband ran down the stairs, took one look at the boy, and grabbed his gun and fired a shot.

The boy wasn't hit, but the homeowner was arrested. And the doorbell camera he'd installed for protection instead provided police with evidence against him, by documenting the encounter and backing the boy's account that he'd done nothing more threatening than ask for directions. The couple saw the boy through the lens of a scary stereotype, and a camera in a doorbell can't remedy that.

Research shows that fear can be a driver of bias, unleashing whatever primal stereotypes make a nervous fourteen-year-old morph into a dangerous man—if that is what your attitudes and experiences have primed you to see. The same fear response that's supposed to keep us safe can activate bias in ways that stigmatize and threaten others. The technology we enlist to shut down threats from outside our homes may also shutter our humanity. In this case, the surveillance equipment captured the thinking that spurred that couple to overreact. "Why did these people choose my house?" the woman was reportedly heard saying. There were no "these people" on her porch that morning, just one lone lost boy.

After law enforcement officials examined the video, county sheriff Michael Bouchard publicly called the homeowner out for putting the boy's life at risk. "The guy stepped out and fired a shotgun because somebody knocked on his door," he told reporters. "If someone is running from your house and you chase them outside and shoot at them, you're going to have criminal charges coming from us."

In October 2018, six months after the homeowner was charged with "assault with intent to murder," he was convicted by a jury of the lesser charge of felony assault and of using a firearm while committing a felony, which has a mandatory two-year prison sentence. It took the jury just three hours to reach a verdict.

From the outset, the sheriff had set the sort of boundaries that allowed justice to be served. He marshaled truth as a weapon against bias, offering clear direction on what is appropriate to do in such circumstances and what is not. He looked at the whole picture, not just at a snapshot gilded by fear and framed by preconceived notions.

That's a fundamentally sound way of dealing with the interference of bias. But it doesn't happen often enough. And some of the measures that are supposed to help us build bridges and blunt bias are turning out to aid and abet the unconscious ways that we discriminate.

• • •

I made the forty-minute drive from Stanford's lush green campus to the grimy congested core of San Francisco to meet with Sarah Leary, one of the founders (with CEO Nirav Tolia) of Nextdoor, an online social networking service that serves as a sort of giant chat room for individual neighborhoods. Tens of millions of people use it, across the country and around the world. Its mission statement conveys its high-minded goal: to provide a trusted platform where neighbors work together to build stronger, safer, happier communities. It sponsors a network of locally based neighborhood online bulletin boards so that neighbors can communicate more easily.

The business is headquartered in a tall, imposing structure, just behind Twitter's main building on Market Street. When I reached the seventh floor and stepped off the elevator and into their office space, it looked just as I would imagine a tech start-up to look: cool and casual. There were no fancy offices with fancy desks. It felt transparent, as if I could see the entire operation from where I stood: a sea of white Formica desks laid out in a wide-open space. Even the founder's desk was mixed in with the masses; there were no dividing walls. We met in a glass-enclosed conference room and sat in rolling plastic chairs. The egalitarian vibe of that physical space is what Nextdoor aims to offer online: a space where people can feel comfortable connecting with neighbors they've never met, whether they're looking for a lost dog or a reliable babysitter, off-loading old furniture or sharing a garden's bounty, warning neighbors about a coyote roaming the block or a stranger who seems out of sync with the prevailing demographic. It's that last option that caused the trouble that brought me to Nextdoor's conference room.

At that time, Nextdoor was working well in more than 185,000 neighborhoods in the United States and another 25,000 around the world. But its "crime and safety" category has become the problem child. There were too many posts with racist overtones, messages that labeled blacks and Latinos "suspicious" for walking down a street, sitting in a car, talking on a cell phone, knocking on a door. When an Oakland-area news outlet wrote about the problem, Sarah and her business partners were horrified by the stories that emerged. And they began hearing similar stories from their own users. Instead of bringing neighbors closer together, the platform exposed raw racial dynamics that generated hurt feelings, sparked hostilities, and fueled fierce online arguments.

The Nextdoor team began scouring the site for signs of racial profiling and digging through the research on how to deal with bias. The number of troubling posts they found was "minuscule" for a site that channels millions of messages every day, Sarah said. "But we were of the mind-set that even one of these is bad. . . . There was a real kind of gut check and soul-searching experience for us."

Her team pored over dense empirical articles, trying to break through the esoteric language and search for techniques that would preserve users' freedom to flag danger when they see it but protect people from being unfairly targeted. "Most people weren't consciously racial profiling," Sarah said. "They couldn't even agree on what it was. They just knew when they'd seen something that made them uncomfortable and compelled them, for safety's sake, to share it. So they're in this heightened state, they put out a message . . . and they think they're doing good by doing that."

Nextdoor needed to find a way to dial back the hair-trigger impulse that makes skin color alone arouse suspicion. Her team wanted to educate, not shame or alienate users who'd stumbled into trouble with awkward or insensitive postings. She found possible solutions in studies that show how bias is most likely to surface in situations where we're fearful and we're moving fast. I visited her office to share my expertise on the subject.

Speed is the holy grail of technology. Most tech products are created with the aim of reducing friction and guiding us through a process rapidly and intuitively. But the very thing that makes technology so convenient also makes it perilous where race and safety are concerned. The goal is to create an online experience for users that's easy, quick, and fluid, allowing them to express themselves instantly. Yet these are exactly the kinds of conditions that lead us to rely on subconscious bias.

To curb racial profiling on the platform, they had to contemplate slowing people down. That meant adding steps to the process of posting about "suspicious people" but not making things so cumbersome that users dropped out. They needed something that would force people to look past the broad category of race and think about specific characteristics. So they developed a checklist of reminders that people have to click through before they can post under the banner of "suspicious person":

Focus on behavior. What was the person doing that concerned you, and how does it relate to a possible crime?

Give a full description, including clothing, to distinguish between similar people. Consider unintended consequences if the description is so vague that an innocent person could be targeted.

Don't assume criminality based on someone's race or ethnicity. Racial profiling is expressly prohibited.

Research supports the notion that raising the issue of race and discrimination explicitly can lead people to be more open-minded and act more fairly, particularly when they have time to reflect on their choices.

The posting process was changed to require users to home in on behavior, pushing them past the "If you see something, say something" mind-set and forcing them to think more critically: if you see something suspicious, say something specific.

Adding friction to the process slowed things down a bit, but it did not lead to the huge drop-off in users that industry observers had predicted. What it did do was reduce the incidence of racial profiling:

Nextdoor's tracking suggests it is down by more than 75 percent. They've even adapted the process for international use, with customized filters for European countries, based on their mix of ethnic, racial, and religious tensions.

The approach offers benefits beyond reducing neighborhood animosity. That friction and the awareness it generates may make people more willing and better equipped to think and talk frankly about race. Conversations about racial issues in interracial spaces can be uncomfortable. It's no wonder people tend to avoid them. Integration is hard work, and threat looms over the process. White people don't want to have to worry that something they say will come out wrong and they'll be accused of being racist. And minorities, on the other side of the divide, don't want to have to wonder if they're going to be insulted by some tone-deaf remark. The interaction required to move past stereotypes takes energy, commitment, and a willingness to let big uncomfortable issues intrude on intimate spaces—your home and your neighborhood.

Research shows that talking about racial issues with people of other races is particularly stressful for whites, who may feel they have to work harder to sidestep the minefields. Their physical signs of distress are measurable: Heart rates go up, blood vessels constrict, their bodies respond as if they were preparing for a threat. They demonstrate signs of cognitive depletion, struggling with simple things like word-recognition tasks.

Even thinking about talking about race can be emotionally demanding. In a study of how white people arranged the physical space when they knew they'd be in conversation with blacks, the arrangements varied based on the subject of those chats. When the study participants were told they'd be talking in small groups about love and relationships, they set the chairs close to one another. When they were told the topic was racial profiling, they put the chairs much farther apart.

Nextdoor can't make the angst go away. But benefits accrue from nudging people to talk about race and consider the harm a thoughtless judgment can do. "What I have found is that this can be a personal journey," Sarah said. "When you raise the issue with people, at first there might be a little bit of 'Oh, come on.' And then you explain and you get 'Oh yeah, that makes sense.' I think right now most people believe 'I can only screw this up, so maybe I shouldn't have that conversation.' But if people believed that having the conversations actually led to better understanding, they'd be more willing."

She saw that happen in Oakland, when people came together to talk about their distress over racially biased posts. "I think people just get closed off, and they try to simplify the world with simple assumptions to get through their day," she said. "But there's a whole canopy of examples of people's lives that are maybe more similar to yours than you assume. When you have direct connections with people who are different from you, then you develop an ability to recognize that." So the scary black teenager in the hoodie in the dark turns out to be Jake from down the block, walking home from swim team practice.

The beauty of Nextdoor's template is that it catches people before they've done anything wrong. "We try and be very mindful of going through the process of assuming good intent," Sarah explained. "I think where it actually gets embarrassing for people is when they had good intentions and they put something out there, and they thought they were helping the neighborhood, and someone comes back and is like, 'You're a racist.'"

The tool gets users to stop and think before they post something that will land them in heated arguments with neighbors. Because once the comment is out there, it's hard to dial things back. It's not a productive conversation if one person is outraged over being labeled a racist and the other is feeling aggrieved about always having to be the person waving the flag and saying, "Do you realize what you just did?" When there's more thoughtfulness and less defensiveness, honest conversations about race are possible.

Ultimately, we see our neighborhoods as an extension of our homes. And home is the place where you let your guard down; where you expect to feel loved, safe, and comfortable. But living with diversity means getting comfortable with people who might not always think like you, people who don't have the same experience or perspectives. That process can be challenging. But it might also be an opportunity to expand your horizons and examine your own buried bias.

• • •

While Nextdoor offers an online platform for sharing information with nearby neighbors, Airbnb provides a platform for sharing our homes with distant travelers. When you subscribe to Airbnb, you are welcomed "to a community that connects global travelers with local hosts across the world." As an alternative to a hotel, Airbnb allows a less expensive and more intimate experience for travelers and a chance for hosts to make money by opening their homes to strangers. In essence, it's a public marketplace for private accommodations. And its core mission is to open the world to people, to let users know that "every community is a place where you can belong."

The idea for the company originated with Brian Chesky and Joe Gebbia, who met at the Rhode Island School of Design. They both wound up in San Francisco in 2007, worrying about how to pay the rent on the small apartment they shared. One weekend, they rented out space in their apartment to techies in town for a conference when the city's hotels were booked, and a new idea was born. It took a while to turn that weekend success into a viable business model. But once they worked out the kinks, the company's growth was astronomical. Today, Airbnb is used by over 150 million people in eighty-one thousand cities across two hundred countries. There are over 5 million homes to choose from—660,000 in the United States alone. By 2018, the once-struggling start-up was worth $31 billion.

Subscribers post a photograph and profile, scroll through home-like places that are available to rent, then book and pay for their lodging online. But unlike booking a room at a hotel, the travelers aren't the only ones doing the choosing. The host can pass on a booking request. So savvy subscribers take pains to sell themselves, with photographs and chatty testimonials that portray them in the best light.

But even a stellar résumé wasn't always enough to secure a booking. Over time, complaints began trickling in from minorities who felt they'd been discriminated against by hosts who declined to accept booking requests from them. By 2016, that trickle had turned into a tsunami as black users took to Twitter, Facebook, and other social media sites to share their stories. Their experiences requesting accommodations—whether in small-town Idaho or cosmopolitan Philadelphia—were remarkably similar: They'd tried to book a place and were told by the owner that it wasn't available. Some had white friends try to book the same place for the same time period, and it suddenly became available. Some users even tried posing as white, changing their photograph and name, and, when they did, found that they could easily book places that were unavailable to them as black.

Researchers at Harvard Business School began digging into the problem and demonstrated how pervasive it was. A rigorous field experiment found that blacks were 16 percent less likely to be accepted as guests than whites, and no manner of adjusting variables beyond race could explain that.

The researchers developed guest profiles by systematically varying the name of the guest so that it sounded either stereotypically white or black. Using those profiles, they contacted the hosts of approximately sixty-four hundred Airbnb listings across five American cities. Racial disparities in bookings were present in every city, with every type of property (whether high end or low) and every category of host (whether they rented often or occasionally; whether they were offering a room or an entire home). It didn't matter if the neighborhood was racially diverse. It didn't even matter if the host was a minority; black hosts discriminated against black people too.

When Airbnb launched its own in-depth investigation, their researchers found evidence that of all the people making booking requests on the platform, requests from blacks were the least likely to be accepted. The company clearly had a race problem. After a sluggish initial response, Airbnb, under the direction of Brian Chesky, began taking aggressive action to curb it. He identified racial discrimination as "the greatest challenge we face as a company. . . . It cuts to the core of who we are and the values that we stand for."

Airbnb brought in Laura Murphy to help them address the challenge. Laura is an African American civil rights attorney who has worked tirelessly to address racial inequality, including in the tourism industry. She spent three months meeting with dozens of stakeholder groups: employees, hosts, elected officials, regulatory agencies, tourism groups, civil rights organizations, and Airbnb users who'd been victims of discrimination.

As a lawyer, she first looked for a legal remedy. That meant figuring out how laws governing public accommodations might apply to this new hybrid situation. Hotels clearly could not deny someone a room based on race; current public accommodations laws forbid it. However, Airbnb is facilitating the advertisement of private accommodations—but on a public platform. How much control should people have in deciding who comes into their home once they have publicly advertised it to make money?

Laura suggested that Airbnb officials go beyond the federal legal requirement and determine for themselves what the rules of conduct should be on the site. She advised the company to strengthen its own nondiscrimination policy and require every user to sign a "community commitment" pact, spelled out in the sign-up process:

> I agree to treat everyone in the Airbnb community— regardless of their race, religion, national origin, ethnicity, disability, sex, gender identity, sexual orientation, or age—with respect, and without judgment or bias. . . . Discrimination prevents hosts, guests, and their families from feeling included and welcomed, and we have no tolerance for it.

Users who aren't willing to sign the commitment can no longer use the platform. And those who violate the antidiscrimination promise can be banned by Airbnb. The commitment provides the company with leverage to uphold core values and dictates terms of use in a manner that is consistent with a traditional civil rights mission. Just as old problems can migrate to new spaces, old agendas can be adapted to support new solutions.

But while policy remedies are a start, getting people to adhere to Airbnb's value statement will only go so far. Even people whose values are appropriately aligned can fail to act in accordance with those values in ambiguous situations. They may not even be aware that they're breaking the rules in those cases. After all, there are non-racial ways to explain away the rejection of a black applicant: *They have young kids, and my home has too many breakable items. They're on spring break, and I don't want people partying all week long.* It's easy to tell yourself that you don't see color, come up with a host of other justifications, and relieve yourself of any self-recrimination for your bias. Laura's job was to focus the company's managers on how these psychological maneuvers worked subconsciously.

The primary problem is not that "people on the platform say, 'Look, I don't want any African Americans,'" Laura said. "The biggest problem to me is the unconscious bias." And it's more difficult to police and remedy that than it is to root out blatant bigotry.

Given that the natural inclination in the tech industry is to remove friction, Airbnb moved toward solutions with this principle in mind. They decided to encourage people to use their "instant book" option, where listings could be arranged without the prior approval of the host. This option is similar to the process that hotels use in the public accommodations arena: if the space is available and the guest can pay, a room is booked without a need for a guest photograph, a profile, or any discussions about hobbies or the reason for their visit. And indeed, Airbnb's analysis showed that when "instant book" was used, racial differences in guest acceptance rates evaporated.

But those results didn't exactly warrant celebration. It turns out that only a tiny fraction of travelers—about 3 percent—opted for the "instant book" process. And blacks were more reluctant to use the option than other groups—perhaps because they wanted to avoid any ugly encounters that might arise from their hosts' surprise. If discrimination has become the expectation—lurking in the shadows of every encounter—then it might be better for the host to know their race ahead of time. So an option designed to disguise race in pursuit of equality also came to signal just how deep the fear of rejection runs.

Another alternative was to add more friction rather than take it away. When hosts are provided with the previous reviews of guests by other hosts, for example, they are more likely to accept them into their homes, and the racial differences in acceptance rate begin to disappear. That's likely because the practice allows hosts to replace vague racial stereotypes of how those guests might behave in their homes with concrete, relevant, factual information about how they have previously behaved. Indeed, decades of research on stereotyping highlight the power of individuating information to mitigate bias.

It's too early in the process to tell whether these tweaks will be enough to wipe out the kind of overt discrimination that prompted complaints. But the company has created a team of engineers, re-searchers, data scientists, and designers whose sole purpose is to root out bias. They've also begun to route complaints of discrimination to investigative specialists and created an Open Doors program that promises to find a comfortable place to stay for anyone who is not able to book a listing because of discrimination.

Laura Murphy is gratified by the changes because she understands "the pain that race discrimination on that platform caused." She knows the stakes are high. And while the platform and the tactics may be new, the problem is as old as America.

She grew up in Baltimore in the 1960s, the daughter of political activists who enlisted their children in civil rights campaigns. Yet her parents feared traveling the country without their *Negro Motorist Green Book,* a legendary travel guide that mapped out safe places for black travelers in almost every state, in an era when businesses—hotels, restaurants, taverns, gas stations, auto repair shops—barred their entry. The *Green Book* promised to provide the information blacks needed to "travel without embarrassment."

In some respects, the *Green Book* served as a mid-twentieth-century version of Airbnb for blacks who were shut out of conventional commercial lodging. It was a cultural response to a structural problem. Yet the problem of the twenty-first century involves managing integration, not segregation. Now that the laws have changed and spaces are being transformed, how do we all find, accommodate, and see one another?

CHAPTER 8
Hard Lessons

Bernice began her education as a six-year-old in Olive Branch, Mississippi, in 1957, in a two-room schoolhouse with no running water and an outhouse for a toilet. She learned from old schoolbooks that white students had discarded, with their names still scrawled across the top. And a few weeks into every school year, the all-black Union School would close its doors so Bernice and her young classmates could spend the next month or two working the fields. They'd watch buses carrying white students to white schools pass them by as they harvested crops.

School segregation had been ruled unconstitutional three years earlier. But for black children in the South, separate and decrepit facilities were still the rule, and the education they received was far from equal to whites'. It wasn't until 1959 that a high school with indoor plumbing was built in Olive Branch for blacks. And it would take another eight years—and a threat to the state's federal funding—for Mississippi to comply with federal law and allow black children to attend school with whites.

At that point, the state developed a "choice" program that gave black students the option of attending white schools in their districts. It avoided the messiness of forced desegregation and banked on the idea that few black children would leave their schools to travel across town and wade into the unknown. Bernice was in high school then. And when a friend decided to make the leap, she agreed to join her. Only four black students, all girls, enrolled that year in the eleventh grade at all-white Olive Branch High. It was 1967 and the first time that Bernice sat in a classroom that included white people.

"It was scary," Bernice recalls now, looking back. "I was really worried because I'd had no interaction with whites. . . . I had obviously been in stores where they were. I had worked in some of their homes. I had worked with my mother at office buildings, cleaning for them, washing dishes, serving them. But I had not sat in an environment where I was a peer."

But it turned out that the white students had no intention of accepting blacks as peers. They called the black girls ugly names and refused to associate with them. The school quickly abandoned long-held traditions and social events, even the prom, to avoid race mixing as soon as the black students arrived. "The atmosphere was very hostile," Bernice recalls.

But she wasn't there to make friends with whites. She was a dark-skinned black girl with a speech impediment, from a poor family. She simply wanted access to the wealth of resources that white schools had and black schools lacked: new textbooks, science labs, well-stocked libraries, guidance counselors, speech therapists. She'd been an honors student at East Side High and never doubted her academic potential. Yet at Olive Branch High, she found that exclusion extended to the classroom.

Some of her teachers were dismissive, and one was downright hostile. In algebra class, where every other student was white, Mr. Jones assigned Bernice a seat at the very front of the room, in a row all by herself. "He would not permit any other students to sit on that row with me," she said. "I was in the classroom, but I was not of the class." It was as though Bernice were willed out of existence yet made into a spectacle all at the same time. For the entire school year, she sat alone, listening to the snide remarks of students in the rows behind her, unable to turn around. Every day, it felt to her that the teacher was enforcing the superiority of her classmates and her own inferiority. He refused to teach to a black person or allow his white students to suffer the indignity of having to sit next to one. He simply taught past her.

"I didn't learn a thing about algebra. I just didn't," Bernice says now. "I would just be so embarrassed and sometimes demoralized sitting there. . . . It was such a horrible experience."

More than skin color set Bernice apart. She was one of ten children of parents who didn't make it much further than elementary school. Her family grew their own food and made their own clothes. Her grandmother worked as a domestic in the home of one of her white classmates.

At her old school, it didn't matter if you showed up with lunch in a molasses bucket or an old burlap sack. No one would judge; everyone was poor. At the white school, though, things were altogether different. There was a shame attached to poverty.

Bernice worked in the school's library as part of a work-study program for students from poor families. Every Friday, she'd be publicly summoned over the school intercom to collect her wages. Her classmates would laugh and make fun of her as she walked out of the room to pick up a check that only she needed to make ends meet. She couldn't help but be embarrassed by her family's financial straits. Her father was a self-taught mechanic who'd pick her up from campus in his old wrecker, greasy and grimy from a long day of work. She found herself praying that he would be late so that her classmates would not see him lumbering up to the school. His presence became yet another indignity to endure, another reminder that she didn't belong.

Bernice didn't complain. She did not want him to feel burdened or powerless. And she especially wanted to steer clear of any action that might ultimately place her father in danger. At the time, he was actively involved in getting black people registered to vote. That alone was enough to trigger threats of violence by whites. So Bernice remained silent.

Did she ever regret the trade-offs she'd made to attend the white high school? "Sometimes I did. But mostly I didn't," Bernice says today. "There were things that I got there that I would never have gotten in my old school. Never."

Her speech impediment was resolved through therapy. Her worldview was expanded by the library's vast selection of books. And at the end of that first year, her grades were so stellar she became the first black student admitted to the Honor Society at Olive Branch High.

Her experience confirms what decades of research have shown. Both black and Latino students do better academically when they attend integrated schools, and white students' academic performance doesn't suffer when their classmates are black and brown. Socioeconomics plays a key role in that outcome: Integrated schools in middle-class and affluent areas tend to be better resourced. They are more likely to have experienced teachers, well-educated parents, and high academic expectations than segregated schools in low-income communities. Tracking test scores, graduation rates, and college success can help us validate the impact of that.

But what's harder to quantify are the social consequences of the sort that Bernice endured. Proponents of school desegregation in the

1950s and 1960s presumed that close personal contact among children of different ethnic groups would make their families and communities more tolerant and ultimately improve race relations.

Back then, racial bias was commonly viewed as the product of ignorance. So, the thinking went, simply bringing people into contact with one another would soften hostile racial attitudes, by allowing everyone to replace broad stereotypes with individual names, faces, and facts. Once the barriers of bias were relaxed, social integration would allow minorities to rise.

Some of that optimism surrounding equal access to education has indeed been borne out. Black students who attended integrated schools for at least five years earn 25 percent more as adults and are in far better health by middle age than their counterparts from segregated schools. And the benefits extend past racial lines and over generations. People of all races who attended racially diverse schools are more likely to have friends of other races, choose to live and raise their children in integrated neighborhoods, and have higher levels of civic engagement than those who did not.

But the promise of school integration as an antidote to prejudice ran into hurdles that advocates didn't expect. As it turns out, simply sitting in the same classroom together isn't enough to remedy time-worn prejudices. The benefits of interracial contact are conditional. As social psychologist Gordon Allport outlined in his 1954 classic, *The Nature of Prejudice*, contact has a much greater chance of piercing bias when the interactions meet a long list of conditions, including that the contact is between people of equal status, is condoned by authorities, and is personal rather than superficial.

When you're stamped with the badge of inferiority—as Bernice was by the physical separation in her algebra class—that stigma is communicated to and absorbed by the people around you. When you're routinely demeaned by a teacher whose authority others trust, the norm of *inequality* is what is being endorsed. When no one is remotely interested in spending time with you, bias isn't challenged and stereotypes endure. And while school desegregation today may not be as traumatizing as it was for Bernice, meeting those conditions is a challenge. Many schools still fall short.

For a long time, even researchers were naive about the power of contact to counteract prejudice. It took Allport's "contact hypothesis" to point out the pitfalls of a simplistic approach. Spending time with groups you're determined to dislike can actually translate in a biased mind to validation: *I thought these people were stupid; now I know they are.* Allport found that contact can exacerbate instead of ameliorate conflict, especially if the contact situations involve competition or create anxiety for those who take part. The encounters need to be long and frequent enough that the groups involved are comfortable with one another and feel they have common goals or bonds. That's what helps dissolve the separation created by out-group distinctions.

And that's what ultimately paved the way to collegiality and acceptance for Bernice. In her senior year of high school, the Honor Society planned a trip to New York City. Because Bernice was an honors student, she was invited along. She was anxious about going. She'd never been away from home before, and the last thing she wanted was to be on a trip with a group of hostile white students. Not that it mattered; she knew her family couldn't afford to send her anyway.

But her mother was as proud as Bernice was worried. She earned a meager income—making clothes, cleaning homes, selling handmade crepe-paper flowers—but she managed somehow to scrape together enough to buy Bernice a plane ticket and pay for her hotel room. She understood that her daughter would have to pay more too, because she wouldn't be able to split the cost of accommodations, as other classmates did. None of those white students were willing to share a hotel room with a colored girl.

So, against all odds, Bernice made the trip. She walked around Manhattan with the group, excited to be in the mix. Like the rest of her southern troupe, she was wired for hospitality. But when the teenagers tried smiling and speaking to strangers, their greetings went unreturned. "We'd be walking down the streets of Manhattan, looking at the New Yorkers, going, 'Hello, hello,'" Bernice recalled. "And they would look at us as if we were Martians. They just kept walking, and they walked very rapidly." Suddenly Bernice and her classmates were all outsiders, demoted collectively in Manhattan to second-class status. That experience was a turning point, she said. "It caused us to focus on what we had in common, more so than how we were different."

That feeling of togetherness lasted the entire trip, allowing her to enjoy at the end what could have been a humiliating restaurant experience. Bernice was the only one in the group who'd never been to a restaurant before. When she wound up dining with her white classmates at New York City's iconic Tavern on the Green, she had no idea what to order. She scanned the menu, looking for something she'd recognize, too embarrassed to ask for help from the waiter or her classmates. "I finally find '*Cornish hen*,' and I thought, 'Hen. That's chicken. I can eat that.' So, I ordered it. I was very proud of myself," she recalled. But when her plate arrived, the entrée looked like a tiny bird. She wouldn't touch it, because she wasn't sure what it was. So she ate her vegetables and passed the hen to a classmate who was happy to polish it off. And no one mocked or teased her. They all sat together, talking and laughing.

Bernice didn't know it then, but she was experiencing the power of context to weaken bias. When we're faced with a common enemy, research has shown, our biases can temporarily dissolve by the urge to band together and survive. Even the harshest of group boundaries can be realigned when we are under threat. Being shunned by those New Yorkers allowed Bernice's classmates to see her, for the first time, as one of them. She finally had a taste of what it felt like to be an equal to whites—and perhaps they experienced what it was like to be outcasts, shunned by the crowd.

WALKING TOGETHER

Gracemount Elementary School in Cleveland was all I knew as a child, and it seemed fine to me. The classrooms were clean, the teachers were okay, the basketball hoops had chain-link nets, and the asphalt playground had room enough to play kickball at recess. But when my parents decided in 1977 to move us from the all-black Lee-Harvard area to the nearly all-white suburb of Beachwood, I entered a new world. The school was modern and spacious, with wide-open classrooms and lush green playing fields. The differences in resources—so stark and so aligned with race—would lead me to develop a lifelong interest in racial inequality. I didn't realize then that my parents' choice would pay such great dividends for me. At twelve years old, I moved from feeling the need to hide my love for learning to a world where my identity as a learner was routinely nurtured and reinforced.

At Beachwood High School, college was viewed as the next step along a well-laid educational path, not an option off-limits to all but the extraordinary few. Though my old neighborhood was only a bike ride away, I feel certain that if we'd stayed there, I would not have earned a college degree, let alone attended graduate school at Harvard. That move changed the course of my life.

Yet that shift was not without costs. Bernice had been perpetually reminded by her teacher that she was an outsider in her southern high school. Sometimes, I got that same sort of message, albeit less blatantly, in my suburban high school.

My pool of friends in Beachwood had grown after middle school. The high school was bigger and a bit more diverse, though every teacher I had was white. There were maybe a few dozen black students, and we enjoyed hanging out.

Beachwood High took pride in its progressive approach to many subjects, including the arts. That's why my friend Mary Norwood and I felt comfortable adopting a social justice theme for the art project we spent months developing during our senior year. Using colored chalk pastels, we created a giant canvas landscape with the support and encouragement of Mr. Scott, our art teacher.

We'd drawn what appeared to be snowcapped mountains but upon closer inspection were actually the hoods of the Ku Klux Klan. What seemed to be a large tree rising up from the mountains was instead a brown hand, veins bulging, reaching through subjugation toward a sun rendered with an image at its center of Dr. Martin Luther King Jr. It was a radical statement for a pair of suburban black teens in the 1980s. And Mr. Scott was so impressed he arranged to have it framed and mounted prominently in the school's main hallway.

Mary and I were proud of what we considered our artistic legacy. Once the framing was complete, we invited several of our girlfriends to the school's basement wood shop to preview the finished product.

We were all still bubbling with excitement when we climbed the stairs from the basement, turned the corner onto the main corridor, and noticed my former algebra teacher, Mrs. Collins, eyeballing us. Her head swiveled to follow our black girl crew. Her eyes narrowed as she walked toward us, her pace quickening with every step. I could feel her disapproval radiating across the space that separated us.

Mrs. Collins began closing in on us, and we kept walking toward the art room. She started hurling black girl names. "Doritia! Tanisha! Sherita! Ieshia!" Nobody turned around. No one in our group had any of those names.

"Don't look behind you!" I commanded our posse, my outrage rising. "Just keep walking unless you hear your name. We don't have to stop!" Mrs. Collins picked up her pace and so did we. And she kept calling out to our backs: "Shaniqua! Derika!" It was just ridiculous, bordering on insulting. There was never a Jennifer, never a Mary. We were nothing more to her than a group stereotype.

We were breaking no rules. We had done nothing wrong. It felt as if walking with other black girls was, in itself, an act of defiance. I was determined that we would not back down. Finally Mrs. Collins gave up and turned around, but I knew there would be a price to pay.

When I reached the art room, I told Mr. Scott what had happened. "We didn't feel we needed to stop when we hadn't done anything wrong. And besides, she couldn't get any of our names right," I said. The art teacher understood what was going on. He was prepared when Mrs. Collins and the principal showed up. They asked me to leave the room so they could talk. I wasn't privy to what he said to her. But I was never punished and made sure never to cross paths with Mrs. Collins again.

Being singled out and chased back to the art room like that soured what had been such a gratifying day. And that kind of bias-based suspicion continues to shape school interactions today, fueling disparities in discipline and academic performance. Fortunately, I had a teacher to trust and turn to. Mr. Scott validated my perspective, my talent, my voice. The value of his encouragement resonates in my life still.

· · ·

Integrated schools promise to turn us into global citizens, appreciative of cultural differences, skilled at navigating diversity. In integrated spaces, we become more practiced at communicating across racial lines. And it is true that personal contact across racial and ethnic lines can often blunt or mitigate bias. But as research suggests and real life demonstrates, integrated spaces can also heighten the threat of becoming the target of bias. And the threat of being devalued because of your racial or ethnic identity can be a burdensome load for a student to carry.

As a black parent whose three sons have attended mostly white schools, I can see the costs as well as the benefits. And I've felt them play out in my children's lives.

When my youngest son, Harlan, was about to enter eighth grade, he adopted a hairstyle popular among his black friends: the high-top fade. He wore the hair at the top of his head in twists and curls with the tips dyed blond. And I must say, he wore the style well.

But when my husband and I returned from a weekend away, the blond tips were gone. He'd had them sheared off, but he wasn't happy about it. He told us one of the school administrators was ready to give him a detention if he didn't get rid of the blond, because the school handbook prohibited students from having "dyed or colored hair."

Harlan's private school had a strict dress code; the hair-color rule was to prevent students from showing up with green or blue or purple hair. But Harlan knew that many of his female classmates were coming to school every day with "dyed or colored" hair. He felt that not only his hairstyle but his very identity was being challenged, that he was being singled out for being different. And in fact many of his classmates agreed. When word spread that he was being forced to ditch his highlighted tips, several girls commiserated. Their hair was highlighted too, they told him, but nobody cited them for breaking the rule. The girls saw it as an issue of basic fairness. My husband and I saw it as an issue of race.

Harlan didn't ask us to get involved. But he did let the administrator know, in an email, how he felt about her edict: "*Since it really matters that much I'll remove my blond hair by Tuesday. I would just like to know why all the white girls at school can dye their hair blond and I can't. I know that some people (not going to say names) have had their hair dyed for years and never been asked about it. Sincerely, Harlan.*"

Our sunny, amicable child had lost something that meant a lot to him. My husband and I decided to meet with the administrator.

She explained to us that she wasn't singling Harlan out but she wasn't willing to make an exception for him either. Her role was to enforce the rules, she said. "I told everybody who came back from summer break with dyed hair to deal with it. And they all dealt with it and Harlan did not." So she'd given him a choice: "Either cut the tips out of your hair, or dye it back to your natural color."

She had no idea which other students might have dyed hair, she admitted. "That's not obvious to me. But it *is* obvious that Harlan has highlights. It really sticks out." In other words, our son faced the threat of punishment because he was unable to hide his transgression. Harlan was the only black boy in his class. So in everything he did, he was bound to stick out. How could it be okay for these girls to violate school policy but our son to merit discipline?

As we talked, the administrator began to develop a clearer picture of what was at stake—and the implications of that shook her up. "The idea that Harlan would think that I'm singling him out . . ." She stopped midsentence; her face grew still and her eyes were wet. She had to grab a tissue before she could continue. "That was not my intention," she said. "I have a good relationship with Harlan. And it just really hurts my heart that he thinks this is a racial issue."

She was caught off guard by our conversation. She'd been trying to enforce the rules in an equal way, not realizing that there was a larger issue at play in Harlan's mind.

We were caught off guard by her tears. I thought back on how kind she had always been to our son, how close he felt to her. I could see this through her administrator's eyes. But I wanted her to see things from our perspective too.

I explained how this transcends hair. There's a larger context within which Harlan experiences being reprimanded in this way. It wasn't as if he simply decided to sport some wacky hairstyle. What might look outrageous to her is a badge of belonging among young black males. In a sense, Harlan was asserting his blackness at an all-white school. That's what diversity is supposed to be about. And when the response to that impulse is a threat to discipline him, that makes him feel as if his only choice is to be invisible; his real self has no value at his school.

By the time I finished that explanation, she was crying so much that it was hard for her to speak. The idea that she had inadvertently wounded Harlan really upset her. She had entered the teaching profession to build up young people—to help them understand that they are loved and supported.

I assured her that we weren't there to blame her. We knew she cared about our son and that she would want to know if there was something she did, unwittingly, that could negatively affect that relationship and his school experience. We also wanted her to see the bigger picture, to understand the challenges that integration brings: treating everyone the same when they're differently situated is not always as fair as you might think.

To her credit and to our relief, she moved skillfully to acknowledge this perspective and validate our son.

She promised to talk to Harlan. She let him know that their relationship mattered to her. She told him she was sorry she hadn't seen the broader context. She said she was open to revisiting the school policy. She even asked Harlan whether he was interested in playing a role as she reconsidered the hair code.

Her actions were a model for how teachers and school administrators should approach difficult conversations about race: with honesty and an open heart. She was willing to let her guard down; she allowed herself to hear us and feel what our son was feeling. She saw things from a new perspective, one she could not have gained without all of us taking the risk of having that racially charged conversation.

I imagine our conversation had an impact on how she now approaches other minority students, or any kid who doesn't quite fit the mold. And I suspect my son learned something that will serve him long after the memories of his blond tips fade: how to stand up for himself and advocate for fairness in diverse, and not so diverse, spaces. Still, it was a hard lesson to learn.

His experience was more than a fashion dilemma. It reflects the value of addressing the social nuances of academic integration that are not as easily measured as test scores or college acceptance rates. Even given its painful moments—and sometimes because of them— integrated schooling can position students to feel better equipped to navigate an integrated world and more convinced that they can succeed.

And despite the stumbles, progress is being made. Back in Olive Branch fifty years ago, Bernice had to endure alone the sanctioned bigotry of a teacher at a white school determined to resist integration. Decades later, I had a small cohort of black friends and a white teacher as allies, willing to deflect any bias thrown my way in a white school firmly committed to integration. Last year, my son enjoyed the support of white classmates and the attention of a thoughtful administrator willing to reconsider policies that might promulgate bias. And just a few months ago, Harlan began his freshman year of high school—sporting dreadlocks. This time in his natural color.

EMERGING DISPARITIES

For the generation of students moving through school in the 1970s and 1980s, integration looked like a success. School districts—often against their will—were required to take affirmative steps to create diversity on their campuses.

But in the last twenty years, school segregation increased as legal rulings whittled away options to counteract the impact of residential segregation—forbidding cross-district busing, terminating court-ordered desegregation plans, and limiting the use of race as a factor in ensuring diversity in magnet schools. The fledgling charter school movement has also added a new force to the mix, with its privately created but publicly funded small-school options that tend to be racially homogeneous. Predominantly white charter enclaves are sprouting in mixed neighborhoods. And in urban areas, where most charters are located, 25 percent of charter campuses are more than 99 percent nonwhite, compared with 10 percent of traditional public schools.

To complicate things, our evolving demographics are making it harder to even agree on what a segregated school looks like. Today only about half of the nation's public school students are white, compared with 80 percent fifty years ago. Latinos now account for about a quarter of public school enrollment. As our country's white population shrinks and ethnic diversity increases, what mix of which students will create the sort of integration that spreads benefits evenly?

Americans still appear to believe in the value of integrated education. A 2017 poll by Phi Delta Kappa, the professional organization for educators, found that 70 percent of parents would like to have their child in a racially diverse school. But 57 percent prize proximity over diversity. Only one-quarter of those who'd like a diverse school say they'd be willing to make a longer commute to get to one. Our persistently segregated neighborhoods make that a challenge across the nation.

As a consequence, the number of intensely segregated schools—where less than 10 percent of students are white—has more than tripled in the past thirty years, according to research by the UCLA Civil Rights Project. The share of black students who attend racially isolated schools has increased by 11 percent. And while black and Latino students tend to be in schools with a substantial majority of poor children, white and Asian students typically attend middle-class schools. Segregation is nearing epidemic levels in the central cities of the nation's largest metropolitan areas, the UCLA study found. The states of New York, Illinois, and California are the top three worst for isolating black students in urban settings. The trend imperils budding academic gains.

And the problems don't end there. Even though black and Latino children perform better in integrated schools than their peers in racially isolated schools, as a group they still lag behind white and Asian students. That long-standing academic achievement gap is linked on a fundamental level to disparities in social class. But a broader mix of forces undermines the performance of black and Latino students, who often perceive the classroom experience differently from their white peers.

Researchers have identified key elements that can improve school performance. They rest on a basic principle: Students need to feel individually valued and respected, connected to both the people and the process involved in their education. Those psychological factors can affect how and how much our children learn.

Some of the classroom interventions that have been shown to work seem deceptively simple but tap into complex psychological processes. Two key studies of middle school pupils used specific exercises that were found to enhance students' sense of competence and connectedness and improve academic performance in lasting and measurable ways.

A team of academics, led by social psychologist Geoffrey Cohen, tested the impact of a "values affirmation" intervention. Beginning in seventh grade, students in two groups regularly wrote structured journal entries—one wrote about values important to them, such as relationships with family and friends or musical interests, and the other wrote about "neutral" subjects, such as their morning routines. The researchers found that the African American students who wrote values-oriented entries earned significantly higher grades than those who did not.

The intimacy built into that basic exercise unleashed students' potential in three ways: It affirmed their own self-image by reminding them of their identity outside the classroom. It allowed them to see school as a supportive place that cared about their beliefs and feelings. It helped teachers to look past stereotypes and understand these students better as individuals.

The research confirms the connection between psychological states and the process of learning—particularly for black students, who display greater psychological vulnerability to early academic failure. The affirmation's benefits were most evident among low-achieving African Americans, the children most undermined by sub-par performance. For them, early failure may register as confirmation of the stereotype that they're not as smart as other kids and won't succeed in school. The values-affirmation exercise helped restore a sense of adequacy, reduce psychological stress, and interrupt the cycle of poor performance. Two years later, those affirmed students were still doing better than the control group.

The second study also considered the potential of trust-building interventions to blunt the threat of bias and unlock the potential of minority students. It's long been clear that constructive feedback is a powerful tool for promoting children's intellectual development. And academic growth requires both praise and criticism. The researchers examined how teachers might convey criticism that leads to improvement, without undermining the motivation of students.

The team, led by Cohen and David Yeager, was particularly interested in the interaction between black students and white teachers. Surveys show that black Americans have lower general trust than other racial groups, particularly when it comes to white Americans. And a large body of research attests to the subtle and not-so-subtle cues—overly harsh discipline, patronizing praise, cold social treatment—that validate that sense of mistrust for black students.

The researchers sought to counteract that by reframing teachers' criticism as an expression of faith in their students' abilities, instead of merely a declaration that the students were falling short. That strategy falls under the label of "wise feedback."

They enlisted middle school students from a school with an almost equal number of whites and blacks and a teacher corps that was virtually all white. The students were given a writing assignment, which their teachers graded and critiqued. Before the papers were handed back, the researchers affixed a note purportedly from their teacher that said either "I'm giving you these comments because I have very high expectations and I know that you can reach them" or "I'm giving you these comments so that you'll have feedback on your paper." The students were then given a chance to revise and resubmit their essays.

The results showed stark differences in student response. The black students' motivation increased significantly when the critical feedback was accompanied by the teachers' assurance that they could meet the higher standards. Four times as many black students from the "wise feedback" group opted to revise and resubmit, as compared with the group that did not get the reassuring comment. And their new drafts were substantially better and earned higher grades than those by the other black students.

The "wise feedback" option led to only a slight rise in the number of white students who revised their essays. The researchers attributed that, in part, to the difference in students' level of trust. "Wise" strategies convey to students that they are not being judged through the lens of a stereotype. White students, as a group, do not need that sort of explicit reassurance; they are free to see criticism as information that can help them improve, rather than as possible evidence of bias.

The success of this intervention rests on whether students feel valued and able to trust adults who hold authority roles. Black students' fears of being unfairly judged by whites can incline them "to view critical feedback as a sign of the evaluator's indifference, antipathy, or bias, leading them to dismiss rather than accept it," the research team noted. And that mind-set can amount to self-sabotage.

But bias isn't always a hazard that's just in the student's mind. Black students are nearly four times as likely to be suspended from school as their white peers, according to a study conducted by the U.S. Office for Civil Rights involving more than ninety-six thousand K–12 public schools. That's a gap that can't be explained by racial differences in student behavior or socioeconomic status. The disparities, in part, are driven by choices made by teachers or administrators in subjective cases. Black students are significantly more likely to be disciplined for relatively minor infractions than any other group.

How do classrooms begin with well-meaning teachers and motivated students and end up with extraordinarily high levels of discipline problems and suspensions involving black students? To explore the role that racial bias might play, Jason Okonofua and I examined the responses of teachers to hypothetical student misbehavior cases. In a set of online studies, we asked practicing teachers in a variety of schools across different parts of the country to read the office-referral record of a middle school student who had misbehaved in some benign way, like sleeping in class. We gave the student either a stereotypically black-sounding name or a white-sounding name. We found that the race of the student did not initially influence how teachers judged the severity of the infraction or what discipline they'd recommend. But when we informed teachers that this same student had misbehaved a second time, everything changed.

Teachers felt more troubled by the second infraction when the student was perceived to be black than when he was presented as white. And they wished to see stronger disciplinary action taken against the black student.

That aligns with earlier research showing that teachers commonly perceive black students to have more negative demeanors and a longer history of misbehavior than whites. Black students are more likely than others to be labeled "troublemakers" after a few minor indiscretions. So when the teachers in our study thought the student was black, they were significantly more likely to see the two minor infractions as fitting a pattern, which led them to view the student as a troublemaker whom they could more easily imagine suspending down the road.

Even very young children can be affected by these kinds of biases. In one study conducted by a team of researchers at the Yale Child Study Center, early education providers were shown a series of videos depicting four preschoolers—a black boy, black girl, white boy, and white girl—sitting together at a table engaging in "traditional classroom activities" for their age. They were told to study the video clips for signs of behaviors that could become problematic. Using eye-tracking devices to monitor their gazes, the researchers found the preschool teachers spent more time looking at the black children, and at the black boys in particular. Before they even enter kindergarten, black children are already considered more likely to misbehave than white children.

That sort of tracking, at such a young age, has serious implications for both the academic achievement and the mental well-being of black students. Over time, those students come to worry about how they could be treated in school environments. And by the time they are in middle school, those concerns can influence their day-to-day interactions with teachers, their academic engagement, their perceived fit at school, and their identity as learners. Thus begins a vicious cycle: As black students pull back, their teachers may become more frustrated with them, and as the teachers' frustration grows, those students become even more inclined to disengage or act out.

Effectively intervening will involve more than focusing on either the bias that teachers possess or the bad behavior that minority students exhibit. Decreasing racial disparities in discipline will require both teachers and students to focus on the relationships they have with each other. It will involve reminding them of what their goals are and showing them paths to achieve those goals. It will also mean drawing their attention to the kinds of relationships they would like to have with one another, rather than bringing into focus the relationships they fear.

With these principles in mind, Jason Okonofua, David Paunesku, and Gregory Walton developed a novel empathy intervention that cut the suspension rate of middle schoolers in half. They assigned 31 middle school math teachers, who collectively taught 1,682 students across five diverse California schools, to participate in either an empathy-building exercise or a similarly structured activity aimed at using technology to promote learning.

During the empathy exercise, teachers learned about the kinds of experiences and worries that could lead to mistrust and misbehavior. They reviewed stories from students describing how they'd been disciplined and the impact that had. They reviewed examples of how other teachers effectively disciplined students. And they provided their own examples of how they could show respect to students in need of discipline. For instance, one teacher wrote, "I NEVER hold grudges. I try to remember that they are all the son or daughter of someone who loves them more than anything in the world."

The researchers found that students of teachers in the empathy group were half as likely to be suspended during the school year than were students in the other group. The drop was particularly dramatic for black and Latino students and for students who'd been suspended before. And when their students were polled, even the views of those who'd been suspended in the past had shifted toward positivity. Those who had a math teacher in the empathy group regarded their teachers as more respectful to them than those whose teachers had no empathy training. That intervention, grounded in the science of relationship building, suggests that an empathetic look at what drives misbehavior could lead to a better result for both students and teachers.

SIDESTEPPING RACE

When it comes to everyday practices that teachers are encouraged to try in school settings to address racial issues, empathy, wise feedback, affirmation, and high-quality contact tend to get short shrift. Instead, one of the most common practices schools foster is the strategy of color blindness. *Try not to notice color. Try not to think about color. If you don't allow yourself to think about race, you can never be biased.*

That may sound like a fine ideal, but it's unsupported by science and difficult to accomplish. Our brains, our culture, our instincts, all lead us to use color as a sorting tool. And yet the color-blind message is so esteemed in American society that even our children pick up the idea that noticing skin color is rude. By the age of ten, children tend to refrain from discussing race, even in situations where mentioning race would be useful, like trying to describe the only black person in a group.

Our adult discomfort is conveyed to our children and our students. When we're afraid, unwilling, or ill equipped to talk about race, we leave young people to their own devices to make sense of the conflicts and disparities they see. In fact, the color-blind approach has consequences that can actually impede our move toward equality. When people focus on not seeing color, they may also fail to see discrimination.

In a study led by social psychologists Evan Apfelbaum and Nalini Ambady, that idea was put to the test. The researchers exposed sixty mostly white fourth- and fifth-grade students from public schools in the Boston area to a videotaped message promoting racial equality. For some of the children, color blindness was encouraged: "We all have to work hard to support racial equality. That means we need to focus on how we are similar to our neighbors rather than how we are different. We want to show everyone that race is not important and we are all the same." For the remaining children, valuing diversity was encouraged: "We all have to work hard to support racial equality. That means we need to recognize how we are different from our neighbors and appreciate those differences. We want to show everyone that race is important because our racial differences make each of us special."

Next, all of the children listened to stories about incidents that involved other children. Some had clear racial components, like the story of a black child being intentionally tripped by another child while playing soccer, simply because he was black. Even in a situation like that, only 50 percent of those in the color-blind mind-set identified the action as discriminatory. In the diversity-minded group, nearly 80 percent saw discrimination as a factor. And when teachers later watched video recordings of the children describing the incidents, the teachers who listened to the descriptions of children in the color-blind mind-set rated the actions as less problematic and were less inclined to intervene to protect the targeted child. Encouraging children to remain blind to race dampened their detection of discrimination, which had ripple effects. Color blindness promoted exactly the opposite of what was intended: racial inequality. It left minority children to fend for themselves in an environment where the harms they endured could not be seen.

• • •

Our children are not blind to the racial and ethnic divisions that have racked this country since its beginnings. Now social media gives them access to every slight, provocation, and indignity: Black men in handcuffs, arrested for not buying anything at Starbucks. White college students in blackface, bellowing fraternity chants laced with racial epithets. Brown children confined in wire enclosures, crying desperately for their border-crossing parents.

We need to help children process the disparities and racial animus they see. We know that close relationships with people unlike ourselves—at school, at work, at church, in neighborhoods—can help mute the impact of prejudice and blur group boundaries.

Journalist Walter Lippmann, who coined the term "stereotypes," said it best: without individual contact that breaks through our categorization, "we notice a trait which marks a well known type, and fill in the rest of the picture by means of the stereotypes we carry about in our heads."

But it takes more than interpersonal connection to break the bonds of institutional bias and promote the sort of equality that allows us all to thrive. That is where education can play an important role. How did certain people or entire social groups land in the positions they are in? Young people need to understand the history that created structural barriers to integration and equity.

History, Lippmann said, is the "antiseptic" that can disinfect the stain of stereotypes by allowing us "to realize more and more clearly when our ideas started, where they started, how they came to us, why we accepted them."

History shapes our view of the present. With a comprehensive history curriculum, well-prepared teachers would be able to offer students context for vexatious issues that roil us today—from the noxious rise of anti-Semitism to the contentious images of black football players kneeling while the national anthem plays. Yet studies show that we are falling short on both accounts: The history lessons that most students receive are woefully inadequate and often dreadfully biased. And teachers are often ill equipped to teach the subject with the breadth and depth it deserves.

According to a survey by the Conference on Jewish Material Claims Against Germany, 22 percent of young Americans who came of age in the twenty-first century said they never heard of the Holocaust. Two-thirds of them—four in ten Americans overall—failed to identify "Auschwitz" as a Nazi death camp.

It can be particularly challenging to teach a racially charged topic like slavery, and because of that it is often simply not taught or watered down beyond meaning. A Southern Poverty Law Center survey of high school seniors and social studies teachers in 2017 found students struggling on even basic questions about the enslavement of blacks in the United States. Only 8 percent of high school seniors could identify slavery as the primary reason the South seceded from the Union. Nearly half of the students said it was to protest taxes on imported goods.

"Teachers are serious about teaching slavery," the survey found. "But there's a lack of deep coverage of the subject in the classroom." Nine in ten high school social studies teachers said they are committed to teaching about slavery, but almost six in ten find their textbooks inadequate. As recently as 2015, one of the nation's largest textbook companies was still publishing a high school geography text in Texas that portrayed slaves as "workers" who'd cruised here on ships from their native Africa to toil in southern agricultural fields.

There's a tendency for textbooks and teachers to shrink or sanitize a subject that stains our nation's legacy. That shields students from the true horror of the institution. But it also deprives them of the opportunity to explore both the brutality of oppression and the bravery of endurance, and to understand how the legacy of slavery still shapes our country's racial dynamic, influencing us in ways we don't even recognize. "Teachers—like most Americans—struggle to have open and honest conversations about race," the survey confirmed. "How do they talk about slavery's legacy of racial violence in their classrooms without making their black students feel singled out? How do they discuss it without engendering feelings of guilt, anger or defensiveness among their white students?"

One teacher in California told the pollster why it's hard. She worries about its emotional effect on the black students, the message it sends to their classmates: "Although I teach it through the lens of injustice, just the fact that it was a widely accepted practice in our nation seems to give the concept of inferiority more weight in some students' eyes. Like if it happened, then it must be true."

BERNICE'S RISE AND RETURN

As I stood in Judge Donald's ornate judicial chambers in Tennessee, I could not stop staring at the painting hung prominently on the dark wood-paneled wall. In autumn shades of red, orange, and stormy grays, it depicted a group of black men in work clothes, loaded down with bales of cotton. They were lined up alongside a cotton field, waiting for white men in suits to weigh their harvest and decide on the value of their labor.

The stark slice of history seemed out of place amid the elegant furniture, expensive rugs, and glossy accolades that Judge Donald had accumulated over her thirty-six years on the bench. But I understood what the painting meant to her.

Bernice Donald had, as a child, been one of those cotton pickers. She'd climbed from the cotton fields of the Mississippi delta to the U.S. Court of Appeals. She was among the first black students to attend the white high school in Olive Branch, her hometown. She was the first in her family to graduate from high school, from college, from law school. And she was the first black woman in the state of Tennessee to be appointed a judge.

Her climb was steep. But Judge Bernice Donald never let go of Bernice from Olive Branch, whose experiences helped propel her forward: The year she spent sitting alone in that high school algebra class, shamed by her teacher and mocked by her classmates. The trip to New York City with the Honor Society, where she finally learned what it felt like to fit in. Her first visit to a college campus, when all the other kids were wearing tie-dyed shirts and jeans and she arrived in heels and a puffy pink dress that her mother had made her for Orientation Day.

She laughs now at that memory of her introduction to higher education. She and her mother were walking around the campus, "and we look like Martians, because everybody is wearing jeans," she recalls. "And I'm in this beautiful pink dress . . . a teenager wearing lace-top socks."

One thing her past had taught her was not to be bothered by whatever her peers thought of her. "I was just really proud," she said. "I met people, and I was excited about it."

Memphis State University was close to home, yet Bernice was unsure of how to navigate the unfamiliar world of college life. She struggled to balance studying with working and being of use to her family. In her freshman year, she was called home by her father for help. He was having trouble getting paid for work he had done for a woman in town. "Bernice," he said, "I want you to put on a suit, and I want you to go with me so that I can get my money. You're going to be my lawyer."

Her years at Olive Branch High had given her the confidence to put on a blue suit, drive to the woman's house with her dad, and inform the woman that her father, Mr. Boyd, was prepared to file a lawsuit if he did not get the money he was owed. The woman looked at them, closed the door, and returned with the money in hand.

When Bernice decided to attend law school, her father was thrilled. "From what he knew, lawyers were the ones who really championed people's rights," she said to me. They were the ones who "stood between oppression and freedom."

As a judge, she sat elevated, facing the room as the ultimate arbiter of justice, surrounded by a supporting cast of lawyers, bailiffs, and minute clerks. As we spoke in the comfort of her chambers, I envisioned Judge Donald being forced to sit alone, with no support, in that algebra class at all-white Olive Branch High. Then she was the object of ridicule, unable to turn back or speak out. After her judicial appointment made history, Judge Donald was invited back to Olive Branch High to be honored. She'd made peace with the injustices of her high school experience, though some things still bothered her.

She'd learned years later that the school principal had forbidden the college counselor to give black students information about scholarships their academic standing had earned. Bernice could have had a fully paid education. Instead, she spent her entire time in college and law school scrambling for jobs to make ends meet.

"The principal was a person who always had a jovial personality," she recalled, "which was kind of deceiving, because you thought that he really believed in equality . . . but he apparently had the perception that none of us was worthy of going beyond high school."

But beyond the deceit, beyond the racial slurs, beyond whatever other negative treatment she was forced to endure, it was the behavior of her algebra teacher—who brought shame down on her daily—that left an indelible scar. A trip back to Olive Branch carried the risk of returning the judge to an uncomfortable past. But it also offered the opportunity to face the past and then move on.

Judge Donald accepted the invitation and addressed a packed room, without anger or bitterness. Afterward, as people lined up to greet her, she recognized her algebra teacher, Mr. Jones, taking a place in the queue. She found his presence unsettling. She wasn't sure what he would say or how she would react. By the time he reached her, the teacher had tears in his eyes. She just stood there, stunned speechless. "Can you forgive me?" Mr. Jones asked softly. "We were so wrong."

She hadn't mentioned the humiliation of algebra class in her speech, and he didn't need to explain what the apology was for. They both knew what he had done. And in that moment, she wasn't ready to offer him absolution. "I think the thing that haunts me is that I knew that I had an obligation to forgive, and I couldn't say the words," she says now. "All I could say was, 'That was a long time ago.' . . . I have forgiven him, but apparently I haven't moved much beyond the hurt."

In that moment, Judge Donald realized that Mr. Jones's actions had left a mark on him too. His tears seemed to reflect the shame his own behavior had brought on himself. Both the biased and the target of bias are forced to dwell in the roles they play.

And I began to understand why this indignity was the hardest to heal from. It was hard because fifty years later there is still no way to resolve it. It was hard because it wasn't yet behind Judge Donald or Mr. Jones. It was hard because it isn't behind us. They are still on the road to healing. And so are we.

CHAPTER 9

Higher Learning

They'd come to start a race war, with weapons hanging from their belts and strapped to their chests. They were yelling Nazi slogans, wearing Confederate gear, and carrying tiki torches in imitation of the white-robed, cross-burning Ku Klux Klan. And their siege of the University of Virginia campus and the city of Charlottesville would shift the conversation around race and bigotry in America in ways that would have been unimaginable a decade before.

For more than twenty years, I had been studying the kind of unconscious bias that operates so quietly that social scientists have to prove that it exists. Now here in my living room were televised images that could have been lifted from a history book. We've been so focused on explaining and eradicating implicit bias that we did not attend adequately to the capacity for implicit bias to become starkly and dangerously explicit again. Now shifting social and political norms are giving once-closeted bigots a mouthpiece and a voice.

I tried to imagine how this must feel to UVA students, who'd come of age in a country that twice elected a black president. Now their campus was ground zero for a newly visible white supremacy movement. The people of Charlottesville turned out in droves to challenge the marchers, but the damage was already done.

Universities, by their very nature, have long been both drivers and reflections of broad social change. Idealistic young people—unchained from parochial views and exquisitely attuned to injustice—are not afraid to challenge authority and eager to change the world.

The civil rights movement leaped onto the national agenda when four black college students in Greensboro, North Carolina, walked into a local Woolworth's in 1960, sat at a "whites only" lunch counter, and refused to leave. That sparked months of protests and led to Freedom Rides and voter registration drives that drew a multiracial coalition of college students from all across the country to battle discrimination in the South.

The antiwar campaign that helped force an end to U.S. involvement in the Vietnam War was rooted in campus activism. When four students were shot to death by National Guard soldiers during a protest at Kent State University in 1970, the nation could not turn away. The wave of demonstrations that followed engaged four million students and shut down more than four hundred college campuses. At New York University, a window banner proclaimed "They Can't Kill Us All."

That sense of agitation is still alive today. In fact, college students' commitment to activism and civic engagement is higher than it's been at any time in the last fifty years, according to surveys of freshman attitudes. And more students rate themselves "liberal" today than at any time since 1973.

But the 2016 election of Donald Trump galvanized liberal students and emboldened right-wing fringe groups, turning college campuses into battlegrounds over whose rights deserve protecting and whose voices are heard.

The clash of values came to a head at the University of Virginia on August 12, 2017, as hundreds of white nationalists, carrying guns and Confederate flags, rallied in downtown Charlottesville, Virginia, to protest the city's proposal to do away with a monument of the Confederate general Robert E. Lee. That march turned into a maelstrom of brawls and beatings; one woman died when a white nationalist plowed through a crowd of counterprotesters in his car.

The night before, more than a hundred torch-bearing neo-Nazis had paraded boldly through the heart of the UVA campus, in a clear challenge to egalitarian norms on race that have been developing in the United States over the last half century.

College is a place where young people discover and reinvent themselves, where the norms that guide our thinking and govern behavior are set and challenged. What starts on campuses migrates out into the larger culture. That makes universities an incubator for nascent social movements and a barometer that can measure where our country is headed.

The violent march in Charlottesville was a throwback to a nation those UVA students were too young to remember. I wondered how that summer of hate was affecting students and professors in and outside the classroom. How were they thinking and talking about bias? What damage did the march leave? What lessons does it carry? How are people attempting to move forward? Those are the questions that compelled me to make my way to Charlottesville on November 1, 2017.

• • •

When my flight landed, it was late and I was tired. I had interviews scheduled with twenty-seven people in the next seventy-two hours, and my mind was on the days ahead. So when my Uber driver asked, "What brings you to town?" I was yanked back to the present, unprepared. The question was typical, but the situation was not.

How do I respond to a middle-aged white man from the South in the South, right on the heels of Nazis marching in the streets, carrying torches and guns and threatening to start a race war? *Could he be one of them?*

"I'm here to talk to people about a book I am writing on racial bias," I answered nervously from the backseat. I couldn't tell how my reply had landed. All I could see was the back of his head, closely cropped graying hair peeking out from under a battered baseball cap.

My answer, apparently, unleashed something in him. He launched into a long story about the woman who had raised him and how much he loved her. Her name was Lyta, she'd just died at ninety years old, and she was black. She was more than a domestic who'd worked for his family for years. She was one of the most important people in his life, a woman who'd cared for him as if he were her child, while his own mother was busy tending to his handicapped sister. I could hear his voice crack and choke as he shared memories of her.

Just thinking about this white man's bond with this black woman made me feel a little less on edge. Then suddenly he went silent. His mood seemed to shift, and he announced in a somber voice: "Bigotry is still in my veins."

Oh, boy. . . . "How do you know?" I asked, trying to tread lightly.

"I can feel it."

"When?" I asked. "When do you feel it?"

He paused for a moment to think that through. "When I'm outnumbered," he said. "I can feel it rising up."

He could feel it rise up when he was the only white person in a setting. Not just with black people in Virginia, but with any group that wasn't his own. He'd spent years living in Florida, surrounded by Latinos, and felt it there as well, he said.

His raw honesty startled me. In the privacy of his car with some-one he saw as an expert at hand, he was beginning to wrestle with something he'd accepted about himself but didn't understand: even though he'd grown up loving this black woman with his whole heart, bigotry was still within him, waiting to be called forth.

By the time he finished unburdening himself, we were pulling up to the entrance to my hotel. I thanked him, left the car, and checked in, still mulling over his words and what they meant.

Our encounter would set the stage for my mission in Char-lottesville. The changing status of whites in America is tinder for the fire of white nationalism. When whites are the mainstream and ev-eryone else the "others," things feel safe and comfortable for men like my driver.

But by the middle of this century, white people are likely to be a minority in this country, according to U.S. Census Bureau projec-tions. And simply reminding some white Americans of their dimin-ishing presence can lead them to express more negative attitudes toward blacks, Latinos, and Asians, according to a series of studies by social psychologists Maureen Craig and Jennifer Richeson.

My driver couldn't explain the bigotry "rising up" in him, but social science can. Feeling outnumbered can signal a threat to the legacy of dominance and the white privilege that affords. That can seed fear and resentment, which can fuel desperate measures to re-claim primacy. Being reminded of an "increasingly diverse racial landscape" leads some whites to express a stronger preference to in-teract exclusively with members of their own racial group, to feel that discrimination against whites is on the rise, and to endorse more politically conservative views and policies.

But social science is only part of the story. To really understand what is happening in Charlottesville and elsewhere, we also need to turn to history.

• • •

The summer of hate began with white nationalists who came to Charlottesville to protest a plan to remove the statue of General Lee from a park in the city's historic downtown core. The proposal was part of a larger effort by the city's elected leaders to examine how history is communicated in public spaces and map out a path to delivering a more complete and accurate story of Charlottesville's past.

UVA history professor John Mason served as vice-chair of the city's Blue Ribbon Commission on Race, Memorials, and Public Spaces. His role was to sift through elements of Charlottesville's history to provide a clearer picture of the circumstances under which the memorials were created and what they were meant to convey.

That meant not only considering the prominence of Confederate symbols but remedying the lack of attention paid to symbols of African American history.

"Virginia was a major slave-exporting state," John noted. In the thirty years before the Civil War, half a million people from Virginia were sold to southern farmers to cultivate cotton crops. "Some of them were marched south. Some of them were shipped south. Some of them went south on railroads. And every one of those people had a story of a family being torn, a community being torn apart, of losing your friends, your family, your connections to everything that you've ever known."

Yet the slave auction block on the city's town square bore only a "small plaque buried on the sidewalk that everybody steps on and overlooks," John bemoaned.

The commission was reevaluating that memorial too. "But when we had our public hearings, the conversation was overwhelmingly about the statues. And when tempers flared, it was overwhelmingly about the statues," he said.

The bronze statue of Robert E. Lee astride his horse had been a town fixture since it was erected in 1924, on parkland donated by a wealthy white Virginia businessman. That was at the height of the Ku Klux Klan's reign of terror and almost sixty years after the end of the Civil War. It was put up as a deliberate act of intimidation and as a reminder of the power of whites: rendered with vile intent, not rose-colored nostalgia.

The idea of doing away with Confederate symbols had been percolating in Charlottesville for several years. The Lee statue was the most visible and vaunted symbol of Virginia's role in the Confederacy and a perpetual reminder of an ethos that deemed blacks fit only for slavery.

White residents challenging its removal considered the statue a gift of immense historical significance. They regaled the Blue Ribbon Commission with "rosy memories" of playing in the park beneath the watchful eye of General Lee, John told me. "There was rarely racist language that was used, but there was a clear identification with white nationalism, southern nationalism. This sense that the history that matters [is] the history of white people in the South, and that to understand southern history in any other way was wrong."

The battle over the statue became a window into the broader issue dividing the city: whether to cling to that sanitized version of history or wrestle publicly with uncomfortable remnants of white supremacy.

"I hadn't appreciated how much the mythology of the war was embedded in the hearts and souls of so many people," John told me.

"How many people take a powerful sense of identity from identifying with the Confederacy as a glorious lost cause, identifying with the defeat of the Confederacy as a terrible tragedy."

Until he served on the commission, the history professor—a descendant of slaves—had failed to understand how what historians call the "lost cause" theory still shapes the consciousness of so many people. "In their minds, to dishonor Robert E. Lee was to dishonor them, was to strike at the soul of their being." That same sentiment, of reverence for Confederate icons, was animating discussions across the country, in Richmond, New Orleans, Atlanta, Baltimore, even Madison, Wisconsin.

In Charlottesville, the public dialogue over the statues had begun to lean away from moving or dismantling them. But that abruptly changed when white progressives began turning up at commission meetings. The local residents were part of a national group called SURJ—Showing Up for Racial Justice—organized "to undermine white supremacy and to work toward racial justice."

"They were more radical than I was," John recalls. "They said, 'No, no, no. None of this transformation business. Get rid of them.' People on the right thought I was some sort of black militant bomb thrower. These folks on the left thought I'm some sort of 'Uncle Tom.' "

Their resistance helped blur the racial divisions. "To hear so many white people talk about white supremacy was really important," John said. "Really, really important." Their skin color insulated them from the typical claims lobbed at blacks. No one could accuse them of playing the race card or sowing racial division.

Ultimately, the commission voted to move the statue out of Lee Park, and the Charlottesville City Council concurred. Court challenges stalled the plan, and its future is uncertain. The statue remains, but in June 2017, one hundred years after it was established, Lee Park was renamed Emancipation Park.

• • •

Diane was unpacking on campus the night the neo-Nazis came. It was the middle of August, and the start of school was a week away, but she'd moved in early because she was so exicited to be one of the chosen few to live in that historic dorm along the Lawn at the center of campus during her senior year.

At 8:30, as night began to fall, her phone flashed a message from the university. What she remembers is the bluntness of the warning: "The Nazis will be here at 9." As if it were announcing a long-awaited visitor.

Everyone knew about a massive Unite the Right march planned for the next day, when hundreds of neo-Nazis and white nationalists were expected to descend on downtown Charlottesville. But no one had expected them to target the campus, two miles away, on that Friday night.

Nine o'clock came and went quietly, so Diane began to relax. Then she heard the chants: "Jews will not replace us! You will not replace us!" She looked out the window at "an angry mob of hundreds and hundreds of people," she said. They were shouting, carrying torches, and marching across the campus Lawn toward her room, close enough that she could see their swastika tattoos.

She took off every piece of jewelry that might identify her as a Jew. Then she fled through a back door into an alley that led to the nearby complex where faculty members live. She would watch the chaos that night from her professor's balcony.

Eventually, another official text arrived. "It's like, 'All clear. They're moving; they're no longer here.' Like, 'Okay, go back to your room and go to bed.' But I couldn't do that; it's like I just didn't want to be in that space," she said. Diane spent the night with the family of a friend who lived in town.

It was new to her, this feeling of being a target. She was a brown-skinned Jewish girl; her mother was white and Jewish, her father Indian and Catholic. Neither race nor religion was talked about in her family. She'd grown up in Maryland, the middle of three girls. "But I think I identify as the most Jewish," she said. "My mom and dad, they just don't understand what it's like to be a person of color just generally." At school, Diane had a multicultural circle of friends. This was the first time that she'd felt like an outsider on campus, at risk and unsafe.

I understood Diane's story on a level deeper than its specific elements. It was more than a visceral fear of bodily harm. She sensed a threat to the UVA self she'd so carefully cultivated in her three years at the school. She was vice president of her class, involved in dozens of activities, a university guide who led visitors and prospective students on historical tours. That was how she had come to define herself.

But we all have multiple selves that we carry around inside us. Which self dominates—to guide our thoughts, feelings, and actions—is, in part, a function of the situations we find ourselves in. The self that emerges at any given moment is not entirely under our control.

Within minutes on that Friday night, Diane's identity shifted from "Ms. UVA" to a Jew who did not belong. She was thrown from the center of campus to its fringes.

• • •

As Diane fled the rallying cries of the marchers, Professor Walt Heinecke ran toward the eye of the storm.

Walt had spent Friday evening firming up plans for alternative events, to counter what felt to many in Charlottesville like a looming alt-right assault. He was heading to St. Paul's Memorial Church, across from the UVA campus, when he spotted "groups of white supremacists" carrying unlit torches moving across the university field. He hustled to the church, where close to one thousand people of every race and religion had gathered that night to fortify themselves.

But just as the sermons and speeches were ending, someone grabbed the mic and told everyone to stay put: "The alt-right is headed here with torches. We don't know what they're planning." The church went on lockdown. It felt to them as if the entire city were under siege.

Walt got out and headed back to campus. He'd learned that the torch-carrying mob had made it to the Rotunda near Diane's historic dormitory and were menacing students who'd linked arms around a statue of Thomas Jefferson, the university's founder. "There were 150 torch-bearing, angry white men yelling, 'You will not replace us! Jews go home!'" Walt told me. "I mean just all the nastiest racial epithets you can imagine.

"Things were escalating by the moment. You could feel the tension and the danger. . . . I was scared out of my wits. I've never been in the midst of that kind of racial hatred and violence."

The students began to chant, "Black lives matter! Black lives matter!!" and the marchers drew in closer screaming, "White lives matter!"

Walt and UVA dean Allen Groves waded through the marchers to get to the students. "I started going around saying, 'Are you okay? Do you want to leave?' Anybody that wanted to leave I was ready to pull them out," Walt said. But none of the students wanted to abandon their comrades.

Suddenly a torch flew from the crowd of marchers, hit Dean Groves, and cut his arm. "And then pretty much quickly, right after that, things were happening like, boom, boom, boom," Walt recalled.

The marchers began dousing the crowd with mace. "A couple of them started beating on the students, hitting and throwing torches at them. It got to be physical and violent at that point," he said.

Then they heard sirens and the police showed up. "The neo-Nazis had started filtering off," he said. "That part was basically over."

But the real terror was about to begin.

SHOWING UP

They held service that Saturday morning, the day of Shabbat, with thirty neo-Nazis circling the synagogue and one man shouting "Heil Hitler" from the sidewalk, his arm raised in a Nazi salute. After they finished praying, the worshippers were forced to leave the temple through a side door.

Still, Geoff was relieved that nothing worse had happened. He was a student at both the law school and the business school at UVA, and his wife was a rabbi at Congregation Beth Israel, Charlottesville's only synagogue. The day before the march, they'd retrieved a sacred eighteenth-century Czech Torah scroll from its synagogue resting space to keep it safe from marauders.

The scroll had been among thousands of religious relics confiscated by Nazis during their European reign of terror. After World War II, hundreds of Czech scrolls were rescued and ultimately made their way to synagogues around the world.

The painful irony of his rescue operation would trouble Geoff for months: "Those [Jewish] communities, they were all exterminated. And now we've got this scroll, and it's being threatened again by Nazis."

That's part of what motivated Geoff and his wife to join a protest against the march after they left the synagogue that Saturday.

"When people say 'Don't go,' that's kind of what we think that our ancestors in Europe were told," Geoff explained. " 'Just let them come. . . . They're just a small group. They're not serious. If we just ignore them, they'll go away.' I think for us, we felt like that has proven itself to be an unsuccessful strategy, so we wanted to go out."

The strategy of turning a blind eye to bias has indeed failed to stem discrimination. But there are powerful currents that pull people away from confronting bias, even when they believe that's the right thing to do. Even small-scale actions that people might take when they see discrimination in play—standing up for a victim or scolding someone for using a racial slur—can require more energy and risk than many people are willing to expend.

Research shows that people tend to grossly overestimate the extent to which they will speak out against prejudice, particularly when they are not the target of the offense. And standing up against racism can be dangerous. The death of Heather Heyer in Charlottesville testifies to that. The thirty-two-year-old woman was killed and dozens of people were injured when a car plowed through a crowd of people protesting the march. Sixteen months later, in December 2018, the driver, twenty-one-year-old James Alex Fields Jr.—a self-professed neo-Nazi from a small town in Ohio—was convicted of murder by a Charlottesville jury that recommended prison, plus 419 years.

During my visit, when the pain was still raw, practically every person I spoke to mentioned Heather Heyer's tragic death. Brick buildings near the spot where Fields mowed her down still bore tributes, scrawled in chalk pastels: "ONE HUMAN RACE. NO MORE HATE. NEVER FORGET. THE MINUTE WE STOP FIGHTING BACK, THAT'S THE MINUTE BIGOTRY WINS."

• • •

On the morning of the march, Geoff and his wife were determined to show up. They made their way to Emancipation Park, where they found an interfaith group of clergy kneeling to counter the rabid displays of hate. One observer told me later that those religious leaders were taunted and spit on by white supremacists as they knelt.

In that southern city where the fault lines of history run black and white, Jews were not only being forced to reckon individually with the visible resurrection of virulent anti-Semitism. The verbal attacks were also meant to signal to everyone else that Jews were no longer to be accepted as white. Their status was probationary—to be threatened in threatening times.

The language of white supremacy has always demonized blacks and Jews in the same medieval style, relying on ancient stereotypes that degrade and dehumanize. The Charlottesville march, with its coalition of radical right-wingers and white nationalists, was intended to mobilize a new generation of haters to return to the good old days, when blacks and Jews knew their place.

According to the Anti-Defamation League, anti-Semitic incidents in the United States jumped almost 60 percent between 2016 and 2017, and much of that increase occurred on college campuses where white supremacist groups have stepped up their activity. Anti-Semitic incidents in schools and universities nearly doubled in that year. And after the wall-to-wall coverage of Charlottesville's violence, reports of threats, vandalism, and attacks on Jewish symbols and institutions spiked across the country for months.

On my visit to Charlottesville, everyone had different ways of referring to the collection of groups under the broad Unite the Right tent. They were white supremacists, Nazis, neo-Nazis, Klansmen, white nationalists, white separatists, the alt-right, or simply a collection of misfits who'd tapped into sentiments that had been percolating underground for years. Divisive political rhetoric and new propaganda tools helped create the momentum that propelled their anger to the surface. Their willingness to brandish blatant symbols of bigotry—torches, Confederate flags, swastikas—risks making the once-unthinkable seem routine, weakening the hold of egalitarian norms that value, or at least tolerate, diversity. That shifting of norms is what allows implicit bias to emerge explicitly.

The Unite the Right rally was the largest public gathering of white supremacists in a generation. Experts who study hate groups say their ranks are growing as social media makes connecting easier and the guardrails that reined in overt displays of racism have begun to come down.

A study of flourishing white supremacist networks on Twitter in 2016 found that two hashtags drew the most retweets: #White Genocide and #DonaldTrump.

• • •

Campbell came to Charlottesville because he loves the South. He'd grown up in Nashville, a white boy with liberal views on race and politics who wanted to study law so he could change the laws that prop up inequality.

He was just beginning his second year of law school at UVA when the white supremacists showed up with their guns and their Confederate flags to stake their claim to his legacy.

Campbell wasn't surprised by their ugly rhetoric or their pride in what he knew were emblems of bigotry. What he felt was more like shame, with a dose of liability.

"Those people are part of my community," he told me. "They could be my cousins, for all I know. . . . So in some ways, [it's] my responsibility and my fault, and taking action to correct that is an important thing."

The night before the march in downtown Charlottesville, Campbell and his classmate Brittany, a black woman from Princeton, New Jersey, were headed to a party when they saw what looked like tiny fires burning near the UVA Lawn. They figured students were holding a vigil, preparing themselves for their roles as counterprotesters the next day.

To a southern man and a black woman, the scene from a distance looked "very KKK-esque," Brittany said. She and Campbell joked about how naive those students must be to mimic what looked "so much like a KKK thing."

Then they realized it was indeed a KKK thing. White supremacists were marching across their campus, brandishing tiki torches, shouting Nazi slogans, and making crude monkey noises.

"I could not wrap my mind around the fact that they were actual torches," Brittany said. It was as if fearsome images of white-robed racists and burning crosses had sprung to life on her college grounds.

Campbell and Brittany cut their partying short that night. "We were out with other people, and it just felt really weird to be out while there were Nazis marching on the Lawn," Brittany explained. "There was just this sense of cognitive dissonance."

For Brittany, it was one of those moments where racial differences become clear and categorical. Her white classmates could hear about that scene and hold it at a distance. "They can say, 'Oh, this is horrible, but I'm not going to let it affect me.' [But] that's not really a choice that I feel like I have," she said.

For Campbell, that dissonance was compounded by crosscurrents of heritage and ideology.

"I felt very weird," he said, "because I knew that I was waking up the next morning to go protest racist anti-Semites, and most of the people at that party weren't. Most people at that party didn't really care."

The "us versus them" lines had begun to shift and blur. The

torches weren't part of a peace vigil; they were instruments of hate. The classmates he'd hoped would stand with him against racism seemed oblivious. And the people he planned to protest against looked eerily familiar to him.

When Campbell arrived to protest the march on Saturday morning, he waded through a sea of men "walking around with guns, wearing camo. . . . It was very hard to tell who the cops were and who the state Virginia Guard was and who the militia members were," he said.

As the conflict heated up and skirmishes broke out, it became harder to cleanly separate the bad guys from the good. Based on later estimates, the counterprotesters who arrived at the march were a couple thousand strong, outnumbering the protesters four to one.

Campbell wasn't afraid, but he was concerned enough to call his dad. "I was like, 'Hey, just FYI, I'm on the downtown mall today. I'm going to be fine, but just in case things go south, you should know that I'm here.'"

The counterprotesters he encountered were an eclectic bunch: clergy and churchgoers, socialists, feminists, pacifists, students, Black Lives Matter activists, militant Antifa warriors, the leftist Redneck Revolt, and a cadre of "de-escalators" trained to stand between warring factions to try to calm things down.

On the other side, marked by their long guns, bulletproof vests, and Confederate insignias, were race-baiting marchers whose uniforms broadcast their ties to the state that Campbell loves.

"There were several guys wearing Tennessee shirts, which my girlfriend pointed out to me," he said. "I'm from Tennessee and a Tennessee fan, so seeing someone who I have a common bond with marching around with a Confederate flag was not surprising, but it was difficult to see." The "them" had become him, it seemed. It was as if Campbell were fighting against himself.

That can raise uncomfortable questions of allegiance and identity. Campbell couldn't sever who he is from where he'd grown up. But he could choose which self he would be.

"If you're a liberal white person in the South, then you can't not grow up constantly wrestling with and thinking about issues of race," he said. "Distancing yourself from that is not something you would want to or could do.

"The people who were surprised by August 12, I think, were mostly not from here and were uniformly white," he said. "It was easy for them to be like, 'Well, I'm going back to New York next year. These southerners are just hicks.'"

• • •

Sophie Trawalter, a psychology professor at UVA, was scheduled to speak at a university event Saturday afternoon. "It was meant to be the counterprotest, but sort of engaging intellectually and thinking about democracy."

But she wanted her young son "to just have one moment where he gets to just have his regular day," she said. So they spent the morning at an indoor playground near their house.

On their drive back, she came across a foreboding sight: a group of men with machine guns, standing on a street corner near her house.

Her four-year-old son was quiet until they got home. Then he asked the question his mother dreaded: "He's like, 'Mom, why did those men have those big guns?'"

Sophie blurted out the first thing that came to her: "Well, you know, there are these people who are in our town today, and I think they're really scared and that's made them angry and they're here to scare people. I think they're here to start fights, and so we're going to stay out of the way, okay?"

Her husband wasn't thrilled with that response. Too much, he thought, for a child that young.

So they dialed it back a bit and widened the frame, to impart the sort of lesson a child could lean on. "We talked to him about how there are people who don't like other people because of the groups they belong to," she said. "And that it's not okay to be mean to people if you're angry, and it's not okay to be angry at people that you don't know just based on what they look like. Nice people look a lot of different ways."

Talking to little children about discrimination can be awkward, particularly for white parents who might not have had to deal with issues around race in their own lives. But the ugly images from Charlottesville forced parents across the country into uncomfortable conversations with their children about hate and race and history.

Under normal circumstances, for many white parents, the instinct is to show your child that race doesn't matter by not talking about it. Being color-blind is what it means to be a good parent; it's a sign of tolerance and a panoply of all the right virtues. But for most black parents, the instinct is to do the opposite: help children to understand how race does matter and show them how to move among people who might be biased. These are the conversations that protect them and prepare them for the world. Indeed, research shows that black parents talk to their children about race much earlier and more often than white parents.

At four, Sophie's son doesn't yet understand the concept of race. "He doesn't get how it functions," she said. But he does know that his babysitter and her daughter are black and that they have less money than his family and they live in a neighborhood that's not as nice as his.

"We've tried to talk to him about these things," Sophie told me. They bought a children's book about Rosa Parks. "We thought that was a good starting point." But her son didn't quite understand. "He was horrified because he thought Ebony, our nanny, still had to sit at the back of the bus. And there was no amount of explaining to him that that was the past." He still cries at the thought of anyone being mean to Ebony because she is black.

Sometimes, Sophie said, her son asks if he's white or black. There's a picture at their local Whole Foods of a little black kid whose smile resembles his. "Every time he sees that poster, he's like, 'Mom, look! That's me!'"

It's hard to tell a boy that innocent that race-baiting neo-Nazis are marching through his town and they hate people like his Jewish father and his black nanny. And that he should still feel safe. But Sophie felt compelled to talk about the march with her son, because "all of this stuff is happening right here and he's seeing it. It's been challenging to frame this for him in a way that he's aware but he's not scared."

It was hard for Sophie herself not to be scared. She had to stifle a scream as she watched live scenes on her cell phone of a "young guy getting beaten up by a group of white supremacists with bats and sticks." A state of emergency had been declared in Charlottesville. The university's talk fest had been scrapped. The attack Sophie saw was three blocks from their house. That afternoon, the family decided to pack up and leave until the marchers were gone.

They had to take a different route than they normally did to get out of town, to avoid driving past the march. Her mother-in-law, who's Jewish, was horrified by that; she wanted them on the front lines, battling anti-Semitism. "She was like, 'I can't believe we have to plot out our escape to avoid Nazis. This is insane.'"

"We all felt sort of that way," Sophie said. "And we were all scared." She was trapped by her dueling identities and the requisite balancing act. The mother in her accepted that it was dangerous to stay and she had a child to protect. But the psychology professor recognized the power in just showing up.

The mother won out. And when I met her three months later, Sophie was still wrestling with that choice.

• • •

For Anne Coughlin, a law school professor who served as a medic during the Saturday march, the weekend was "devastating" in ways that unexpectedly complicated her life.

She and her husband both volunteered to serve as medics during the march. They had a van, water, bandages, and a few medical supplies. They tended to people who had been teargassed, had been beaten up, or were simply so shaken by what they'd seen and heard that they could not stop crying. For days, the chemical taste of tear gas lingered in her mouth, and thoughts of those wounded bodies and souls were stuck in her head.

As a criminal law professor with a social justice bent, she'd prodded students to think about systemic racial bias. But as the marchers and counterprotesters clashed on the sidewalk outside a church, those racial dynamics became more than academic.

She saw "waves of vehicles carrying neo-Nazis and alt-right people, you could just tell. . . . Really scary people." And too many Nazi and Confederate flags to count. But what shook her up was not the folks "who looked like the *Duck Dynasty* guy" but the earnest young men who looked as if they belonged in her criminal law class, except that they were carrying weapons and wearing hateful expressions.

For weeks after that, "every time I see a white guy, I was having startled reactions," she said. "I would see an undergraduate [and think] maybe he was an alt-righter. . . . A white guy's walking down Fraternity Row and he's wearing a blue blazer and slacks and I'd have this startled reaction. Because that's what some of the alt-right guys were wearing, dressed like proper young gentlemen of the South."

She'd been primed by that march to link white skin with violence—just as we are primed all our lives to see random black men in that light. It was as if someone had flipped the script of her life, and the nice white lady lawyer was suddenly looking at life through a black-person lens.

The church that served as a gathering spot for the resistance was checking visitors for weapons with metal-detector wands. "They let everybody else through, but my husband got wanded," Anne told me. "They said to him, 'We're sorry, but all white guys are getting . . .' And then they realized, 'Whoa! We're racially profiling white guys.' So they start wanding everybody, which I thought was kind of hysterical."

But it stopped being funny when one of the white supremacist marchers outside the church was spotted with a gun. Anne tried to help hustle all the young black men inside so they would be safe. "And one of those guys just became enraged," she told me. "He was very close to me, in my space but not making eye contact, and screaming at me about how 'We have guns too!' Black guy. 'We have guns too.' And I thought, 'Okay. Just get in the church.'"

Then the young man lit into Anne and her do-gooder crew. "He started saying that the worst in the world were the white liberals. 'You are the people who have let us down. You did not get our backs. Fuck you! The Nazis, at least we know who we're dealing with when we're dealing with the KKK. But it's you white liberals . . .'

"And then there was this young Jewish man, and I know he was Jewish because he was wearing a yarmulke . . . and he turned to the African American man and said, 'You're right. We've done a terrible job. We need to do better.'

"That's my story," Anne said. "How do I do that?"

THE AFTERMATH

Anne seemed shaken to her core. I had come to Charlottesville on a quest for information. Yet I found myself absorbing Anne's pain along with the information she delivered. Simply being a witness to the aftermath exposed me to more than I had imagined. I saw human struggle, and violence, and its effects, up close.

For decades, Anne had been an advocate of movements to promote equality. But that didn't seem to matter much during the summer of hate. "I like to think of myself as an ally," she told me. "I don't know anymore. . . . They think I'm a fake ally. Oh, God. I don't know what to do. What do I do?" After everything she'd been through in Charlottesville, she seemed most worried that her efforts were misguided—that in the end, they'd failed. The young black man's denouncement of "white liberals" had clearly pierced her.

But black people are wondering about failed efforts too, I said to her. Black people who stood up during the civil rights movement, who marched and held steady when met with violence, felt as if they won and the whole world were about to open up. My parents' families fled the South so we would not grow up under the tyranny of Jim Crow. They looked to us—their children—to carry the baton across the finish line. Now many in my generation feel as if we were asleep at the wheel. What happened here in Charlottesville is about all of us.

The mistake we keep making—the mistake we all keep making—is in thinking that our work is done. That whatever heroic effort we've made will keep moving us forward. That whatever progress we've seen will keep us from sliding back to burning crosses and hiding Torah scrolls.

But this moment in Charlottesville is our lot, our inheritance. This is where our history and our brain machinery strand us—time and time again. Moving forward requires continued vigilance. It requires us to constantly attend to who we are, how we got that way, and all the selves we have the capacity to be.

• • •

In the aftermath of that summer of hate, getting back to normal teaching at UVA was hard. Students were feeling rattled and raw. Professors wanted to make the march a teachable moment but didn't want to prolong or intensify the trauma.

It was difficult "for the faculty to really know what our responsibility is in response to these events," Sophie said. "I've really struggled with that, because it's not clear what action is going to make a difference."

Many of the courses she taught dealt with issues that made it particularly hard to dodge fraught themes. "I talk about race and gender and social class and status in all of my classes," she told me. "This year more than ever, it's been really challenging."

Just one week after the Unite the Right march, she began teaching a class on values and bias to eighty-five UVA undergraduate public policy majors. The students seemed to her more ready to engage than in any other semester she had taught the course. But not every student saw the march and the issues it raised through the same lens.

Some could hold it at arm's length and wanted to talk about its intellectual meaning, as a test of our commitment to freedom of speech or a symbol of the cyclical sway of history. Others saw it as a challenge to their very existence. To them, it was an irredeemably ugly and emotional experience, a wholesale assault akin to terrorism.

Still, she was pleased that her students were willing to engage across that gap. "But I will say that this semester, more than any other semester I've ever taught, I've had situations where things got more heated than I'm comfortable with in the classroom."

Like those at most universities, UVA's student body leans liberal. But it's more conservative than the average college, and within its spectrum the conservative students tend to be "quite conservative . . . students for whom this is a really hard topic because they feel very easily targeted," Sophie said. "I take it as a victory in my class that those students feel comfortable speaking out."

In fact, there was so much speaking out that class discussions devolved into heated arguments. Some students would walk out in the middle of class because they were so angry or upset. "And then they'll come back," she said. "I get the sense that all my students are just sort of bubbling under the surface and just small things can lead to eruptions."

Her goal was to allow them to process what happened before, during, and after the march by making space for the emotion of it. As a social psychologist, she also considered those discussions a tool that would allow her students to understand the value of science. "It's really useful, in my mind, to have them debate these things because the whole point of this class is that we have values and biases that shape how we come up with public policy," she said. Typically, students could see the role of bias come into focus as the discussion unfolds "and then be able to say, 'Okay, talk to me about the psychology of this.'"

But the post-march discussions didn't always work out that way. It was harder than before to set boundaries that would let students boldly explore the role of alternate perspectives without leaving someone feeling angry, wounded, or insulted.

Her ground rules were the same as they'd always been, simple and straightforward: be respectful in the tone and the content of your comments. But this time, she said, "it was amazing that students really struggled with that and couldn't do it." Their arguments were too polarizing and their emotional investment too strong.

• • •

Students from the law school at UVA were having a tough time too. I met with a dozen students in two discussion groups during the last day of my visit. For hours we talked about what happened and what, in the aftermath, needed tending. A recurring theme they raised had to do with the notion of free speech, protected by the First Amendment of the U.S. Constitution. In fact that was the dominant frame for the march I heard all across the campus: First Amendment rights need to be protected, even when we despise and dispute the messages we hear. In that context, some felt the university was a champion of constitutional rights, and the students' emotional wounds were mere collateral damage.

But you can condemn what people say without condemning their legal right to say it. That's intrinsic to the success of many history-making campus movements. And many students felt there wasn't enough support for those who resisted and tried to douse the marchers' rhetorical fires. It was as if the moral high ground belonged to those who exercised their free speech rights and not to those who acted to protect the rights of others to live with dignity.

University administrators and leaders across the country are trying to find a balance, but often seem more concerned about emphasizing the value of the legal standards than the value of the lives that are being diminished, demeaned, and dehumanized. There is a rush to protect the law but more foot-dragging when it comes to protecting egalitarian norms on their campuses.

I understand why professors are conflicted about weighing in and why universities don't want to fan the flames or encourage uncivil disputes. But numerous students told me that what they perceived as biased or insensitive comments made by their classmates often went unchallenged in class. When those comments are ignored, an opportunity for educating everyone is missed.

Brittany, the black law student from Princeton, shared with me a friend's experience in a constitutional law course, where a classmate impugned black students during a discussion about affirmative action, implying that the black students in the class weren't qualified for their law school spots.

The comment was "completely unaddressed by the professor," she said. "To say that all black people in this school are not qualified to be here or to imply that they're somehow biologically deficient is factually incorrect. So there's definitely a way for you, as a teacher, to push back on that without it being, 'I'm showing my biases' or 'I'm pushing my agenda.'" Instead, marginalized students were left to defend themselves. "That's just not a burden," Brittany said, "that they should have to bear."

Or as another student, in her final year of law school, told our group, "Only a person that's never had to sit through a class in elementary school learning about slavery as the only black person in the class would not understand how hard and how uncomfortable that has to be."

That kind of identity threat, left unaddressed, can affect students' attachment to the school and their ability to function within it. It's hard to learn when people are challenging your right to be in the space. That takes a toll on grades, and it takes a toll on the soul.

Brittany, who'd helped the university with recruitment and developed a broad circle of friends, found herself pulling back from all things UVA. "It's a struggle to engage with the school in the same way that I had," she said. "Because all I see is just a lot of active dissociation from something that is very, very relevant. . . . I can't dissociate, and so it just feels very isolating because I'm not going to forget what happened anytime soon and I'm not going to feel secure about any of it anytime soon."

• • •

The Unite the Right rally might have been the largest public gathering of white supremacists in a generation. But it didn't come out of nowhere. And it could have been reined in before someone died.

That was the conclusion of a report commissioned by the City of Charlottesville and conducted by Tim Heaphy, a UVA graduate and former U.S. Attorney. The police took too long to take the threat seriously and were wary of being seen as heavy-handed if they waded in to break up scattered battles, his investigation found.

That confirmed the perceptions of many Charlottesville residents, who had accused police of being unresponsive and not sufficiently prepared. Some residents presumed they just didn't care, and others thought they were siding with the race-baiting terrorists.

A month before the August 12 march, the Ku Klux Klan had held a Charlottesville rally. Forty Klansmen showed up and were greeted by one thousand people protesting their presence. The rally lasted only forty-five minutes before the police shut it down and escorted the Klansmen away, to cheers and celebrations by counterprotesters. But when that crowd failed to disperse quickly enough, the police returned, declared an unlawful assembly, and began teargassing them.

In an interview, Tim told me that translated to a narrative embraced by the counterprotesters: "You protect these racists by giving them an escort into the event and out, then you give us tear gas." The police department was lambasted then for being overly aggressive.

So when August 12 rolled around, the police stood down. There seemed to be no official plan to protect anyone. The marchers and counterprotesters were not adequately separated. And as people were taunted, threatened, and beaten, officers on the scene declined to get involved. And given that breach, an armed, militant wing of counterprotesters under the Antifa banner stepped in. For some, that was a surreal turn of events that amplified how mixed up everything had become.

When a church hosting an interfaith group came under an alt-right attack, "there were police just on the corner [who] didn't get involved at all," Geoff, the rabbi's husband, recalled. "I'm a business student and a law student, and I was being protected by communists and anarchists," he said.

The investigation confirmed the public safety breach. "There's just awful body cam footage where you have officers standing behind barricades twenty feet away from a brawl in the street, and they're not moving in," Tim told me. "I think people come out of this feeling just unsafe. . . . And there's a long-term impact of that."

His report was released on December 1, 2017. Less than three weeks later, the Charlottesville police chief stepped down. Tim's position has changed as well. He is now university counsel at UVA, his alma mater, and is eager to serve what he believes to be "the best public university in the nation."

Until that summer, Tim told me, people had regarded Charlottesville as "this idyllic community . . . a safe place. It's harder to say that now."

That feeling of insecurity engulfed the entire town. Many white counterprotesters felt so unsafe and unprotected by police at the march that they got a hint of what it's like to experience the world as black people often do.

In fact, Professor Walt Heinecke said as much to me: he "finally . . . had an inkling of what it must be like for a nonwhite person to live in this society and be always worried about your safety—always having that on the forefront of your mind. I felt that viscerally that day."

• • •

That's the feeling that settled deeply into Diane after the neo-Nazis marched outside her dorm, carrying torches and yelling anti-Semitic chants. Three months later, it was still "really hard to navigate," she said. "Because sometimes it feels perfectly normal, and then, sometimes, if I'm walking down the Lawn at night, I picture the flames."

She felt "mentally and emotionally exhausted and traumatized." Even innocent gestures of like-minded students could trigger the sort of panic that made her feel afraid again. On more than one occasion, she saw a candlelight vigil or heard muffled chants and thought the invaders had returned, only to find out that they were rallies for peace and justice.

And those fears followed her into the classroom. Reflexively, she found herself "suddenly counting how many people of color are in the class. . . . Counting how many Jewish people are in the class."

Diane had always felt aware of herself as a nonwhite person in a predominantly white space, but now she felt threatened by that status. "Psychological safety in the classroom is a thing," she said. It didn't just make her anxious. Diane gave me a sense of other ways it affected her too, like "not being able to focus my eyes and pay attention in class, because I'm so distracted by the fact that all these white people just can move on with their lives where I'm just reeling in the aftermath."

I tried to imagine what it felt like to experience an unexpected loss of safety. I thought of my father's death, twenty-six years ago. He died suddenly at fifty-five when I was in graduate school, trying to train my mind to think like a psychologist. His death was deeply destabilizing. I came to realize that my sense of safety was tied to my father's presence in my life. It was as if I'd gone through life with him holding out an invisible force field that would protect me no matter where I was on earth. That force field dissolved the instant he died. What Diane described to me felt familiar in this way. At the broadest level, her story seemed to be about the death of security and freedom.

And yet Diane remained attached and committed to UVA. She wasn't going to let the terrorists win. "I just love this place too much to see it be known and remembered for the alt-right coming and not for how great this university is. It breaks my heart because I have to justify. People are like, 'Charlottesville? UVA? Why would you go there? Aren't there a bunch of really bad people there?'"

Diane managed to go back to giving university tours, and she learned how to talk about the summer of hate. On tours for prospective

257

applicants, "I am very upfront and very open about being here that day and being terrified," she said. But she also talks about new and better safety measures the university has planned and about the courage and compassion of students on the campus.

Still, the historical tours she conducts are more difficult to command. Her narrative used to have a "wonderful arc" where she would recognize the ugliness of Charlottesville's and UVA's pasts—slavery, racial subjugation, segregation, and discrimination—then focus on how far the city and the university have come. Now it feels hollow to talk about how good it feels to see the progress that's been made. She's forced instead to acknowledge the hazards we still face and highlight the fact that we can slip back.

• • •

L ocals like to say that Charlottesville is as far north as southerners are willing to go and as far south as northerners are willing to go. It's a place where different worlds collide and coexist. And there in the middle of it all is the University of Virginia—the school that Thomas Jefferson built and where he still stands atop a marble base in the ornate university Rotunda, holding court.

I could feel his presence on the campus, where he is discussed, consulted, and regularly engaged in lectures, formal presentations, and daily conversations. I saw his image, read his name, or heard his thoughts each day I set foot on the campus. Here, Jefferson is kept alive—his spirit supported and nurtured as a guiding light. The author of the Declaration of Independence was not only the founder of UVA; he was the visionary and the architect. He brought into being an institution where human progress is stirred and cultivated. And every day, his patrons praise and bow to him.

The "academical village" that Jefferson forged landed in the eye of the struggle in August 2017. UVA was poised to celebrate two hundred years since its founding when the torch-wielding neo-Nazis came marching through its cherished Lawn to face the founder and his students who locked arms around him.

The marchers had come to start a race war. But in many respects, that race war was seeded more than two hundred years ago, and Jefferson himself was the embodiment of its warring principles. The man who preached independence and equality held more slaves in bondage than almost any white man in the state of Virginia. He wrote "all men are created equal" but believed in white supremacy, contending that blacks were inferior to whites in both "body and mind." Jefferson the intellectual believed in the power of science to advance human progress, yet he also believed that blacks were incapable of intellectual growth.

Jefferson built UVA with black enslaved labor. White students enrolled and the institution ran with the support of black slaves, who were, by Jefferson's design, hidden from view, placed in pavilion basements and pushed into work yards where they lived behind serpentine walls. Jefferson used a similar architectural plan at his Monticello home, where slave quarters and work areas were built into an embankment at the back of the property, in a separate, subterranean world. Blacks were removed from sight so that free people could live in peace.

As a country, even as we have attempted to move steadily toward Jefferson's egalitarian ideals and away from his notions of white supremacy, bias has sought refuge inside us. In Charlottesville, it ripped through the pact we've made to pretend that blatant bigotry is a relic of the past. In truth, bias has been biding its time in an implicit world—in a place where we need not acknowledge it to ourselves or to others, even as it touches our soul and drives our behavior.

In this country, blacks have become a reminder of the racial bias that we refuse to see. Indeed, blacks have become symbolic of the unwanted. And this is even apparent on college campuses, the setting for the construction of a new generation. "African American students have always felt alienated and unwelcome at this university," Professor John Mason said of UVA. "It's hard for them to articulate why, and I think a lot of it has to do with our history. . . . Slavery is really embedded here."

I talked with black students who felt exhausted from fending off narratives that question their humanity. Those dehumanization narratives may be felt most acutely in a place where the bones of slaves are buried, but they are still operating across the country and around the world. They circulate in our minds and animate our culture. They still work to help free people live in peace.

CHAPTER 10

The Bottom Line

I got my first lesson in economics in 1976, when I was eleven years old. It was delivered by my father, after I wound up underwater in my first business venture.

I'd landed a paper route in my Cleveland neighborhood, with dozens of customers. Every day my boss would drop a twine-wrapped bundle of newspapers on a corner near my house. I would head there straight from school, unravel the twine, place the bundle on my head, brace it with my hands on both sides, and travel my delivery route on foot. Once I mastered the process, I could distribute all my papers in less than an hour.

Then, once a week, I'd collect the money subscribers owed and turn it over to my boss. He'd dole out my cut, which couldn't have been more than $10 but felt like a fortune to me.

I was so proud to have a paying job. I'd negotiated the entire thing myself. It felt as if I were doing something big—keeping records, delivering papers, handling money, and dealing with the hazards I faced, from snow-clogged sidewalks to snarling dogs.

But there was one hazard I couldn't negotiate. Every Friday my newspaper bundle would be ransacked by local teenagers who'd pil-fer the weekly TV guides, a valuable commodity if you wanted to know what to watch on the handful of television channels we had access to back then.

That meant I didn't have enough TV guides for all my paying customers. So I made what I thought was a shrewd business decision: I would deliver the TV guides I had to some customers and make sure the ones I'd skipped got one the following week. But when I made my rounds on Mondays to collect for the previous week, the custom-ers who'd been stiffed would refuse to pay me a cent. If they hadn't received their TV guides, my week's work didn't count for anything to them.

I still had to pay my boss for each customer's subscription, so almost every week I'd come up short. To make up the difference, I'd have to ask my father for an advance on my allowance.

Before long, my dad sat me down to talk about the bottom line. "Let me explain something to you about how this all works and what it means to have a job," he said. "The idea is to make money, not owe money." The advances were going to stop. "You've got to figure it out or quit that job."

I didn't want to quit, so I had to find a way to protect my product and keep my customers satisfied. I realized that the only safe place for those newspaper bundles was in my backyard. My boss agreed to drop them there; after all, his income depended on whether kids like me could do the job.

I spent the next several months delivering papers to happy subscribers—and raking in enough cash to buy all the candy I wanted at Gardell's, our neighborhood store. With my business out of the red, I was living the life.

Even then, on some level, I realized that employment could be a major mechanism to propel my life forward and raise my standard of living. What I didn't realize was how hard it would be for the young people who came after me. Today, the unemployment rate for black teens and young adults is about twice as high as it is for whites. At a time of life when critical work habits and life skills are developed, black teens in low-income neighborhoods—where businesses, restaurants, and retail outlets are sparse—have fewer options and face adult competition for entry-level jobs.

Just as where we live and what schools we attend help chart the trajectory of our lives, the jobs we take on can provide us not only with financial resources but with opportunities to stretch, set goals, and thrive. The work we do becomes a part of who we are and how we come to experience the world. Yet the employment arena is also a place where racial gaps loom large.

Historically, not only are blacks less likely to be employed than whites; they have worse jobs and earn less money. Many factors contribute to these disparities, including the quality of the applicant's social networks marshaled to secure employment as well as the level of education, skills, or experience certain jobs require.

But research has made clear that racial bias is also a factor that influences the choices employers make and how minorities fare in the job search and in the workplace.

In a now-classic study of discrimination in the U.S. labor market, economists Marianne Bertrand and Sendhil Mullainathan set out to document the impact of race on the job application process. They constructed fictitious résumés that matched qualifications of actual help-wanted ads listed in newspapers in Chicago and Boston. They signaled the race of applicants on identical résumés by using names that sounded either black or white and sent five thousand of them to thirteen hundred posted jobs.

When they tallied the responses, they found that Tyrone, Jamal, Keisha, and Tamika got far fewer calls for interviews than Geoffrey, Brad, Emily, and Jill, even though their credentials and experience were exactly the same.

The applicants with black-sounding names were 50 percent less likely to get a callback than applicants with white-sounding names. The racial difference emerged regardless of the applicant's gender, regardless of where the ad was placed (Chicago or Boston), regardless of the occupational category of the job (sales, administrative support, clerical, or customer service), and regardless of whether the position was entry level or management.

Even having a "high quality" résumé, featuring more experience and skills, didn't do much to heighten interest in black candidates. In fact, highly qualified black applicants were less likely to be called back than less-qualified whites. And companies labeling themselves "equal opportunity employers" were no less likely to discriminate.

The hypothetical white applicants received one callback for every ten applications sent out, while the black applicants needed fifteen tries to generate one response. That puts blacks at a disadvantage at the first point of entry in the hiring process. Fewer of them ever make it out of the gate.

The study was published in 2003, but the results have held up over time. And stark racial differences in callback rates are not limited to the United States. Employment discrimination against nonwhites has been shown in Australia, Europe, and across North America. In Canada, researchers using a similar methodology found strong evidence of bias toward applicants with foreign experience or those with Chinese, Indian, Pakistani, and Greek names. In Australia, résumés with Middle Eastern and East Indian names were most likely to be ignored.

In the United States, an evaluation of data from two dozen studies that have been conducted over the last twenty-six years found that both blacks and Latinos are disadvantaged by bias in the job search process. The meta-analysis, led by sociologist Lincoln Quillian, involved more than fifty-four thousand applicants who applied for more than twenty-five thousand jobs. The research team found that whites received 36 percent more callbacks than blacks and 24 percent more than Latinos. The disparities persisted even when controlling for gender, education level, job categories, and labor market conditions. The role of racial bias in hiring decisions seems to have changed little in the last quarter century.

• • •

We've spent decades talking about affirmative action and preaching diversity in the United States, but even our country's most promising minority college students are still forced to wrestle with prejudice as they try to launch their careers.

Beginning in 2013, a team of researchers tested the perceptions of college students by interviewing dozens of black and Asian university students who were actively job hunting. Social scientists Sonia Kang, Katherine DeCelles, András Tilcsik, and Sora Jun wanted to know how they planned to present themselves during the application process. The research team was following up on previous studies that have shown that blacks and Asians are subject to stereotypes that could resonate unfavorably with employers or recruiters.

The students they spoke with were surprisingly matter-of-fact about their concerns that bias might hold them back. In fact, many had taken pains to scrub their résumés of references that could draw attention to their race in ways that might trigger damaging stereotypes.

They Anglicized their names, relying on nicknames or initials to avoid identifying as Zhong or Jamal. They toned down or omitted ethnic affiliations and commitments, like heading the Black Students Association or volunteering with a Korean health-care group. Some added interests, like wilderness treks, typically associated with white people.

"Ultimately you want to do as much as you can to be familiar, relatable" to prospective employers, a young Asian man looking for a job in finance told the researchers.

This particular practice of fitting in is so widespread that it even has a name: Whitening the Résumé. Two-thirds of the students the team interviewed either engaged in the practice or knew someone who did. In the same way that minorities on the home-stay platform Airbnb might curate their profiles to increase their odds of booking a spot, these students—all from top-tier private universities—curate their résumés to keep from getting knocked out of the job process in the very first round.

These young women and men are at an age when idealism is presumed to reign. But they've also lived long enough to know that race matters and that discrimination comes in different forms.

Anyone can be influenced by bias, particularly when it comes to intimate decisions like who is going to stay in your home or join your team on the job. When someone seems foreign or unfamiliar or un-predictable, your gut reactions prepare you to be wary. That is when out-group bias can surface instinctively.

In fact, neuroimaging studies show that our brains work harder to process positive information about out-group members than neg-ative information. And we do just the opposite with in-group mem-bers. Several of my colleagues, Brent Hughes, Nalini Ambady, and

Jamil Zaki, have found that this even extends to money. Giving money to an out-group member really gets the attention of the brain systems involved in executive functioning. It's as if an all-systems alert were fired off, just to underscore the danger: be careful now.

These young people were trying to sidestep that instinct. One young Korean woman bluntly explained her fears to the research team: "I think they do perceive me as an 'other' despite the fact that my English is perfect. Like, I grew up in America. I am a U.S. citizen. . . . But there is—it's still like very stigmatizing to be Asian."

For Asian students, the goal was to seem less foreign and closer culturally to white Americans, "to fit a more American or Western friendly kind of persona," as one student put it.

"You want to kind of Americanize your interests," explained a male college student of Bangladeshi descent who was born and raised in the United States and has worked for the federal government. "You don't want to be too multicultural. . . . So a lot of people will put, you know, hiking or snowboarding or things that are very common to America or Western culture."

For black students, the challenge was to not be seen as radical or a rabble-rouser, but project instead the image of a nonpolitical person uninterested in racial causes.

A black college senior shared his perspective on that rationale: "In the real world I think people . . . want to have like an awesome black worker, but they want one who they feel like fits within a certain box. . . . [Someone who] will conform and lay low and just kind of do what's expected of them."

The students were employing what legendary social scientist Erving Goffman called an "assimilative technique." You restrict information about the aspects of your identity that are most likely to become a basis for discrimination. By toning down their minority status, they were trying to "send reassuring signals of conformity to the white majority." It was hard for me to read the contortions students still went through in the twenty-first century to comfort that white majority.

A black student interested in investment banking concealed his involvement with the National Society of Black Engineers because "they would automatically know that I am or could be black."

A leader in the university's Black Christian Fellowship called it simply the Christian Fellowship.

A student of Chinese descent loaded the "interests" section of her résumé with risk-taking endeavors, "to distinguish myself and not just be the perfect cookie-cutter Asian."

A black college senior planning a career in education even omitted a prestigious scholarship he'd received because it's widely known that it goes only to minority students.

The bias they face is so ingrained that even college counselors and corporate mentors advised them to play down the salience of race.

One young woman was encouraged to whiten her résumé by the campus Career Services center. "In freshman year, I put my legal name, which is very Chinese-sounding," she said. A career counselor suggested she use her American nickname instead, because "it's just more relatable if you're more American-sounding." The résumé with her Chinese name got no responses, she said. After she changed it, "I got interviews."

Another black student about to graduate was advised by "a black guy at Goldman Sachs" to tone down references to his work with black middle school students, because a "life skills" class he taught included a session on dealing with authoritarian police. "I was told . . . to remove [that] from my résumé because of how controversial it could look," he said. Activities that "don't fit the corporate image" could work against him, he was warned.

He made the change but was conflicted about the personal cost: "It just goes to show . . . that to get ahead, some parts of our race need to be only talked about at certain times. Some parts of my racial identity need to be squashed or held back."

The students who resisted the impulse to whiten their résumés had a variety of reasons. Some found it hypocritical, particularly when their career plans involved working with marginalized groups. Others worried that scrubbing their résumés of volunteer work or leadership roles would make them appear less qualified than they really were. Many said they didn't want to work at a place that tolerated discrimination, so they saw no need to keep their real selves under wraps. And some clung to the notion of America as a meritocracy, where their accomplishments would be evaluated fairly without regard to race.

I was struck by their determination to fit in to what they imagine the business world to be. "Diversity" has been a corporate watchword since before they were born. That's supposed to reflect an enthusiastic embrace of new perspectives and a willingness to hear and accommodate previously marginalized voices. Instead, it seems to have become a numbers game. Companies want to check the boxes but not change their culture. So young people are desperately tailoring themselves to fit in to those boxes. And I'm left wondering what will happen to those selves they jettison in the process.

That kind of mild subterfuge makes the role of implicit bias even more complicated in the hiring and management sphere. The employers with hiring power are probably not bigots, trashing black résumés and crossing off Asian names. But they are part of a process that is skewed toward prioritizing a comfortable fit and away from valuing differences. They are practicing in-group favoritism rather than out-group derogation. And that's the sort of mind-set that allows bias to flourish, under the radar and unchecked.

After the research team finished interviewing the students, they generated their own bank of résumés and sent matched pairs of whitened and unwhitened résumés to employers advertising real jobs that matched the fictional qualifications they'd created.

A clear pattern emerged across both groups: The whitened résumés led to more callbacks than unwhitened résumés. The gap was particularly large when applicants "whitened" both their names and their experiences. The disparity suggests that signaling racial assimilation and conformity is a key strategy for minorities trying to find work in white-dominated industries.

Even when the employers' job posts declared a commitment to diversity, the researchers found that those companies were just as likely to reject the candidates whose race was most obvious. The students who trusted the diversity language wound up being disadvantaged. That led the researchers to conclude that whitening "presents a dilemma rather than a solution" for minorities.

The research findings and the experiences of those students run counter to views on race that have been percolating in this country for years: *Affirmative action has tilted the playing field so that minorities have the advantage on everything. White people are losing ground economically because of our society's infatuation with diversity.*

More than half of white Americans—55 percent—believe there is discrimination against white people in the United States today, according to a 2017 survey by Harvard University's School of Public Health, the Robert Wood Johnson Foundation, and National Public Radio. "If you apply for a job, they seem to give the blacks the first crack at it," one middle-aged white man from Ohio told interviewers. "It's been going on for decades, and it's been getting worse for whites." He was disgruntled because a black man made the finals for a promotion he didn't get. The job wound up going to a white man many years younger than he.

. . .

The students who whitened their résumés were trying to level the playing field, to get over that first hurdle so they could remain in the race. But even if they make it to the next step in the career competition, bias is liable to infiltrate the process. And again, this can happen in places beyond the United States. For example, in a study conducted in Sweden, researchers found that the interview questions developed by professional recruiters varied based on the applicant's ethnicity. Recruiters prepared to ask those with Arab-sounding names questions that focused on their "cultural fit." In contrast, the questions they prepared for those with Swedish-sounding names were directed at "job fit" (for example, "what previous experience do you have that is most relevant to this job?"). And the interview questions matter. In a separate study, recruiters indicated that the questions they found the most useful were those aimed at understanding an applicant's qualifications.

Yet sometimes, having impeccable qualifications is still not enough to shield people from bias in the workplace. Even in the high-stakes world of entrepreneurial markets, minorities and women are held to higher standards than white men in competing for investment dollars.

My colleague Hazel Markus and I co-direct SPARQ, a center at Stanford designed for the purpose of bringing researchers and practitioners together to tackle such issues. Recently, we partnered with Daryn Dodson, who leads a private investment firm, to begin isolating the causal role race might play in the investment market. We designed a series of studies and recruited asset allocators, whose job is to determine what businesses to invest in, to participate. In one study, we presented the allocators with a description of a highly qualified venture-capital team, using photographs to depict the managing partner of the team as either black or white. We found that the more qualified the black-led team appeared to be, the more bias they faced. Asset allocators evaluated the track record of the highly qualified black-led team more negatively and perceived them to be less capable of "executing on strategy" than a white-led team with identical qualifications. In an investment world that is 99 percent white and male, it may turn out that blacks are turned away not because they are less qualified than white men but because they are equally qualified.

Bias is activated against women in much the same way as it is against racial minorities—whether they are at the beginning of their careers or at the pinnacle, whether they are seeking a low-wage job or one that is highly paid. Research has shown that résumés from men generate more callbacks than identical résumés from female candidates, leading some women to use gender-neutral names on their résumés, in the same way that the black and Asian students tried to seem less ethnic and less threatening.

For women, being too smart can be a turnoff too. A study by sociologist Natasha Quadlin found that résumés from men with high GPAs generate nearly twice the rate of callbacks as résumés from women with the same grades. And when math is their major, the male-female gap is three to one. Quadlin followed up by surveying hiring managers and concluded that "gendered stereotypes" were to blame.

"Employers value competence and commitment among men applicants, but instead privilege women applicants who are perceived as likable," Quadlin explained. "This standard helps moderate-achieving women, who are often described as sociable and outgoing, but hurts high-achieving women, whose personalities are viewed with more skepticism."

The men were expected to be high achievers in the workplace; the women were expected to get along with everyone. Those expectations shape what people focus on and what they perceive.

Reams of studies have shown that judgments of women in the labor market are more likely to be based on factors that have little to do with professional competence: weight, appearance, hairstyle, style of dress, perceptions of personality. Confidence in a man is arrogance in a woman. A strong-willed man is a leader; an outspoken woman is difficult. Bias determines who gets to shine, who's allowed to stand out, who is lauded for being a "disrupter," and who is sidelined for being disruptive.

One of the most intriguing examples of how gender perceptions can color evaluations of professional competence comes from a study of auditions for positions with America's most renowned symphony orchestras.

Economists Claudia Goldin and Cecilia Rouse examined gender bias in the hiring practices of orchestras in 2000. Historically, female classical musicians have been stereotyped in ways that downgrade their talent and cast them as undeserving prima donnas: they have "smaller techniques than men," are "more temperamental," require "special attention or treatment," and produce "poorer sound."

The researchers wondered what impact those widespread perceptions might have on audition outcomes for women judged by male musicians and what changes in the hiring process might mitigate bias.

They had an ideal set of circumstances to study, built on history. In the 1970s, stung by criticism over the paucity of female musicians, many orchestras began using what they called "blind" auditions, with candidates performing behind an opaque curtain to mask their identity. Goldin and Rouse acquired audition records of the leading orchestras in the United States and examined more than seven thousand candidates in more than fourteen thousand rounds of auditions to gauge the effectiveness of the intervention.

The screens, often hung from the ceiling rafters of the symphony hall, were made of heavy sound-porous fabric. As an extra precaution, carpets could be rolled across the wooden floor to "muffle footsteps that could betray the sex of the candidate."

The researchers found that blind auditioning increased the probability that a woman would make it past the preliminary round by 50 percent. And of those women who advanced to the final round, the ones who auditioned behind the screens were 33 percent more likely to be hired by the symphony than those who played in the open. In fact, the subset of women who auditioned more than once—with a screen and without—almost always fared better when the screen hid their gender. Ultimately, the blind audition process increased the likelihood that a woman would be hired to join the orchestra by 25 percent.

But the process does more than blunt the impact of bias. It raises provocative questions that reach beyond the concert hall and move us to consider the interplay among stereotypes, performance, and basic sensory functioning. How you are seen may affect how you are heard.

Given the pervasive and persistent stereotypes about the performance of women, might the concerto actually sound different to the audition judge's ear when he knows that the instrument is being played by a woman? To what extent might the audience in the symphony hall experience a concert solo by a female musician as less sharp, less skillful, less resonant, less emotionally moving? And to what extent might that woman actually perform differently when she knows that her identity attaches to every note she hits?

Those are the sorts of questions that animate the study of bias and the complicated relationship between the subconscious messages our minds emit and the way our brains register subjective experience. How we perceive a talent or a trait can depend on who carries it.

For example, when it comes to corporate leadership roles, the mental associations between whiteness and leadership have contributed to the scarcity of minorities at the helm of powerhouse corporate entities. But research by social psychologists Robert Livingston and Nicholas Pearce suggests that the same physical features that can handicap white men on their corporate climb can help a black man rise to the top of the corporate hierarchy.

Studies have long held that grown men with "baby faces" are apt to be perceived as naive, submissive, or weak—not exactly the traits that align with leadership potential. But it turns out that a baby face may be an asset instead of a liability for professional black men. Black male CEOs of Fortune 500 companies are more likely than their white counterparts to sport the smooth round face, large wide-set eyes, and small nose and chin that conjure up a baby's visage. And they are more likely to make higher salaries and lead companies with higher prestige than black CEOs who look more mature.

Brain-imaging studies show that our neurons activate in much the same pattern whether we're looking at babies' faces or baby-faced men. Our primitive minds equate those features with being trustworthy, docile, and warm. And that perception can have a "disarming" effect by neutralizing stereotypes that tag black men as aggressive or threatening. It scrambles the perceptions that tend to drive racial bias.

THE TRAINING IMPULSE

It was my middle son, Everett, who showed me the video of what would come to be known as the Starbucks incident. Two young black men, Donte Robinson and Rashon Nelson, were waiting to meet a business acquaintance in a Starbucks near Philadelphia's tony Rittenhouse Square when they were handcuffed and arrested by police. Their offense? Trying to use the restroom without buying anything first.

My sixteen-year-old son watched the scene unfold on a cell phone video: the police asking the men to leave, the business partner demanding to know why, "What did they do?," the police leading them out of the coffee shop and into the backseat of their cruiser. Everett thought it must be some kind of prank. "I just thought, like, this can't be real," he said. The two men were simply sitting there waiting. "They actually got kicked out, and the cops came just because they were there." The whole thing—from bathroom request to public arrest—went down in less than ten minutes. "It was just really surprising to me," my son said.

But I wasn't sure what he found surprising about it. For months, Everett had been sharing posts of racially offensive advertisements that popped up on his Instagram feed. And two years earlier, we'd both been shocked by the live-streamed death of a man shot by a police officer who'd stopped him because his taillight was out.

Perhaps the Starbucks incident was most surprising to him because what the two black men did was what people do routinely: walk into a Starbucks, sit down, and wait for a friend. It was so surprising precisely because it was so ordinary.

Black people regularly encounter racial bias in all types of businesses and in all types of routine interactions. They attract out-sized attention from sales and security personnel, who follow them around in retail stores. They pay more than whites for cars at auto dealerships, even when they have equivalent credit histories. They wait longer to be helped at restaurants. They receive poorer service. And as social media has so graphically made clear, individual black consumers are often subjected to racial epithets from other customers, insulted by clerks, and challenged—or even physically removed—by police.

The Starbucks incident crystallized all that, in ways that made it hard to dismiss. The video that Everett watched had garnered more than three million viewers in the two days before the Starbucks CEO weighed in. It was a striking tableau of the force of bias to empower, enrage, divide, unite, humiliate, and leave us shaken and confused.

The barista imagined a threat where none existed when she reported the men for trespassing because they hadn't yet purchased anything. The young black men were quiet and polite as they were questioned, scolded, and handcuffed by police. The white business-man they were there to meet rose to their defense. The black police chief said they deserved to be arrested, because they refused to leave. And a few disgusted white patrons wondered aloud why they them-selves had been allowed to sit unbothered in Starbucks for hours without buying anything. "This doesn't happen to white people," the white woman who filmed the incident told CNN.

The uproar ultimately led the Starbucks CEO to fly to Philadel-phia to personally apologize to Donte and Rashon. The company policy was changed so that every Starbucks visitor can have access to the bathrooms.

Starbucks also did what no other company had done before: it held a nationwide training on implicit bias for all its 175,000 employees. On May 29, 2018, eight thousand company stores were shuttered for the four-hour session, which included a series of short films featuring black people of all ages talking about how discrimination in public places makes them feel. The store closures were estimated to cost Starbucks $12 million in lost revenue, but were hailed as a smart business move for the brand.

The world is more transparent today than ever before. Mistreatment of customers can be captured on cell phones and shared instantly. Social media platforms allow disgruntled employees to reach millions with stories of sexism, bigotry, or other wrongdoing. And research suggests that the millennial generation, more than seventy million strong, places a higher value on ideals like corporate responsibility and workplace diversity. Companies are bound to respond to the pressure those factors create.

Millennials make up almost 40 percent of the American workforce today and are on the verge of passing baby boomers as the nation's largest living generation. They are also the most diverse adult generation in American history. About one-third are foreign born and almost half are nonwhite. Eradicating bias in the workplace has both philosophical and personal significance for them.

"Bias training" is the new watchword in human-resource programs. A growing number of private companies are creating and pitching training modules that range from brief online videos to weeklong seminars. Their clients run the gamut from big money-making corporations to cash-strapped government entities, private not-for-profits, and high-minded philanthropic foundations. Some want to understand the role that bias may play in the decisions their companies make. Some organizations are being pushed by clients, constituents, or communities to train employees to behave more equitably. And some businesses view implicit bias training as a way to signal to their base that they care about these issues and value egalitarian ideals.

The promise of bias training is not to magically wipe out prejudice but to make us aware of how our minds work and how knee-jerk choices can be driven by stereotypes that cloud what we see and perceive. Done well, training can make employees more mindful of how they interact with co-workers and customers. The intent is genuine, and the programs have stirred up a lot of surprising reactions among employees who had no idea about some of their own behaviors.

But implicit bias can be layered and complicated. It's simple to explain, but not so easy to see or to rectify. And the value of training, with all its variables, is often hard to quantify. The vast majority of implicit bias trainings are never rigorously evaluated, in part because measuring their worth is hard. There are no agreed-upon metrics developed by scientists for evaluating training effectiveness. Should the training lead to an immediate reduction in implicit bias? That's a tall order considering that these implicit associations have been practiced over a lifetime. What would a reduction in implicit bias even look like? Should the training lead to better employee decision making? Should it lead to improvements in customer satisfaction? And how would we measure and parse blame or credit for any of that?

Although this is an area that seems ripe for scientific discovery, many researchers are hesitant to get involved. They are concerned that the trainings are not evidence based, that they overpromise, and that they could even leave us worse off. From this perspective, everyone needs to just slow down until we can get the science right.

I have a different perspective. It's not that social scientists are too fast to act; we are too slow. There is so much concern over the prospect of acting before we know enough about a phenomenon that we never get around to taking action. And because the scientific enterprise is iterative, we never seem to get to the point where we think we know enough. Social scientists fret so much about the purity and precision of science that we rarely throw ourselves into the messy problems of the world. From my perspective, engaging in the world, tackling thorny problems, can open the way to scientific discovery. If we don't know enough as scientists to shed light on a problem, sometimes it is because we simply aren't close enough to it.

As a scientist, I don't arrive on the scene with the answers. I arrive with questions. And my goal is to engage practitioners and encourage them to get involved in the business of putting the puzzle pieces together.

Even beyond the difficulty of evaluating the effectiveness of training are the high financial stakes involved with declaring success or failure. Bias training is a fast-growing for-profit business, and finding fault with results could affect the bottom line of the trainers. Better to just check the box that says "Yes, we've trained our employees" and call it victory.

Most trainers in the business today are not scientists trying to solve the mysteries of the mind but entrepreneurs trying to deliver a message and sell a product that is in high demand. In fact, given the stakes, it may be simpler not to know whether the training works or why it may be less likely to work under certain conditions.

The organizations that solicit training, likewise, have little incentive to spend the time and money it would take to measure the effectiveness. If a primary incentive for them is to signal to their stakeholders and to the world more broadly that they are doing something to curb bias, being presented with a finding of the limited effects of training is a risk they don't need.

For businesses, there are big upsides to training. But there are also downsides. The first has to do with the importance of norms in guiding behavior. The vast majority of implicit bias trainings stress how pervasive bias is. Bias is presented as a part of normal human functioning. That is something I have done as a trainer in the policing industry, and it is something I have stressed in this book. It's true that we are wired for bias. But the problem with narrowly settling for that perspective is that it can lead us to care less about the danger associated with bias, instead of more.

When something is regarded as a norm, people cease to judge it harshly. They are not only inclined to believe that the norm is just "the way things are"; they are inclined to believe that something normative is "the way things *should* be." They feel less agency and less motivation to change.

Norms pose a problem even for behaviors that are unwanted, unsafe, or unhealthy. In a classic study of drinking behavior on college campuses, for example, social psychologists Dale Miller and Deborah Prentice at Princeton University found that the more alcoholic beverages male Princeton students thought others were drinking, the more they drank themselves. Their own behavior was tethered to what they perceived the campus norm to be, even when their perception of the norm was inaccurate. Likewise, a research group led by Chris Crandall, a social psychologist at the University of Kansas, found that people are more likely to endorse stereotypes about out-groups—from racists to drug users to porn stars to trash collectors—when they believe those stereotypes are widely held in society.

But trainers stress the prevalence of bias for a good reason: They want the people they're training to engage with the topic in a personal way. It's difficult to stay engaged if what you are hearing is accusatory and threatening. Race is such a loaded topic it's easy to shut down if you feel that owning up to bias makes you a bad person and a source of evil in the world. So the trainers try to make the employees feel better, or at least less uniquely bad; after all, it's something that everyone is vulnerable to. But too much focus on how good innocent people can be biased without intention can sap people's motivation to do something about it. So, teaching and learning about bias is a balancing act that has to be expertly calibrated to have the appropriate impact.

The second place where bias training can go wrong has to do with what social psychologists call moral credentialing. "People are more willing to express attitudes that could be prejudiced when their past behavior has established their credentials as nonprejudiced," say Benoît Monin and Dale Miller, two social psychologists. It's the "some of my best friends are black" hall pass. If you've stored enough credits in the bank of equality, you're entitled to behave badly.

Two researchers, Margaret Ormiston and Elaine Wong, recently followed up on this idea to find out whether Fortune 500 firms rely on moral credentialing. Indeed, they found that companies that touted "corporate social responsibility" in a specific arena—for example, by improving their safety records—were significantly more likely to behave irresponsibly down the road, maybe by ignoring important safety warnings. It was as though responsible behavior handed them a license to behave recklessly. That suggests that companies that offer bias training might be loosening the reins in ways that set prejudice free. The worry is that groups that sign on to the easy, socially responsible training might be less likely to attempt to mitigate bias and address inequities later, especially when it's hard—when it involves changes in cultural practices and policies, for example.

We may not ever know whether the training Starbucks offered

to its employees was effective. And although the training was sparked by the poor decision of one barista in one store in Philadelphia, what happened in that coffee shop is a commentary on something bigger than one employee's bias.

When she called the police to have Donte and Rashon forcibly removed, perhaps she was simply looking out for the company's bottom line—doing her part to protect the brand. Perhaps she reasoned that other people would be less likely to enter the store—or would not want to linger for long if they did—with those two young black men sitting there. And maybe she guessed correctly. If that is the case, was it her bias she acted on or ours?

. . .

Just one month after the Starbucks incident, another video popped up on Everett's Instagram feed. This one homed in on Kevin Moore, a black firefighter who was on duty, in full gear, performing a standard exterior inspection of a home in Oakland Hills when a resident phoned 911 to report him. The state-mandated summer inspections occur at the same time each year and are conducted to control the growth of hazardous brush that could contribute to the spread of wildfires.

The same day, another resident emailed the police department with video footage he had taken with his home security camera. The video simply showed Moore doing what he was trained to do: ringing the doorbell of a home and, when no one answered, yelling out, "Oakland Fire Department," and then proceeding with the outside inspection. Yet the resident feared Moore was up to something sinister.

And that was not the only time Moore had been questioned and videotaped by residents who didn't trust him on their property—even when he was dressed in firefighter gear, even when he showed them his firefighter ID, and even when he pointed out his big red fire truck parked on the street. "It's unfortunate that somebody would mistake an Oakland firefighter, a professional who would go into harm's way every day to protect citizens, as someone who was there for criminal intent. Kevin's out there doing his job well and representing the Oakland Fire Department with the highest integrity," the supervisor of the inspection program said.

One of Moore's colleagues, who was contacted by a police dispatcher to verify his status, said she will pair up with Moore for future inspections because a white woman in fire fighter gear won't generate suspicion. She and her white colleagues have never been reported to the police for doing their jobs.

"It's our work to do with other white people, to check our implicit biases and racism," she told reporters. "It's not fair to him, and it's actually not safe for him to be going into these backyards due to the sociopolitical climate."

Now my son Everett is wondering what is safe for him. He is already expressing concern about how race might influence the way people see and treat him in the future, in whatever profession he chooses: "Sometimes I feel like it'll just be a lot harder for me when I get a corporate job or something that's normally dominated by white people."

That worry is what keeps him tuned to social media, with its endless stream of racial incidents. He studies the videos as if they hold the key to his own security. He is looking for clues that will help him understand how to manage his fears—and defuse the fears others might feel when they look at him.

BEYOND TRAINING

Understanding how implicit bias works and what it impacts is a good first step. But the real challenge—for both companies and individuals—is learning how to keep bias in check. Bias is not something we exhibit and act on all the time. It is conditional, and the battle begins by understanding the conditions under which it is most likely to come alive.

Among those conditions, speed and ambiguity are two of the strongest triggers of bias. When we are forced to make quick decisions using subjective criteria, the potential for bias is great. Yet more often than not, these are the very conditions under which hiring managers make initial decisions about job candidates. Due to the volume of applications and inevitable time constraints, managers may spend an average of only six seconds reviewing each résumé they receive. That may lead them to resort to hunches and rely on familiar patterns to assist them in making rapid judgments about the applicant's fit for the job. And when something as basic as a candidate's name triggers unfavorable unconscious stereotypes, the bar to employment can rise.

There are proven techniques that women and minority candidates can use to avoid being swept into the reject pile by employers' preconceived ideas. To increase the probability of a favorable decision, applicants are advised by professionals to be concrete about their accomplishments, providing numbers and metrics and specific successes that relate to the position at hand. For example, instead of saying you grew the client base, say you produced a 50 percent increase in sales over a six-month period. Introducing objective standards can help neuter the subjective influence of stereotypes. Recruiters could minimize bias as well—through the use of structured interviews with a set of standard questions asked of all applicants.

Bias is also more likely to flare up when our decisions are left unmonitored, when there are no checks and balances on the spur-of-the-moment choices we make. That's been borne out in a particularly high-stakes situation: when umpires are calling balls and strikes in Major League Baseball games.

In a study evaluating all 3,524,624 pitches in regular-season Major League Baseball games from 2004 to 2008, economist Christopher Parsons and his team found that umpires typically made the right call. However, in situations that were close calls, when the ball flew across the plate right on the border of the strike zone, the umpires were more likely to exhibit racial bias—calling a strike when the pitcher was the same race as the umpire and a ball when the pitcher was of a different race. But in ballparks where playback cameras tracked the trajectory of every ball thrown and the footage was available to assess umpires' calls, that racial bias disappeared. This suggests that the awareness that they were being monitored led umpires to make more sound judgments—judgments that could withstand the influence of extraneous factors threatening to seep in to corrupt their decision-making process in subtle ways.

Monitoring certainly helps, but bias can endure even in situations that are closely scrutinized—if the right incentives are not in place. Let's stick with baseball on this one. No baseball game ends in a tie. So, as anyone who has watched Major League Baseball can attest, once a game goes into extra innings, there is no telling when it will end. That can take a toll on the players and the fans alike. It also takes a toll on the umpires, who are not paid a penny for their labor during unlimited overtime. This led researchers Michael Lopez and Brian Mills to examine whether the umpires' interest in restricting the amount of time they work without pay could bias their calls. They found that in "too close to call" situations, umpires were more likely to make a call that would end the game—whether that call was a ball or a strike, whether it meant the home team would win or not. Bias was generated by the way the baseball industry structured employee incentives.

. . .

In addition to situational influences like time, money, and the prospect of accountability, personal connections can override the power exerted by implicit bias, especially when those relationships involve intimacy, mutual dependence, or working together toward a shared goal.

My niece Tanisha is a nurse in a Jewish convalescent home in Ohio. She's worked there for more than fourteen years. When she began, all the residents were Jewish, most of them Orthodox; the nurses were white, and the aides, housekeepers, and kitchen crew were black. Tanisha was an aide but enjoyed the job enough to go back to school and train to be a nurse.

In the last ten years, the mix of patients and employees has become more diverse, but Tanisha's mission hasn't changed. "When you're doing nursing for long-term [care], you've got to keep them thriving, making sure they're eating and making sure their everyday needs are met."

And because most patients are nearing the end of life, her job has morphed into a cross between medical professional and trusted confidante. "If you're with this person every day for eight hours a day, you're going to form some kind of bond," she said. "And when they get to that state, race and religion go out the window. People don't look at it like that anymore because it's life and death."

Research shows that close attachments between people from

different groups can puncture holes in stereotypic beliefs and negative attitudes. Patients and family members can overlook the "otherness" of a caregiver they depend on because their own needs push back against the pull of bias. And the openness of that relationship can leave a mark that lasts well beyond the moment and extends past that particular person.

Tanisha's role at this specific juncture of her patients' lives brings her into the families' orbit and blurs lines that might naturally divide. "It's more like a unity-type thing," she said. "You'd be surprised how many people get attached to people they've never known before." Even if those people belong to a group they've spent their life trying to avoid.

Some of the home's residents "have been racist for years," Tanisha acknowledged. But they've also been mentally or physically ill. "They have dementia, they have Alzheimer's . . . and they have no recollection that they're not in the 1950s anymore," she said. Tanisha's been called names, insulted, ordered around: " '*You black, you-know-what, go out there and get me some cotton.*' But I don't take it personal because they're not mentally there. Even if that was what they were like back then, right now they have a condition. . . . You can't be mean to them. They have no idea, no idea what's going on." She's willing to overlook racial slights because she looks past the act and at the actor.

Although she's learned to let insults from patients roll off her back, off duty she keeps her stethoscope hanging from the mirror of her car, to signal that her identity doesn't stop with "black." And she finds that skin color tends to pigeonhole her at work with people she doesn't know, where she's often mistaken for an aide or a cleaning lady.

"Still to this day, I'll get family members and even people who work here who might not know me, and they'll walk up to me and say, 'Hey, I need to talk to the nurse. Is the nurse here?' I'm like, 'Yeah, she's right here.' They'll be like, 'Oh, I'm sorry. I had no idea you were the nurse.' I'm like, 'My badge says charge nurse. I'm sitting in the nurse's station. I'm on the computer. I don't know what else you need to know.'"

She recalls when the daughter of a patient walked right past her, cornered a young white woman working as an aide, and interrogated her about the patient's care. "The poor little white girl was like, 'I don't know, Tanisha. I don't know why she came to me. You're sitting right there. You have on a [nurse's] uniform.' I didn't want to tell her, 'Because you're white.'" When the patient's daughter realized her error, she apologized to Tanisha. "She said, 'I don't know why I walked past you and automatically assumed that she's the nurse.' I'm like, 'Yeah, it kind of happens all the time, but it's okay.' That happens a lot, a lot."

But what also happens are spontaneous eruptions of love and appreciation for the woman caring for a vulnerable relative. Tanisha lives not far from the convalescent home and often encounters family members of patients she's cared for over the years. They hug her, gush over her, and sometimes cry as they share memories. "I'll be at Walmart and it's 'Oh my God. Tanisha. I love you so much.'" It's embarrassing but also fortifying, she said.

Science has shown that intense relationships that cross racial, religious, or ethnic boundaries can quickly undo fundamental associations that have built up slowly over time. For the patients and their family members who come within Tanisha's orbit, blackness becomes associated with dedication instead of laziness; with competence, not stupidity; with tenderness, not aggression; with love, not fear.

• • •

Institutional values, norms, and practices both dictate and reflect the cultural forces that shape society. They can be a resonant force for the sorts of social changes that help derail bias, but it won't be simple, cheap, or without stumbles and scorn.

Starbucks is a case in point: three years before the arrest of two black guys in a Philadelphia Starbucks made "bias training for everyone" a corporate strategy to rally around, the world's best-known coffee company was trying to make race easier to talk about.

But its "Race Together" labeling of coffee cups was so widely mocked that the campaign lasted only about a week. It had been conceived as a way to jump-start a national dialogue about race, after a series of police shootings of unarmed black men in 2014.

"Our objective from the very start of this effort . . . was to stimulate conversation, empathy and compassion toward one another," CEO Howard Schultz explained in a letter to employees as he called the whole thing off.

It might have been tone-deaf or superficial, as critics claimed. But there was indeed a message in that white cup with "Race Together" scrawled in black by your barista: "Hey folks, this is something important. We care about this, and we hope you do too." That was a strong values statement, even if it fell on deaf ears. And it set the stage for the company's response to the bogus arrests of the two young black men at that Starbucks in Philadelphia several years later.

The company made sure it got our attention by closing its stores to train all of its employees to recognize and resist implicit bias. Of course, a four-hour series of lessons and movies isn't going to render anyone bias free. But that kind of bold, broad stroke by an industry leader can legitimize efforts to end the sort of discrimination that's subtle, subjective, and happening all around us.

And that's what puts values on the route to becoming societal norms. Starbucks was, in essence, trying to align the company's norms with the values it has set by requiring everyone to attend the class on bias.

Resetting norms isn't easy, for a country or a company. But the next step—revamping company practices that allow or sustain bias—is where things really get complicated. That covers everything from recruiting and hiring to who gets invited to play golf with the boss.

Businesses say they are making inroads in ways that weren't possible a generation ago. They're modifying job descriptions to remove gender-biased language and using online writing tools to construct new ones. They're relying on video platforms that analyze interviews with job applicants—the content of their answers, their body language, the intonation of their voices—to assess the sorts of "soft skills" that conventional tests find hard to measure. It's like a technological arms race, to get out in front of bias.

And then there are the old-fashioned measures, repurposed to serve new means, like the practice of having classical musicians audition behind a heavy curtain that obscures their identity. That has short-circuited bias well enough that the number of women hired by top-tier orchestras jumped significantly. Now curtain interviews have become the norm, leveling the playing field by hiding a multitude of factors—weight, skin color, physical handicap—that might trigger bias. For many symphony orchestras, that has led to more diversity and a broader musical palette.

Increasing diversity has long been hailed as the conventional remedy for implicit bias: all that working together will surely counter the power of stereotypes and erase our outdated ways of thinking about one another.

It turns out that diversity itself is not a remedy for, though it may be a route to, eliminating bias. But we have to be willing to go through the growing pains that diversity entails. We've learned that diverse groups are more creative and reach better decisions, but they aren't always the happiest group of people. There are more differences, so there is apt to be more discord. Privilege shifts, roles change, new voices emerge.

Success requires us to be willing to tolerate that discomfort as we learn to communicate, get to know one another, and make deeper efforts to shift the underlying cultures that lead to bias and exclusion.

It doesn't just come down to "Am I a bigot, or am I not? Can I or can I not get trained out of this?" Bias is operating on a kind of cosmic level, connecting factors and conditions that we must individually make an effort to comprehend and control. And it deserves a cosmic response, with everyone on board.

When it comes to combating bias, it's not enough to be alarmed by white supremacists and Nazis, but ignore the ways we rely on stereotypes to marginalize the unfamiliar "others" among us.

The battle against explicit bias is taking place on a very public stage, where icons are being brought down for what might have been indulged a generation ago.

The founder of the Papa John's pizza chain was forced to step down from the company he built for using a racial slur during a conference call in 2018. John Schnatter's face was wiped off his company's logo and ads, and the NFL dropped Papa John's as its official pizza.

A few months before that, ABC had abruptly pulled the plug on the country's most popular television show because its star Roseanne Barr had likened Valerie Jarrett—a high-profile adviser to Barack Obama—to an ape in a late-night tweet. Barr first blamed Ambien, then said she didn't know that Jarrett was black. "I mistakenly thought she was white," Barr claimed, invoking the "I just don't see color" defense.

Yet it took network officials only a few hours to decide to cancel Barr's show as advertisers threatened boycotts and Barr's co-stars began blasting her on social media.

The move was expected to cost ABC tens of millions of dollars, but the network leaders looked past that and considered the inevitable damage to their brand if they didn't take a stand.

That speaks volumes about the power of muscle flexing by a citizenry that is losing its tolerance for explicit displays of bigotry and racism. Implicit bias may not be as easy to recognize and fight, but it can be addressed. And as it turns out, believing that it can be addressed is a critical ingredient to progress.

Conclusion

A gang shooting had just ravaged an Oakland neighborhood, leaving five people wounded and one nearly dead. I was at police headquarters, wrapping up a training on implicit bias, when an officer rushed into the auditorium, moving against the traffic filing out.

He was a tall, dark-skinned black man in full uniform, heading straight for the podium where I stood. When he reached me, I could tell he was agitated by the way he waved his hands as he began to speak. His voice was thick with anguish.

He described for me the chaos at the hospital where the victims of the mass shooting were being treated. Their friends and family members had descended on the emergency room—noisy, angry, and afraid. They were wailing, sobbing, and screaming at the hospital staff. But when the officer waded in with questions that might help ID the gunmen, he was met with stony silence. Even in their grief, they wanted nothing to do with cops.

He wanted me to know, he said, what it was like to face victims and survivors of violent crime and be unable to make them whole.

What it felt like to be rebuffed or insulted when you tried to help. What it meant to have to swim upstream all the time, trying to save lives weighed down by apathy and distrust.

He told me about the "shots fired" call that led him to a nine-year-old girl who'd been sitting in her living room when a bullet tore through the wall of her house and left her paralyzed. There was nothing that could be done by the time the officer arrived.

He shared an encounter he had with a little black girl he'd spotted on a crowded residential street, clutching a quilt stitched with a tribute to a murdered loved one: "*May He Rest in Peace.*" The officer began to speak to her, to express sympathy, but her elders warned her not to say a word. As if he were the one who had extinguished that life.

As he spoke, my eyes were drawn to a huge gash on the top of his glistening bald head. Fresh blood was still darkening and clotting around the stitches straining to hold his skin together.

And as he moved his hands through the air, describing all the shooting, stabbing, and killing going on, I noticed a much older wound. Part of his pinkie finger had been lopped off at the joint, leaving it dangling and out of sync with the movement of the fingers that remained intact. He was putting himself on the line every day. And the streets seemed to be taking him one piece at a time.

I could feel his frustration, but also his sense of mission. These police officers were mired in something bigger than any training could resolve. What they were experiencing on the streets was the fallout of racial disparities that reflect and generate biases that keep the cops and the community divided.

When people feel they are being treated unjustly, they aren't likely to cooperate when it counts—when a call to police might help stop a crime or track a violent criminal. That lack of goodwill stalls investigations and lets crimes go unsolved, which sours the perceptions of police and community members alike.

Discussions about bias typically revolve around the gymnastics of our mental processing as we sort and judge and categorize. But the role of obvious racial disparities can't be overlooked. Disparate outcomes in the criminal justice system—who gets stopped and searched, how suspects get charged, who sits in jail to await trial, and who winds up with a prison sentence—shape a mind-set that leads to biases in thought. When members of the broader public witness these disparities, many conclude that blacks are simply more crime prone and therefore deserve the negative treatment they receive. Disparities are the raw material from which we construct the narratives that justify the presence of inequality.

Those narratives spring to life to justify unequal treatment not just in the criminal justice arena but in our neighborhoods, schools, and workplaces. They explain why black families are steered away from white neighborhoods. They lead us to remain undisturbed as our schools continue to fail poor children in minority communities. They allow us to accept the shortage of women in the tech industry, as if that were the natural order of things.

The narratives that prop up inequality can help us to live less troubled in a troubling world. But they also narrow our vision and strand "others" on the wrong side of the opportunity divide. When our comfort comes at their expense, that's a social cost that ultimately shortchanges everyone.

So addressing bias is not just a personal choice; it is a social agenda, a moral stance. Every society has disadvantaged groups that are the targets of bias. When that disadvantaged status is blamed on those groups' imagined faults, our incipient biases can feel warranted. Those biases will continue to be reproduced until we understand and challenge the disparities that fuel them. And the first step toward ending those disparities is to discard the assumption that they are inevitable.

Nowhere has this been made clearer to me than in Oakland, where the police department had a toxic relationship with the public for generations until it was ordered by the court to make sweeping changes. Through shifts in policies and practices over the last ten years, the department has not only improved police-community relations but also made it easier to curtail bias among officers.

It adjusted to its foot pursuit policy so that officers could no longer follow suspects as they ran into backyards or disappeared into blind alleys. Instead, officers were instructed to step back, slow down, call for backup, and think it through. The policy change not only has led to fewer civilians being shot but also has made cops safer. Injuries among officers dropped by 70 percent, and the number of officer-involved shootings fell dramatically, from an average of eight every year to a total of eight in the past five years, even while the arrest rate held steady and crime levels have fallen.

That small policy adjustment reduced the potential for bias to influence officers' decision making. Because whether we are in the workplace, in the classroom, or on the streets, bias is most likely to have an impact on our thinking in high-stress situations where we feel we have limited options and are pressed to act quickly.

The Oakland Police Department was an early adopter of body-worn cameras, which are now used by most urban police departments and have been shown to influence officer behavior. Since the cameras were introduced in 2010, both citizen complaints and police use of force have declined sharply in Oakland. The cameras hold officers accountable, reminding them to raise the standard for their own behavior. And they empower communities by providing a visual record of the action in the field.

Oakland's use of technology goes beyond body cameras. Our research team from Stanford helped create new metrics for police stops and sophisticated algorithms for analyzing body-camera footage. The metrics push officers to rely on credible information rather than gut feelings during routine stops, because those hunches often fail to yield anything worth the conflict they're liable to create. And the analysis of body-camera footage is allowing the department to dissect how community relations can be imperiled by even ostensibly benign officer conduct, such as the language they use during routine traffic stops.

Technology and data have helped the department move toward a more transparent form of precision policing. Officers on the streets in Oakland are being encouraged to think more deeply about why they are making some stops and not others. And the department's top executives are thinking about how to protect those officers from the conditions that make acting on bias most likely.

Law enforcement agencies across the country used to encourage officers to make as many stops as possible, with little regard for the negative impact this could have on communities. That was considered good policing. Now—driven by court orders, government mandates, expensive lawsuits, and the activism of community members—they are beginning to embrace principles that drive crime down without imperiling their relations with the public.

Working with the police department convinced me that major institutional change can occur even in places where conflict seems most intractable. And those changes can help keep bias at bay.

. . .

We all have the capacity to make change—within ourselves, in the world, and in our relationship to that world.

My son Everett is now a teenager. Just this past summer, he was on Stanford's campus, riding his bike home from the gym, when he came upon a young Asian woman jogging toward him along the same wide path. When she looked up and saw him, she veered off the path.

And that simple gesture got Everett's attention. "I just felt kind of weird, and I didn't know if she was scared of me," Everett explained when we discussed the encounter.

"And you don't think she was just trying to give you more room?" I asked.

"No," Everett insisted. "There was a lot of room."

"Well, maybe she was moving off the path to stay safe—to avoid a collision," I suggested.

Everett had already considered that. "Seems like jogging in the middle of the street would be more dangerous than the path," he said. "Even if I'm there."

"It made me feel like . . ." Everett hesitated as he fought to find a way to capture this new experience. Then the words came: ". . . maybe more self-conscious about my actions and how I come off to other people." He paused. "It made me sad too, kind of."

It made me sad too. Whether on a high-crime street in Oakland or in a leafy green neighborhood on the edge of Stanford's campus, my son now has to manage how he is seen. He has to grow accustomed to the fact that people may experience fear at the sheer sight of him. Already, at sixteen, he has begun to sense their discomfort— even as he struggles to name it.

This is my same son who, when he was five, had casually presumed the lone black male passenger on our plane might be a dangerous robber. He doesn't even remember that. Now, eleven years later, he is becoming the target of his own perceptions.

The shift in that jogger's trajectory led Everett and me down a track that neither of us wanted to be on. And it surfaced our own fears about what lay ahead.

I thought about those middle-aged Chinese women in Oakland who became fearful of the young black men who might snatch their purses—young men they couldn't tell from one another. My son had now joined that broad demographic that ignites the sort of primal fears that fuel implicit bias.

But with new appreciation, I also recognized that the capacity for growth comes from our willingness to reflect, to probe in search of some actionable truth.

I thought about my niece Tanisha, whose clarity on who she wants to be in the world—a healer—insulates her from bias and transforms those around her.

I thought about the thousands of people in Charlottesville who went out to stand against racism, to fight for their community, for the values of our democracy. I thought about the Uber driver in that same city who recognized the bigotry in his veins and unburdened himself to me. I thought about Judge Donald's algebra teacher, who apologized for his own bigotry decades after the fact, and Judge Donald herself, who endured, triumphed, and returned to face the past that had threatened to confine her there.

I thought about the challenges facing the criminal justice system and those mired in it: The inmate at San Quentin who never stopped wondering how free people think. Deputy Chief Armstrong, who never stopped fighting to redeem the city he loves. That German officer I met at a training who reflected on how he came to see black men as dangerous. And Tiffany Crutcher, who is dedicating her life to understanding how bias operates and to reforming police practices after her twin brother was shot and killed by an officer in Tulsa, Oklahoma.

So many people among us are probing, reaching, searching to do good and to be good in the best way they know how. And there is hope in the sheer act of reflection. This is where the power lies and how the process starts.

My son, in his own way, is discovering that. "I'm not really sure," Everett told me at the end of our talk about why the jogger avoided him. "But I think she maybe just got nervous."

After the woman passed, Everett looked back and noticed that she had returned to the path. He moved ahead with his journey too. He kept pedaling, heading home to get ready for a new day.

ACKNOWLEDGMENTS

First, let me thank Doug Abrams and his entire team at Idea Architects. Thank you for finding me, for reaching out to me, for recognizing that the world was ready for this book. You saw in me a storyteller as well as a social scientist and had an unshakable faith in my capacity to write for a broad audience. Through you, I have learned to see the world differently and come to better appreciate the power of books to change lives. I never had a book agent before, but I cannot imagine anyone as great as you. When this book was just an idea, you were there. And here you remain. I will be forever grateful.

And, of course, there is the Viking publishing team led by Brian Tart. You've supported this book in so many ways. I still remember the excitement I felt when I met you all for the first time. Carolyn Coleburn in publicity has been amazing. And Wendy Wolf, my editor, has been with me every step of the way, keeping the book moving forward and on track, even when I made her job difficult, which was frequently. Thank you for your dedication and direction.

I'd also like to recognize Tom Avery, my editor in the UK, who was an early champion of this work, as well as the foreign rights co-agents—Caspian Dennis and the team at Abner Stein, Camilla Ferrier and the team at the Marsh Agency—who believed this book could be of interest to those beyond American shores.

To my writing coach (and sister-in-law!), Sandy Banks, you were a gift. You saved me so many times. Because of you, I found my writing voice. You opened the door and stood by my side. You taught me how to bring the emotion back to the page after decades of practice at removing it from every single thing I published. To work with a master writer, a renowned *Los Angeles Times* journalist, a person who really gets race, who is intrigued by science, who knows me—what else could I have asked for? Nothing. You brought it all. I am immensely grateful for the opportunity to have taken this journey with you.

I want to acknowledge those who participated in the creation of the scientific knowledge that I cover in the book—my colleagues in the field of social psychology and beyond, my research collaborators who have worked with me directly in an effort to bring scientific findings on race and racial bias to the world. From the laboratory research at Stanford University to the field research in Oakland, California, I have had many partners. I would like to single out two colleagues who have made invaluable contributions to this work. Benoît Monin brilliantly demonstrated how data can be used to transform institutional culture. Dan Jurafsky showed us all how to use sophisticated language-based tools to analyze police body-worn camera footage. Both worked tirelessly in their efforts to improve police-community relations.

Thank you to the Stanford SPARQ staff. We like to call ourselves a "do tank" rather than a "think tank." We are researchers working in direct collaboration with practitioners to address significant social problems in criminal justice, education, economic development, and health. My hope is that this book can be of benefit to the many people working in those spaces to improve society. I am also grateful to those who have funded SPARQ projects and some of the more recent work noted in the book—funders such as the John D. and Catherine T. MacArthur Foundation, the Prudential Foundation, and the William and Flora Hewlett Foundation. To the many stakeholders in the city of Oakland who believe science matters, I acknowledge you as well.

I could not have produced such a book without the incredible research assistance that Maggie Perry provided at Stanford. Her attention to detail was invaluable as I began compiling the information needed to draft the book. She is extremely sharp, capable, productive, meticulous, and passionate about the capacity of science to inform our everyday lives. During this project, she was also patient, calm, and always willing to go the extra mile. Thank you, Maggie.

My appreciation goes out to Hazel Markus (also a key collaborator), Claude Steele, Linda Darling-Hammond, Rebecca Hetey, Nick Camp, Daphna Spivack, and Amrita Maitreyi for reading an earlier draft of the book. Thank you for your wisdom and your kind words. My dear friend Syma, thank you for being there every step of the way, as a reader and a listener. Whenever we talk, I learn more about the world and myself. You are my "go to" person—always.

I'd like to give special recognition to those who shared their stories with me and allowed me to share them with the world. You inspire me. You are calming forces in troubling times.

To my siblings, Harlan Jr., Kevin, Justin, and Stephanie: growing up, I looked up to you all in different ways, and still do. To my father and mother, Harlan and Mary Eberhardt: your love and sacrifice changed everything. I so wish you were alive today. I still miss you dearly.

To my boys, Ebbie, Everett, and Harlan: thank you for the stories and memories. To Everett, I am especially grateful for the attention you gave mom's book, always thinking of ways to contribute to the work.

And, finally, to Rick, my partner, my love, you've blessed me with your commitment, guidance, support, and patience throughout this project and our partnership. You are incredible.

SOURCES

Chapter 1: Seeing Each Other

THE SCIENCE OF RECOGNITION

Anzures, Gizelle, Paul C. Quinn, Olivier Pascalis, Alan M. Slater, James W. Tanaka, and Kang Lee. "Developmental Origins of the Other-Race Effect." *Current Directions in Psychological Sciences* 22, no. 3 (2013): 173–78.

Cassia, Viola Macchi, Marta Picozzi, Dana Kuefner, and Monica Casati. "Why Mix-Ups Don't Happen in the Nursery: Evidence for an Experience-Based Interpretation of the Other-Age Effect." *Quarterly Journal of Experimental Psychology* 62, no. 6 (2009): 1099–107.

Chiroro, Patrick, and Tim Valentine. "An Investigation of the Contact Hypothesis of the Own-Race Bias in Face Recognition." *Quarterly Journal of Experimental Psychology* 48A, no. 4 (1995): 879–94.

de Heering, Adélaïde, Claire de Liedekerke, Malorie Deboni, and Bruno Rossion. "The Role of Experience During Childhood in Shaping the Other-Race Effect." *Developmental Science* 13, no. 1 (2010): 181–87.

Meissner, Christian A., and John C. Brigham. "Thirty Years of Investigating the Own-Race Bias in Memory for Faces." *Psychology, Public Policy, and Law* 7, no. 1 (2001): 3–35.

Sangrigoli, Sandy, Christophe Pallier, Anne-Marie Argenti, Valerie A. G. Ventureyra, and Scania de Schonen. "Reversibility of the Other-Race Effect in Face Recognition During Childhood." *Psychological Science* 16, no. 6 (2005): 440–44.

Sangrigoli, Sandy, and Scania de Schonen. "Recognition of Own-Race and Other-Race Faces by Three-Month-Old Infants." *Journal of Child Psychology and Psychiatry* 45, no. 7 (2004): 1219–27.

Scott, Lisa S., Olivier Pascalis, and Charles A. Nelson. "A Domain-General Theory of the Development of Perceptual Discrimination." *Current Directions in Psychological Science* 16, no. 4 (2007): 197–201.

IMAGING RACE

Doidge, Norman. *The Brain That Changes Itself: Stories of Personal Triumph from the Frontiers of Brain Science.* New York: Penguin Books, 2007.

Golby, Alexandra J., John D. E. Gabrieli, Joan Y. Chiao, and Jennifer L. Eberhardt. "Differential Responses in the Fusiform Region to Same-Race and Other-Race Faces." *Nature Neuroscience* 4, no. 8 (2001): 845–50.

Haxby, James V., Elizabeth A. Hoffman, and M. I. Gobbini. "The Distributed Human Neural System for Face Perception." *Trends in Cognitive Sciences* 4, no. 6 (June 2000): 223–33.

Kanwisher, Nancy, Josh McDermott, and Marvin M. Chun. "The Fusiform Face Area: A Module in Human Extrastriate Cortex Specialized for Face Perception." *Journal of Neuroscience* 17, no. 11 (1997): 4302–311.

Maguire, Eleanor A., David G. Gadian, Ingrid S. Johnsrude, Catriona D. Good, John Ashburner, Richard S. J. Frackowiak, and Christopher D. Frith. "Navigation-Related Structural Change in the Hippocampi of Taxi Drivers." *Proceedings of the National Academy of Sciences* 97, no. 8 (2000): 4398–403.

Maguire, Eleanor A., Hugo J. Spiers, Catriona D. Good, Tom Hartley, Richard S. J. Frackowiak, and Neil Burgess. "Navigation Expertise and the Human Hippocampus: A Structural Brain Imaging Analysis." *Hippocampus* 13 (2003): 250–59.

Maguire, Eleanor A., Katherine Woollett, and Hugo J. Spiers. "London Taxi Drivers and Bus Drivers: A Structural MRI and Neuropsychological Analysis." *Hippocampus* 16 (2006): 1091–101.

Chapter 2: Nurturing Bias

Brown, Thackery I., Melina R. Uncapher, Tiffany E. Chow, Jennifer L. Eberhardt, and Anthony D. Wagner. "Cognitive Control, Attention, and the Other Race Effect in Memory." *PLOS One* 12, no. 3 (2017): 1–21.

Dweck, Carol S. *Mindset: The New Psychology of Success.* New York: Random House, 2006.

Eberhardt, Jennifer L., Nilanjana Dasgupta, and Tracy L. Banaszynski. "Believing Is Seeing: The Effects of Racial Labels and Implicit Beliefs on Face Perception." *Personality and Social Psychology Bulletin* 29, no. 3 (2003): 360–70.

Grill-Spector, Kalanit, Richard Henson, and Alex Martin. "Repetition and the Brain: Neural Models of Stimulus-Specific Effects." *Trends in Cognitive Science* 10, no. 1 (2006): 14–23.

Hughes, Brent L., Nicholas P. Camp, Jesse Gomez, Vaidehi S. Natu, Kalanit Grill-Spector, and Jennifer L. Eberhardt. "Neural Adaptation to Faces Underlies Out-Group Homogeneity Effect." Manuscript in preparation.

Levin, Daniel T. "Classifying Faces by Race: The Structure of Face Categories."

Journal of Experimental Psychology: Learning, Memory, and Cognition 22, no. 6 (1996): 1364–82.

MacLin, Otto H., and Roy S. Malpass. "Racial Categorization of Faces: The Ambiguous Race Face Effect." *Psychology, Public Policy, and Law* 7, no. 1 (2001): 98–118.

Miller, Arthur. *Focus.* New York: Penguin Books, 2001.

THE MECHANICS OF BIAS

Banaji, Mahzarin R., and Anthony G. Greenwald. *Blindspot: Hidden Biases of Good People.* New York: Bantam Books, 2016.

Executive Order No. 9066, 3 C.F.R. (1942).

Green, David B. "This Day in Jewish History 1974: A Giant of Punditry Who Never Admitted Being a Jew Dies." *Haaretz*, December 14, 2016. Accessed September 30, 2018. www.haaretz.com/jewish/.premium-1974-a-giant-of-punditry-who-never -admitted-being-a-jew-dies-1.5473466.

Hugenberg, Kurt, and Galen V. Bodenhausen. "Facing Prejudice: Implicit Prejudice and the Perception of Facial Threat." *Psychological Science* 14, no. 6 (2003): 640–43.

———. "Ambiguity in Social Categorization: The Role of Prejudice and Facial Affect in Race Categorization." *Psychological Science* 15, no. 5 (2004): 342–45.

Lippmann, Walter. "1919—Introductory Note." In *The Chicago Race Riots, July, 1919*, by Carl Sandburg, xix–xi. New York: Harcourt, Brace and Howe, 1919.

———. *Public Opinion.* New York: Harcourt, Brace, 1922.

Regalzi, Francesco. "Democracy and Its Discontents: Walter Lippmann and the Crisis of Politics (1919–1938)." *E-rea* 9, no. 2 (March 15, 2012). Accessed September 30, 2018. https://journals.openedition.org/erea/2538.

"The War Relocation Camps of World War II—Reading 1." National Park Service. Accessed September 30, 2018. www.nps.gov/nr/twhp/wwwlps/lessons/89manzanar /89facts1.htm.

THE TRANSMISSION OF BIAS

Duranton, Charlotte, Thierry Bedossa, and Florence Gaunet. "When Facing an Unfamiliar Person, Pet Dogs Present Social Referencing Based on Their Owners' Direction of Movement Alone." *Animal Behaviour* 113 (2016): 147–56.

Greenwald, Anthony G., Debbie E. McGhee, and Jordan L. Schwartz. "Measuring Individual Differences in Implicit Cognition: The Implicit Association Test." *Journal of Personality and Social Psychology* 74, no. 6 (1998): 1464–80.

Sinclair, Stacey, Elizabeth Dunn, and Brian S. Lowery. "The Relationship Between Parental Racial Attitudes and Children's Implicit Prejudice." *Journal of Experimental Social Psychology* 41 (2005): 283–89.

Skinner, Allison L., Andrew N. Meltzoff, and Kristina R. Olson. "'Catching' Social Bias: Exposure to Biased Nonverbal Signals Creates Social Biases in Preschool Children." *Psychological Science* 28, no. 2 (2017): 216–24.

Weisbuch, Max, Kristin Pauker, and Nalini Ambady. "The Subtle Transmission of Race Bias via Televised Nonverbal Behavior." *Science* 326, no. 5960 (2009): 1711–14.

Chapter 3: A Bad Dude

Franklin, Dallas. "Read Full Letter from Jury That Acquitted Tulsa Police Officer in Fatal Shooting of Terence Crutcher." Oklahoma's News 4, May 22, 2017. Accessed September 30, 2018. kfor.com/2017/05/22/read-full-letter-from-jury-that-acquitted -tulsa-police-officer-in-fatal-shooting-of-terence-crutcher/.

"Police Shootings 2016 Database." *Washington Post.* Accessed September 30, 2018. www.washingtonpost.com/graphics/national/police-shootings-2016/.

"Prosecutors: Tulsa Officer Charged in Death of Unarmed Black Man 'Reacted Un-reasonably.'" *Chicago Tribune,* September 22, 2016. Accessed September 30, 2018. www.chicagotribune.com/news/nationworld/ct-tulsa-police-shooting-charges -20160922-story.html.

Stelter, Brian. "Philando Castile and the Power of Facebook Live." CNN, July 7, 2016. Accessed September 30, 2018. money.cnn.com/2016/07/07/media/facebook -live-streaming-police-shooting/index.html.

"Tamir Rice Autopsy Report." Cuyahoga County Medical Examiner's Office, December 11, 2014. Accessed September 30, 2018. www.documentcloud.org /documents/1378708-tamir-rice-autopsy-report.html.

"Tamir Rice Investigation Report." The Marshall Project, June 15, 2015. Accessed September 30, 2018. www.themarshallproject.org/documents/2102450-tamir-rice -investigation-report.

Wagner, Laura, and Merrit Kennedy. "Grand Jury Declines to Indict Police Officers in Tamir Rice Investigation." NPR, December 28, 2015. Accessed September 30, 2018. www.npr.org/sections/thetwo-way/2015/12/28/461293703/grand-jury -declines-to-indict-police-officers-in-tamir-rice-investigation.

Weber, Tom. "Yanez Juror: 'Nobody Was OK with It.'" MPR News, June 23, 2017. Accessed September 30, 2018. www.mprnews.org/story/2017/06/23/74-seconds -yanez-juror.

Yan, Holly, Justin Gamble, and Darran Simon. "Tulsa Officer on Trial Tells of Killing Unarmed Black Man." CNN, May 16, 2017. Accessed September 30, 2018. www .cnn.com/2017/05/15/us/oklahoma-betty-shelby-officer-trial/index.html.

THE SCIENTIFIC LENS

Berman, Mark. "What the Police Officer Who Shot Philando Castile Said About the Shooting." *Washington Post,* June 21, 2017. Accessed November 11, 2018. https ://www.washingtonpost.com/news/post-nation/wp/2017/06/21/what-the -police-officer-who-shot-philando-castile-said-about-the-shooting.

Bor, Jacob, Atheendar S. Venkataramani, David R. Williams, and Alexander C. Tsai. "Police Killings and Their Spillover Effects on the Mental Health of Black Americans: A Population-Based, Quasi-Experimental Study." *Lancet* 392, no. 10144 (2018): 302–10.

Correll, Joshua, Bernadette Park, Charles M. Judd, and Bernd Wittenbrink. "The Police Officer's Dilemma: Using Ethnicity to Disambiguate Potentially Threatening Individuals." *Journal of Personality and Social Psychology* 83, no. 6 (2002): 1314–29.

Correll, Joshua, Bernadette Park, Charles M. Judd, Bernd Wittenbrink, Melody S. Sadler, and Tracie Keesee. "Across the Thin Blue Line: Police Officers and Racial

Bias in the Decision to Shoot." *Journal of Personality and Social Psychology* 92, no. 6 (2007): 1006–23.

Duncan, Birt L. "Differential Social Perception and Attribution of Intergroup Violence: Testing the Lower Limits of Stereotyping of Blacks." *Journal of Personality and Social Psychology* 34, no. 4 (1976): 590–98.

Eberhardt, Jennifer L., Phillip Atiba Goff, Valerie J. Purdie, and Paul G. Davies. "Seeing Black: Race, Crime, and Visual Processing." *Journal of Personality and Social Psychology* 87, no. 6 (2004): 876–93.

Ellison, Ralph. *Invisible Man.* New York: Random House, 1952.

Jones-Brown, Delores, Jaspreet Gill, and Jennifer Trone. *Stop, Question & Frisk Policing Practices in New York City: A Primer.* New York: Center on Race, Crime, and Justice at John Jay College of Criminal Justice, 2010.

Larson, John. "Behind the Death of Timothy Thomas." NBC News. April 10, 2004. Accessed November 11, 2018. http://www.nbcnews.com/id/4703574/ns/date line_nbc-dateline_specials/t/behind-death-timothy-thomas/#.W-kR3y2ZMcg.

McFadden, Robert D. "Four Officers Indicted for Murder in Killing of Diallo, Lawyer Says." *New York Times*, March 26, 1999. Accessed November 11, 2018. https ://www.nytimes.com/1999/03/26/nyregion/four-officers-indicted-for-murder -in-killing-of-diallo-lawyer-says.html.

The People of the State of New York v. Kenneth Boss, Sean Carroll, Edward McMellon and Richard Murphy (2000).

Sagar, H. Andrew, and Janet Ward Schofield. "Racial and Behavioral Cues in Black and White Children's Perceptions of Ambiguously Aggressive Acts." *Journal of Personality and Social Psychology* 39, no. 4 (1980): 590–98.

Van Derbeken, Jaxon. "Johannes Mehserle Says He Feared Oscar Grant Was Going for Gun." *SFGate,* June 14, 2014. Accessed November 11, 2018. https://www.sfgate.com /default/article/Mehserle-says-he-fired-after-Grant-made-digging-5551691.php.

Wilson, John Paul, Kurt Hugenberg, and Nicholas O. Rule. "Racial Bias in Judgments of Physical Size and Formidability: From Size to Threat." *Journal of Personality and Social Psychology* 113, no. 1 (2017): 59–80.

SAYING GOOD-BYE

Bor, Jacob, Atheendar S. Venkataramani, David R. Williams, and Alexander C. Tsai. "Police Killings and Their Spillover Effects on the Mental Health of Black Americans: A Population-Based, Quasi-Experimental Study." *Lancet* 392, no. 10144 (2018): 302–10.

Chapter 4: Male Black

AB-953: The Racial and Identity Profiling Act of 2015 (California). leginfo.legislature .ca.gov/faces/billTextClient.xhtml?bill_id=201520160AB953.

Abrams, David. "Report of David Abrams, Ph.D." *Charles Collins et al. v. City of Milwaukee et al.* U.S. District Court, Eastern Division of Wisconsin, Milwaukee Division, February 20, 2018.

Alpert, Geoffrey P., Elizabeth Becker, Mark A. Gustafson, Alan P. Meister, Michael

R. Smith, and Bruce A. Strombom. "Pedestrian and Motor Vehicle Post-stop Data Analysis Report." Analysis Group, Inc., Los Angeles, July 2006.

Borooah, Vani K. "Racial Disparity in Police Stop and Searches in England and Wales." *Journal of Quantitative Criminology* 27 (December 2011): 453–73.

DeFao, Janine. "Oakland Settles 'Riders' Suits: Record $10.5 Million Payout—Police Reforms Required." *SFGate,* February 19, 2003.

Eberhardt, Jennifer L., ed. "Strategies for Change: Research Initiatives and Recommendations to Improve Police-Community Relations in Oakland, Calif." SPARQ: Social Psychological Answers to Real-World Questions, Stanford University, 2016.

Fagan, Jeffrey, Anthony A. Braga, Rod K. Brunson, and April Pattavina. "An Analysis of Race and Ethnicity Patterns in Boston Police Department Field Interrogation, Observation, Frisk, and/or Search Reports," June 15, 2015.

Foster, Lorne, Les Jacobs, and Bobby Siu. "Race Data and Traffic Stops in Ottawa, 2013–2015: A Report on Ottawa and the Police Districts." Submitted to Ottawa Police Services Board and Ottawa Police Service, October 2016.

Garone, Liz. "Oakland's Police 'Riders' on Trial." *Washington Post,* January 26, 2003.

Hetey, Rebecca C., Benoît Monin, Amrita Maitreyi, and Jennifer L. Eberhardt. "Data for Change: A Statistical Analysis of Police Stops, Searches, Handcuffings, and Arrests in Oakland, Calif., 2013–2014." SPARQ: Social Psychological Answers to Real-World Questions, Stanford University, 2016.

"Investigation of the New Orleans Police Department." U.S. Department of Justice Civil Rights Division, Washington, D.C., March 16, 2011.

Meng, Y., S. Giwa, and U. Anucha. "Is There Racial Discrimination in Police Stop-and-Searches of Black Youth? A Toronto Case Study." *Canadian Journal of Family and Youth* 7, no. 1 (2015): 115–48.

Monmaney, Terence. "Rampart-Like Scandal Rocks Oakland Justice System, Politics." *Los Angeles Times,* December 11, 2000.

President's Task Force on 21st Century Policing. "Final Report of the President's Task Force on 21st Century Policing." Washington, D.C.: Office of Community Oriented Policing Services, 2015.

Zamora, Jim Herron. "With Charges Dismissed, Oakland Riders Want Jobs Back." *SF Gate,* June 11, 2005.

THE POLICE RESPONSE

Banks, R. Richard. "Beyond Profiling: Race, Policing, and the Drug War." *Stanford Law Review* 56, no. 3 (2003): 571–603.

———. "Race-Based Suspect Selection and Colorblind Equal Protection Doctrine and Discourse." *UCLA Law Review* 48 (2001): 1075–124.

Johnson, Chip. "Oakland Crime Issue Goes Far Deeper Than Racial Profiling." *SFGate,* March 28, 2014.

PROCEDURAL JUSTICE

Chabris, Christopher F., and Daniel J. Simons. *The Invisible Gorilla: And Other Ways Our Intuitions Deceive Us.* New York: Crown, 2010.

Gilbert, Daniela, Stewart Wakeling, and Vaughn Crandall. "Notes from the Field:

Strengthening Community-Police Relationships: Training as a Tool for Change."
California Partnership for Safe Communities, Oakland, 2016.

———. "Procedural Justice and Police Legitimacy: Using Training as a Foundation for Strengthening Community-Police Relationships." Working paper, California Partnership for Safe Communities, Oakland, 2015.

Kunard, Laura, and Charlene Moe. "Procedural Justice for Law Enforcement: An Overview." Washington, D.C.: Office of Community Oriented Policing Services, 2015.

Leovy, Jill. Ghettoside: A True Story of Murder in America. New York: Spiegel & Grau, 2015.

Meares, Tracey L., Tom R. Tyler, and Jacob Gardener. "Lawful or Fair? How Cops and Laypeople Perceive Good Policing." Journal of Criminal Law and Criminology 105, no. 2 (2015): 297–344.

National Initiative for Building Community Trust and Justice. "Procedural Justice." Community-Oriented Trust and Justice Briefs. Washington, D.C.: Office of Community Oriented Policing Services, 2015.

Skogan, Wesley G., Maarten Van Craen, and Cari Hennessy. "Training Police for Procedural Justice." Journal of Experimental Criminology 11, no. 3 (September 2015): 319–34.

Tyler, Tom R., Phillip Atiba Goff, and Robert J. MacCoun. "The Impact of Psychological Science on Policing in the United States: Procedural Justice, Legitimacy, and Effective Law Enforcement." Psychological Science in the Public Interest 16, no. 3 (December 2015): 75–109.

Tyler, Tom R., and Yuen Huo. Trust in the Law: Encouraging Public Cooperation with the Police and Courts. New York: Russell Sage Foundation, 2002.

AN IMPERFECT SHIELD

Du Bois, W. E. B. The Souls of Black Folk. Chicago, Il: A. C. McClurg, 1903.

Chapter 5: How Free People Think

Camp, Nicholas P., Vinodkumar Prabhakaran, Dan Jurafsky, Rebecca C. Hetey, Benoît Monin, and Jennifer L. Eberhardt. "Mining Traffic Stop Narratives Reveals Pervasive Racial Disparities in Discretionary Stops." Manuscript in preparation.

Eith, Christine, and Matthew R. Durose. "Contacts Between Police and the Public, 2008." Washington, D.C.: Bureau of Justice Statistics, U.S. Department of Justice, 2011.

Epp, Charles R., Steven Maynard-Moody, and Donald P. Haider-Markel. Pulled Over: How Police Stops Define Race and Citizenship. Chicago: University of Chicago Press, 2014.

Fishman, Nancy, Kaitlin Kall, Rebecca Silber, Jessi LaChance, Hanna Dershowitz, and Stephen Roberts. Report to the Greater Oklahoma City Chamber Criminal Justice Task Force. Report. December 2016. Accessed November 18, 2018. https://storage
.googleapis.com/vera-web-assets/downloads/Publications/oklahoma-city-chamber
-criminal-justice-task-force-report/legacy_downloads/OK-chamber-final
-report.pdf.

Langton, Lynn, and Matthew Durose. "Police Behavior During Traffic and Street Stops, 2011." Washington, D.C.: Bureau of Justice Statistics, U.S. Department of Justice, 2013.

Lowery, Wesley. "A Disproportionate Number of Black Victims in Fatal Traffic Stops." *Washington Post*, December 24, 2015. Accessed September 30, 2018. www .washingtonpost.com/national/a-disproportionate-number-of-black-victims -in-fatal-traffic-stops/2015/12/24/c29717e2-a344-11e5-9c4e-be37f66848bb _story.html?utm_term=.09d7579a63d3.

U.S. Department of Justice, Civil Rights Division. "Investigation of the Ferguson Police Department." Washington, D.C.: U.S. Department of Justice, 2015.

Voigt, Rob, Nicholas P. Camp, Vinodkumar Prabhakaran, William L. Hamilton, Rebecca C. Hetey, Camilla M. Griffiths, David Jurgens, Dan Jurafsky, and Jennifer L. Eberhardt. "Language from Police Body Camera Footage Shows Racial Disparities in Officer Respect." *Proceedings of the National Academy of Sciences* 114, no. 25 (June 20, 2017): 6521–26.

NOT QUITE FREE

Angwin, Julia, Jeff Larson, Surya Mattu, and Lauren Kirchner. "Machine Bias." ProPublica, May 23, 2016. Accessed September 30, 2018. www.propublica.org/article /machine-bias-risk-assessments-in-criminal-sentencing.

"A Deal You Can't Refuse: The Troubling Spread of Plea-Bargaining from America to the World." *Economist*, November 9, 2017.

The Disappearing Trial. Report. Fair Trials, 2017. Accessed October 11, 2018. www .fairtrials.org/wp-content/uploads/2017/12/Report-The-Disappearing-Trial.pdf.

Koseff, Alexei. "Jerry Brown Signs Bill Eliminating Money Bail in California." *Sacramento Bee*, August 28, 2018. Accessed September 30, 2018. www.sacbee.com /news/politics-government/capitol-alert/article217461380.html.

Rahman, Insha. "Against the Odds: Experimenting with Alternative Forms of Bail in New York City's Criminal Courts." Vera Institute of Justice, New York, September 2017.

Silver-Greenberg, Jessica, and Shaila Dewan. "When Bail Feels Less Like Freedom, More Like Extortion." *New York Times*, March 31, 2018.

STILL NOT QUITE FREE

Alameda County Probation Department, 2018. *Percentage of African Americans in Oakland.*

Banks, Ralph Richard. *Is Marriage for White People? How the African American Marriage Decline Affects Everyone.* New York: Penguin Group, 2011.

"Gate Money by State." Hard Time: Life After Prison. Accessed October 11, 2018. americanradioworks.publicradio.org/features/hardtime/gatemoney/index .html.

The Health and Well-Being of Children: A Portrait of States and the Nation, 2011–2012. Report. Health Resources and Services Administration, U.S. Department of Health and Human Services, Rockville, Md., 2014.

Nerbovig, Ashley. "License to Clip." The Marshall Project, July 10, 2018. Accessed September 30, 2018. www.themarshallproject.org/2018/07/10/license-to-clip.

Pager, Devah. "The Mark of a Criminal Record." *American Journal of Sociology* 108, no. 5 (2003): 937–75.

Pager, Devah, Bruce Western, and Naomi Sugie. "Sequencing Disadvantage: Barriers to Employment Facing Young Black and White Men with Criminal Records." *Annals of the American Academy of Political and Social Science* 623, no. 1 (April 15, 2009): 195–213.

Western, Bruce. *Punishment and Inequality in America*. New York: Russell Sage Foundation, 2006.

THE INCARCERATED

Alexander, Michelle. *The New Jim Crow: Mass Incarceration in the Age of Colorblindness.* New York: New Press, 2010.

Baldus, David C., George Woodworth, David Zuckerman, and Neil Alan Weiner. "Racial Discrimination and the Death Penalty in the Post-Furman Era: An Empirical and Legal Overview with Recent Findings from Philadelphia." *Cornell Law Review* 83, no. 6 (1998): 1643–770.

Claiborne, William. "California Only State Applying Three Strikes' Law Extensively." *Washington Post,* September 10, 1996. Accessed September 30, 2018. www.washingtonpost.com/archive/politics/1996/09/10/california-only-state-applying-three-strikes-law-extensively/b5d67ee5-e9cb-4bd5-854d-677e268746c4/?utm_term=.be1bb0978773.

Davis, Lois M., Jennifer L. Steele, Robert Bozick, Malcolm V. Williams, Susan Turner, Jeremy N. V. Miles, Jessica Saunders, and Paul S. Steinberg. *How Effective Is Correctional Education, and Where Do We Go from Here?* Report. Safety and Justice Program, RAND Corporation, 2014. Accessed October 11, 2018. www.rand.org/content/dam/rand/pubs/research_reports/RR500/RR564/RAND_RR564.pdf.

Eberhardt, Jennifer L., Paul G. Davies, Valerie J. Purdie-Vaughns, and Sheri Lynn Johnson. "Looking Deathworthy: Perceived Stereotypicality of Black Defendants Predicts Capital-Sentencing Outcomes." *Psychological Science* 17, no. 5 (2006): 383–86.

Hetey, Rebecca C., and Jennifer L. Eberhardt. "Racial Disparities in Incarceration Increase Acceptance of Punitive Policies." *Psychological Science* 25 (2014): 1949–54.

Jeffries, John Calvin, Jr. *Justice Lewis F. Powell, Jr.: A Biography*. New York: Fordham University Press, 2001.

Kennedy, Randall. "Race, Law, and Punishment: The Death Penalty." In *Race, Crime, and the Law*, 311–50. New York: Vintage Books, 1997.

Kirchmeier, Jeffrey L. "The Supreme Court's Legacy on Race and Capital Punishment in *McCleskey v. Kemp.*" *Human Rights Magazine,* November 9, 2015. Accessed September 30, 2018. https://www.americanbar.org/publications/human_rights_magazine_home/2015—vol—41-/vol—41—no—1—-lurking-in-the-shadows—the-supreme-court-s-qui/the-supreme-courts-legacy-on-race-and-capital-punishment-in-mccl/.

Latane, Bibb, and John M. Darley. "Group Inhibition of Bystander Intervention in Emergencies." *Journal of Personality and Social Psychology* 10, no. 3 (1968): 215–21. doi:10.1037/h0026570.

Western, Bruce. *Punishment and Inequality in America.* New York: Russell Sage Foundation, 2006.

Chapter 6: The Scary Monster

THE SCIENCE OF THE SCARY MONSTER

Broca, Paul. "Sur les projections de la tête et sur un nouveau procédé de céphalométrie et d'anthropométrie." In *Mémoires d'anthropologie,* 79–105. Paris: C. Reinwald, 1871.

Cohen, Adam. "This Jigsaw Puzzle Was Given to Ellis Island Immigrants to Test Their Intelligence." *Smithsonian Magazine,* May 2017. Accessed September 30, 2018. www.smithsonianmag.com/history/puzzle-given-ellis-island-immigrants -test-intelligence-180962779/.

Darwin, Charles. *On the Origin of Species by Means of Natural Selection; or, The Preservation of Favoured Races in the Struggle for Life.* London: J. Murray, 1859.

Eberhardt, Jennifer L. "Imaging Race." *American Psychologist* 60, no. 2 (2005): 181–90.

Fredrickson, George M. *The Black Image in the White Mind: The Debate on Afro-American Character and Destiny, 1817–1914.* New York: Harper & Row, 1971.

Gould, Stephen Jay. "Flaws in a Victorian Veil." *New Scientist,* August 31, 1978, 632–33.

———. *The Mismeasure of Man.* New York: W. W. Norton, 1996.

Menand, Louis. "Morton, Agassiz, and the Origins of Scientific Racism in the United States." *Journal of Blacks in Higher Education,* no. 34 (2001): 110–13.

Morton, Samuel George. *Crania Americana; or, A Comparative View of the Skulls of Various Aboriginal Nations of North & South America.* Philadelphia: J. Dobson, 1839.

Nott, Josiah Clark, and George R. Gliddon. *Types of Mankind.* Philadelphia: Lippincott, Grambo, 1854.

Samelson, Franz. "From 'Race Psychology' to 'Studies in Prejudice': Some Observations on the Thematic Reversal in Social Psychology." *Journal of the History of the Behavioral Sciences* 14, no. 3 (1978): 265–78.

White, Charles. *An Account of the Regular Gradation in Man, and in Different Animals and Vegetables; and from the Former to the Latter.* London: C. Dilly, 1799.

THE NEW SCIENCE OF DEHUMANIZATION

Bain, Paul G., Jacques-Philippe Leyens, and Jeroen Vaes. *Humanness and Dehumanization.* New York: Psychology Press, 2014.

Browning, Lexi, and Lindsey Bever. "'Ape in Heels': W. Va. Mayor Resigns amid Controversy over Racist Comments About Michelle Obama." *Washington Post,* November 16, 2016. Accessed October 11, 2018. www.washingtonpost.com /news/post-nation/wp/2016/11/14/ape-in-heels-w-va-officials-under-fire-after -comments-about-michelle-obama/.

Capehart, Jonathan. "Going Ape over Racist Depiction of Obama." *Washington Post,* April 19, 2011. Accessed October 11, 2018. www.washingtonpost.com/blogs /post-partisan/post/going_ape_over_racist_depiction_of_obama/2011/03/04 /AFvrOs5D_blog.html.

Glover, Scott, and Dan Simon. "'Wild Animals': Racist Texts Sent by San Francisco

Police Officer, Documents Show." CNN, April 26, 2016. Accessed September 24, 2018. www.cnn.com/2016/04/26/us/racist-texts-san-francisco-police-officer/index .html.

Goff, Phillip Atiba, Jennifer L. Eberhardt, Melissa J. Williams, and Matthew Christian Jackson. "Not Yet Human: Implicit Knowledge, Historical Dehumanization, and Contemporary Consequences." *Journal of Personality and Social Psychology* 94, no. 2 (2008): 292–306.

Ignatiev, Noel. *How the Irish Became White.* New York: Routledge, 1995.

Independent Commission on the Los Angeles Police Department. *Report of the Independent Commission on the Los Angeles Police Department (Christopher Commission Report).* 1991. archive.org/details/ChristopherCommissionLAPD.

Jablonski, Nina G. *Skin: A Natural History.* Berkeley: University of California Press, 2006.

Jackson, Allison. "The Ugly, Racist Trend of Tossing Bananas at Black Soccer Players Continues." Public Radio International, May 13, 2014. Accessed September 23, 2018. www.pri.org/stories/2014-05-13/ugly-racist-trend-tossing-bananas-black -soccer-players-continues.

James, William. *The Principles of Psychology.* New York: Henry Holt, 1890.

Klein, Christopher. "When America Despised the Irish: The 19th Century's Refugee Crisis." History.com, March 16, 2017. Accessed September 30, 2018. www.history .com/news/when-america-despised-the-irish-the-19th-centurys-refugee-crisis.

Newton, Jim. "Jim Newton: Change in Black and White in L.A." *Los Angeles Times,* March 6, 2011. Accessed September 30, 2018. articles.latimes.com/2011/mar/06 /opinion/la-oe-newton-rodney-king-20110306.

Rattan, Aneeta, and Jennifer L. Eberhardt. "The Role of Social Meaning in Inattentional Blindness: When the Gorillas in Our Midst Do Not Go Unseen." *Journal of Experimental Social Psychology* 46, no. 6 (2010): 1085–88.

Reisman, Sam. "FoxNews.com Closes Comment Section on Malia Obama Article After Avalanche of Racism." Mediaite.com, May 3, 2016. Accessed October 11, 2018. www.mediaite.com/online/foxnews-com-closes-comment-section-on-malia -obama-article-after-avalanche-of-racism/.

Wood, Tracy, and Sheryl Stolberg. "Patrol Car Log in Beating Released: Police: The Officers' Messages Include Racial Slurs About an Earlier Case. 'A Big Time Use of Force' Against Rodney King Is Referred to in the Transcript." *Los Angeles Times,* March 19, 1991. Accessed September 30, 2018. articles.latimes.com/1991-03-19 /news/mn-487_1_patrol-officer.

Chapter 7: The Comfort of Home

SEGREGATED SPACE

Bobo, Lawrence, and Camille L. Zubrinsky. "Attitudes on Residential Integration: Perceived Status Differences, Mere In-Group Preference, or Racial Prejudice?" *Social Forces* 74, no. 3 (1996): 883–909.

Bonam, Courtney M., Hilary B. Bergsieker, and Jennifer L. Eberhardt. "Polluting Black Space." *Journal of Experimental Psychology: General* 145, no. 11 (2016): 1561–82.

SOURCES

Chetty, Raj, Nathaniel Hendren, and Lawrence F. Katz. "The Effects of Exposure to Better Neighborhoods on Children: New Evidence from the Moving to Opportunity Experiment." *American Economic Review* 106, no. 4 (2016): 855–902.

Farley, Reynolds, and William H. Frey. "Changes in the Segregation of Whites from Blacks During the 1980s: Small Steps Toward a More Integrated Society." *American Sociological Review* 59, no. 1 (1994): 23–45.

Quillian, Lincoln, and Devah Pager. "Black Neighbors, Higher Crime? The Role of Racial Stereotypes in Evaluations of Neighborhood Crime." *American Journal of Sociology* 107, no. 3 (2001): 717–67.

———. "Estimating Risk." *Social Psychology Quarterly* 73, no. 1 (2010): 79–104.

Reardon, Sean F., Demetra Kalogrides, and Kenneth Shores. "The Geography of Racial/ Ethnic Test Score Gaps." *American Journal of Sociology*, 2017. Accessed November 18, 2018. https://cepa.standford.edu/sites/default/files/wp16-10-v201712.pdf.

Rothstein, Richard. *The Color of Law: A Forgotten History of How Our Government Segregated America.* New York: Liveright, 2017.

Sampson, Robert J., and Stephen W. Raudenbush. "Seeing Disorder: Neighborhood Stigma and the Social Construction of 'Broken Windows.'" *Social Psychology Quarterly* 67, no. 4 (2004): 319–42.

U.S. Commission on Civil Rights. *Understanding Fair Housing.* 1973. Accessed October 1, 2018. www2.law.umaryland.edu/marshall/usccr/documents/cr11042.pdf.

Williams, David R., and Chiquita Collins. "Racial Residential Segregation: A Fundamental Cause of Racial Disparities in Health." *Public Health Reports* 116, no. 5 (2001): 404–16.

POLLUTED PEOPLE

"Anti-Muslim 'Incidents' Surge in Germany, Spain." *Al Jazeera,* March 4, 2018. Accessed October 1, 2018. www.aljazeera.com/news/2018/03/anti-muslim-hate-crimes-surge-germany-spain-180303142227333.html.

Bianchi, Emily C., Erika V. Hall, and Sarah Lee. "Reexamining the Link Between Economic Downturns and Racial Antipathy: Evidence That Prejudice Against Blacks Rises During Recessions." *Psychological Science* 29, no. 10 (2018): 1584–97.

Ellison, Ralph. *Invisible Man.* Franklin Center, Pa.: Franklin Library, 1980.

Harris, Lasana T., and Susan T. Fiske. "Dehumanizing the Lowest of the Low." *Psychological Science* 17, no. 10 (2006): 847–53.

Hirschman, Charles. "The Impact of Immigration on American Society: Looking Backward to the Future." Institute for Human Sciences, 2007. Accessed October 1, 2018. www.iwm.at/transit/transit-online/the-impact-of-immigration-on-american-society/.

Huang, Julie Y., Alexandra Sedlovskaya, Joshua M. Ackerman, and John A. Bargh. "Immunizing Against Prejudice: Effects of Disease Protection on Attitudes Toward Out-Groups." *Psychological Science* 22, no. 12 (2011): 1550–56.

Jefferson, Thomas. *Notes on the State of Virginia.* Philadelphia: Pritchard and Hall, 1788.

Marcus, Kenneth L. *Fact Sheet on the Elements of Anti-Semitic Discourse.* Report. Louis D. Brandeis Center for Human Rights Under Law. Accessed October 1, 2018. www

.ohchr.org/Documents/AboutUs/CivilSociety/ReportHC/75_The Louis D. Brandeis Center _Fact Sheet Anti-Semitism.pdf.

ABSORBING SPACE

Jablonski, Nina G. *Skin: A Natural History.* Berkeley: University of California Press, 2006.

Sherman, Gary D., and Gerald L. Clore. "The Color of Sin." *Psychological Science* 20, no. 8 (2009): 1019–25.

MIGRATING

Blackmon, Douglas A. *Slavery by Another Name: The Re-enslavement of Black People in America from the Civil War to World War II.* New York: Anchor, 2008.

Cotter, Holland. "A Memorial to the Lingering Horror of Lynching." *New York Times,* June 1, 2018. Accessed November 18, 2018. https://www.nytimes.com /2018/06/01/arts/design/national-memorial-for-peace-and-justice-montgomery -alabama.html.

Robertson, Campbell. "A Lynching Memorial Is Opening. The Country Has Never Seen Anything Like It." *New York Times,* April 25, 2018. Accessed November 18, 2018. https://www.nytimes.com/2018/04/25/us/lynching-memorial-alabama.html.

Wilkerson, Isabel. *The Warmth of Other Suns: The Epic Story of America's Great Migration.* New York: Random House, 2010.

FIGHTING BIAS IN NEW PLACES

Airbnb. Accessed November 13, 2018. www.airbnb.com/.

Associated Press. "Detroit-Area Man Shoots at Black Teen Who Asked for Help." Fox News, April 13, 2018. Accessed October 1, 2018. www.foxnews.com/us/detroit -area-man-shoots-at-black-teen-who-asked-for-help.

A.W., "More Airbnb Customers Are Complaining About Racism." *Economist,* June 27, 2016. Accessed September 23, 2018. www.economist.com/gulliver/2016/06/27 /more-airbnb-customers-are-complaining-about-racism.

Badger, Emily. "Airbnb Says It Plans to Take Action to Crack Down on Racial Discrimination on Its Site." *Washington Post,* June 2, 2016. Accessed September 23, 2018. www.washingtonpost.com/news/wonk/wp/2016/06/02/airbnb-says-it-wants -to-take-action-to-crack-down-on-racial-discrimination-on-its-site/?utm _term=.184cdb5bcb29.

Doubek, James. "Black Teenager Shot at After Asking for Directions." NPR, April 15, 2018. Accessed October 1, 2018. www.npr.org/sections/thetwo-way/2018/04/15 /602598119/black-teenager-shot-at-after-asking-for-directions.

Dovidio, John F., and Samuel L. Gaertner. "Aversive Racism." *Advances in Experimental Social Psychology* 36 (2004): 1–52.

Edelman, Benjamin, Michael Luca, and Dan Svirsky. "Racial Discrimination in the Sharing Economy: Evidence from a Field Experiment." *American Economic Journal: Applied Economics* 9, no. 2 (2017): 1–22.

The Editorial Board. "America's Federally Financed Ghettos." *New York Times,* April 7, 2018. Accessed October 1, 2018. www.nytimes.com/2018/04/07/opinion/sunday /americas-federally-financed-ghettos.html.

Fiske, Susan T., and Steven L. Neuberg. "A Continuum of Impression Formation, from Category-Based to Individuating Processes: Influences of Information and Motivation on Attention and Interpretation." *Advances in Experimental Social Psychology,* 1990, 1–74.

Fortin, Jacey. "A Black Teenager Asked for Directions. A Man Responded with Gunfire." *New York Times,* April 14, 2018. Accessed October 1, 2018. www.nytimes.com/2018/04/14/us/michigan-teen-shot-directions.html.

Goff, Phillip Atiba, Claude M. Steele, and Paul G. Davies. "The Space Between Us: Stereotype Threat and Distance in Interracial Contexts." *Journal of Personality and Social Psychology* 94, no. 1 (2008): 91–107.

Green, Victor H. *The Negro Motorist Green Book.* New York: Victor H. Green, 1948.

Hannah-Jones, Nikole. "Living Apart: How the Government Betrayed a Landmark Civil Rights Law." ProPublica, June 25, 2015. Accessed October 1, 2018. www.propublica.org/article/living-apart-how-the-government-betrayed-a-landmark-civil-rights-law.

Karimi, Faith, and Eric Levenson. "Man to Spanish Speakers at New York Restaurant: 'My Next Call Is to ICE.'" CNN, May 17, 2018. Accessed October 1, 2018. www.cnn.com/2018/05/17/us/new-york-man-restaurant-ice-threat/index.html.

Levin, Sam. "Racial Profiling via Nextdoor.com." *East Bay Express,* October 7, 2015. Accessed September 23, 2018. www.eastbayexpress.com/oakland/racial-profiling-via-nextdoorcom/Content?oid=4526919.

Mendes, W. B., J. Blascovich, B. Lickel, and S. Hunter. "Challenge and Threat During Social Interactions with White and Black Men." *Personality and Social Psychology Bulletin* 28, no. 7 (2002): 939–52.

Murphy, Laura W. *Airbnb's Work to Fight Discrimination and Build Inclusion.* Report. September 8, 2016. Accessed September 23, 2018. blog.atairbnb.com/wp-content/uploads/2016/09/REPORT_Airbnbs-Work-to-Fight-Discrimination-and-Build-Inclusion_09292016.pdf.

Nextdoor. Accessed November 13, 2018. nextdoor.com/.

"Report: SC Woman Hit Black Teen and Told Him to Leave Pool Because 'He Didn't Belong.'" ABC11 News, June 29, 2018. Accessed October 1, 2018. abc11.com/report-sc-woman-hit-black-teen-told-him-he-didnt-belong-at-pool/3662114/.

Richeson, Jennifer A., and J. Nicole Shelton. "Negotiating Interracial Interactions: Costs, Consequences, and Possibilities." *Current Directions in Psychological Science* 16, no. 6 (2007): 316–20.

Rothstein, Richard. *The Color of Law: A Forgotten History of How Our Government Segregated America.* New York: Liveright, 2017.

Solon, Olivia. "Airbnb Host Who Canceled Reservation Using Racist Comment Must Pay $5,000." *Guardian,* July 13, 2017. Accessed October 1, 2018. www.theguardian.com/technology/2017/jul/13/airbnb-california-racist-comment-penalty-asian-american.

Tolia, Nirav. "Reducing Racial Profiling on Nextdoor." *Nextdoor* (blog), August 24, 2016. Accessed September 23, 2018. blog.nextdoor.com/2016/08/24/reducing-racial-profiling-on-nextdoor/.

Chapter 8: Hard Lessons

Allport, Gordon W. *The Nature of Prejudice*. Cambridge, Mass.: Addison-Wesley, 1954.

Aronson, Elliot, and Diane Bridgeman. "Jigsaw Groups and the Desegregated Classroom: In Pursuit of Common Goals." *Personality and Social Psychology Bulletin* 5, no. 4 (1979): 438–46.

Gaertner, Samuel L., John F. Dovidio, Phyllis A. Anastasio, Betty A. Bachman, and Mary C. Rust. "The Common Ingroup Identity Model: Recategorization and the Reduction of Intergroup Bias." *European Review of Social Psychology* 4, no. 1 (1993): 1–26.

Pettigrew, Thomas F. "Intergroup Contact Theory." *Annual Review of Psychology* 49, no. 1 (1998): 65–85.

Pettigrew, Thomas F., and Linda R. Tropp. "A Meta-analytic Test of Intergroup Contact Theory." *Journal of Personality and Social Psychology* 90, no. 5 (2006): 751–83.

Wagner, Chandi. *School Segregation Then and Now: How to Move Toward a More Perfect Union*. Report. Center for Public Education, January 2017. Accessed October 1, 2018. www.centerforpubliceducation.org/research/segregation-then-now.

Wells, Amy Stuart, Lauren Fox, and Diana Cordova-Cobo. "How Racially Diverse Schools and Classrooms Can Benefit All Students." Century Foundation, February 9, 2016. Accessed October 1, 2018. tcf.org/content/report/how-racially-diverse-schools-and-classrooms-can-benefit-all-students/.

EMERGING DISPARITIES

Cohen, Geoffrey L., Julio Garcia, Valerie Purdie-Vaughns, Nancy Apfel, and Patricia Brzustoski. "Recursive Processes in Self-Affirmation: Intervening to Close the Minority Achievement Gap." *Science* 324, no. 5925 (2009): 400–403.

"The 49th Annual PDK Poll of the Public's Attitudes Toward the Public Schools." *Phi Delta Kappan* 99, no. 1 (August 29, 2017): NP1–NP32. Accessed October 1, 2018. https://journals.sagepub.com/doi/abs/10.1177/0031721717728274.

Gilliam, Walter S., Angela N. Maupin, Chin R. Reyes, Maria Accavitti, and Frederick Shic. *Do Early Educators' Implicit Biases Regarding Sex and Race Relate to Behavior Expectations and Recommendations of Preschool Expulsions and Suspensions?* Issue brief. Child Study Center, Yale University, September 28, 2016. Accessed September 23, 2018. medicine.yale.edu/childstudy/zigler/publications/Preschool Implicit Bias Policy Brief_final_9_26_276766_5379_v1.pdf.

Moreno, Ivan. "US Charter Schools Put Growing Numbers in Racial Isolation." Associated Press, December 3, 2017. Accessed October 1, 2018. www.apnews.com/e9c25534dfd44851a5e56bd57454b4f5.

Okonofua, Jason A., and Jennifer L. Eberhardt. "Two Strikes: Race and the Disciplining of Young Students." *Psychological Science* 26, no. 5 (2015): 617–24.

Okonofua, Jason A., David Paunesku, and Gregory M. Walton. "Brief Intervention to Encourage Empathic Discipline Cuts Suspension Rates in Half Among Adolescents." *Proceedings of the National Academy of Sciences* 113, no. 19 (2016): 5221–26.

Okonofua, Jason A., Gregory M. Walton, and Jennifer L. Eberhardt. "A Vicious

Cycle: A Social-Psychological Account of Extreme Racial Disparities in School Discipline." *Perspectives on Psychological Science* 11, no. 3 (2016): 381–98.

Orfield, Gary, Erica Frankenburg, Jongyeon Ee, and John Kuscera. *Brown at 60: Great Progress, a Long Retreat, and an Uncertain Future.* Report. Civil Rights Project, UCLA, May 2014. Accessed October 1, 2018. civilrightsproject.ucla.edu/research /k-12-education/integration-and-diversity/brown-at-60-great-progress-a-long -retreat-and-an-uncertain-future/Brown-at-60-051814.pdf.

Reardon, Sean F., Demetra Kalogrides, and Kenneth Shores. "The Geography of Racial /Ethnic Test Score Gaps." *American Journal of Sociology*, 2017. Accessed November 18, 2018. https://cepa.standford.edu/sites/default/files/wp16-10-v201803.pdf.

Skiba, Russell J., Robert S. Michael, Abra Carroll Nardo, and Reece L. Peterson. "The Color of Discipline: Sources of Racial and Gender Disproportionality in School Punishment." *Urban Review* 34, no. 4 (2002): 317–42.

Steele, Dorothy M., and Becki Cohn-Vargas. *Identity Safe Classrooms: Places to Belong and Learn.* Thousand Oaks, Calif.: Corwin, a Sage Company, 2013.

U.S. Department of Education. *Civil Rights Data Collection*, March 23, 2012. Accessed September 23, 2018. ocrdata.ed.gov/.

U.S. Department of Education, Office for Civil Rights, *2013–2014 Civil Rights Data Collection: A First Look.* June 7, 2016. Accessed December 17, 2018. https://www2 .ed.gov/about/offices/list/ocr/docs/2013-14-first-look.pdf.

Yeager, David S., Valerie Purdie-Vaughns, Julio Garcia, Nancy Apfel, Patricia Brzus-toski, Allison Master, William T. Hessert, Matthew E. Williams, and Geoffrey L. Cohen. "Breaking the Cycle of Mistrust: Wise Interventions to Provide Critical Feedback Across the Racial Divide." *Journal of Experimental Psychology: General* 143, no. 2 (2014): 804–24.

SIDESTEPPING RACE

Apfelbaum, Evan P., Kristin Pauker, Nalini Ambady, Samuel R. Sommers, and Mi-chael I. Norton. "Learning (Not) to Talk About Race: When Older Children Underperform in Social Categorization." *Developmental Psychology* 44, no. 5 (2008): 1513–18.

Apfelbaum, Evan P., Kristin Pauker, Samuel R. Sommers, and Nalini Ambady. "In Blind Pursuit of Racial Equality?" *Psychological Science* 21, no. 11 (2010): 1587–92.

Costello, Maureen. "Teaching Hard History." Southern Poverty Law Center, January 31, 2018. Accessed October 1, 2018. www.splcenter.org/20180131/teaching-hard-history.

Lippmann, Walter. *Public Opinion.* New York: Harcourt, Brace, 1922.

"New Survey by Claims Conference Finds Significant Lack of Holocaust Knowledge in the United States." Claims Conference. Accessed October 1, 2018. www.claimscon .org/study/.

Chapter 9: Higher Learning

Clukey, Abby. "Facing the Legacy of Paul Goodloe McIntire." *Cavalier Daily*, No-vember 16, 2017. Accessed September 23, 2018. www.cavalierdaily.com/article /2017/11/facing-the-legacy-of-paul-goodloe-mcintire.

Colby, Sandra L., and Jennifer M. Ortman. *Projections of the Size and Composition of the U.S. Population: 2014 to 2060*. U.S. Census Bureau, U.S. Department of Commerce Economics and Statistics Administration, March 2015. Accessed September 23, 2018. www.census.gov/content/dam/Census/library/publications/2015/demo/p25-1143.pdf.

Craig, Maureen A., and Jennifer A. Richeson. "Information About the US Racial Demographic Shift Triggers Concerns About Anti-White Discrimination Among the Prospective White 'Minority.'" *PLOS One* 12, no. 9 (2017): e0185389.

———. "More Diverse Yet Less Tolerant? How the Increasingly Diverse Racial Landscape Affects White Americans' Racial Attitudes." *Personality and Social Psychology Bulletin* 40, no. 6 (2014): 750–61.

———. "On the Precipice of a 'Majority-Minority' America: Perceived Status Threat from the Racial Demographic Shift Affects White Americans' Political Ideology." *Psychological Science* 25, no. 6 (2014): 1189–97.

Eagan, Kevin, Ellen Bara Stolzenberg, Hilary B. Zimmerman, Melissa C. Aragon, Hannah Whang Sayson, and Cecilia Rios-Aguilar. *The American Freshman: National Norms Fall 2016*. Report. Higher Education Research Institute, UCLA, 2017.

Gallagher, Gary W., and Alan T. Nolan. *The Myth of the Lost Cause and Civil War History*. Bloomington: Indiana University Press, 2010.

James, William. *The Principles of Psychology*. New York: Henry Holt, 1890.

Report to City Council. Report. Blue Ribbon Commission on Race, Memorials, and Public Spaces, City of Charlottesville, December 19, 2016. Accessed September 23, 2018. www.charlottesville.org/Home/ShowDocument?id=48999.

"Showing Up for Racial Justice." Showing Up for Racial Justice. Accessed September 24, 2018. www.showingupforracialjustice.org/.

Wallace, Jerry L. "The Ku Klux Klan in Calvin Coolidge's America." Calvin Coolidge Presidential Foundation, July 14, 2014. Accessed September 23, 2018. coolidgefoundation.org/blog/the-ku-klux-klan-in-calvin-coolidges-america/.

SHOWING UP

Berger, J. M. *Nazis vs. ISIS on Twitter: A Comparative Study of White Nationalist and ISIS Online Social Media Networks*. Report. Program on Extremism, George Washington University, September 2016. Accessed October 1, 2018. cchs.gwu.edu/sites/g/files/zaxdzs2371/f/downloads/Nazis v. ISIS Final_0.pdf.

Du Bois, W. E. B. *The Souls of Black Folk*. New York: Dover, 1903.

Hamm, Jill V. "Barriers and Bridges to Positive Cross-Ethnic Relations." *Youth and Society* 33, no. 1 (2001): 62–98.

Hughes, Diane, James Rodriguez, Emilie P. Smith, Deborah J. Johnson, Howard C. Stevenson, and Paul Spicer. "Parents' Ethnic-Racial Socialization Practices: A Review of Research and Directions for Future Study." *Developmental Psychology* 42, no. 5 (2006): 747–70.

Kawakami, Kerry, Elizabeth Dunn, Francine Karmali, and John F. Dovidio. "Mispredicting Affective and Behavioral Responses to Racism." *Science* 323, no. 5911 (2009): 276–78.

Lamont, Michèle, and Virág Molnár. "The Study of Boundaries in the Social Sciences." *Annual Review of Sociology* 28, no. 1 (2002): 167–95.

Spencer, Margaret Beale. "Children's Cultural Values and Parental Child Rearing Strategies." *Developmental Review* 3, no. 4 (1983): 351–70.

2017 Audit of Anti-Semitic Incidents. Report. Anti-Defamation League, February 27, 2018. Accessed October 1, 2018. www.adl.org/resources/reports/2017-audit-of-anti -semitic-incidents.

THE AFTERMATH

"Ferguson Grand Jury Testimony and Reports. *State of Missouri v. Darren Wilson*." November 2014. Accessed September 23, 2018. arks.princeton.edu/ark:/88435 /dsp014q77ft580.

Gordon-Reed, Annette. "Charlottesville: Why Jefferson Matters." *New York Review of Books*, August 19, 2017. Accessed September 23, 2018. www.nybooks.com /daily/2017/08/19/charlottesville-why-jefferson-matters/.

Heaphy, Timothy J. *Independent Review of the 2017 Protest Events in Charlottesville, Virginia*. Report. November 24, 2017. Accessed September 23, 2018. www.huntonak .com/images/content/3/4/v4/34613/final-report-ada-compliant-ready.pdf.

Markus, Hazel, and Paula Nurius. "Possible Selves." *American Psychologist* 41, no. 9 (1986): 954–69.

Parker, Diantha. "Protests Around the Country Mark the Moment of Ferguson Shooting." *New York Times*, December 1, 2014. Accessed September 23, 2018. www.nytimes.com/2014/12/02/us/protests-around-the-country-mark-the -moment-of-ferguson-shooting.html.

Steele, Claude M. *Whistling Vivaldi: And Other Clues to How Stereotypes Affect Us*. New York: W. W. Norton, 2011.

Steele, Claude M., Steven J. Spencer, and Joshua Aronson. "Contending with Group Image: The Psychology of Stereotype and Social Identity Threat." *Advances in Experimental Social Psychology* 34 (2002): 379–440.

Xia, Rosanna. "Hate Speech vs. Free Speech: Where Is the Line on College Campuses?" *Los Angeles Times*, June 5, 2017. Accessed September 23, 2018. www.latimes .com/local/lanow/la-me-berkeley-free-speech-20170605-story.html.

Chapter 10: The Bottom Line

Bertrand, Marianne, and Sendhil Mullainathan. "Are Emily and Greg More Employable Than Lakisha and Jamal? A Field Experiment on Labor Market Discrimination." *American Economic Review* 94, no. 4 (2004): 991–1013.

Booth, Alison L., Andrew Leigh, and Elena Varganova. "Does Ethnic Discrimination Vary Across Minority Groups? Evidence from a Field Experiment." *Oxford Bulletin of Economics and Statistics* 74, no. 4 (2012): 547–73. doi:10.1111/j.1468-0084.2011.00664.x.

Devos, Thierry, and Mahzarin R. Banaji. "American—White?" *Journal of Personality and Social Psychology* 88, no. 3 (2005): 447–66.

Fryer, Roland G., Jr., Devah Pager, and Jörg L. Spenkuch. "Racial Disparities in Job

Finding and Offered Wages." *Journal of Law and Economics* 56, no. 3 (August 2013): 633–89.

Goffman, Erving. *Stigma: Notes on the Management of Spoiled Identity.* Englewood Cliffs, N.J.: Prentice-Hall, 1963.

Goldin, Claudia, and Cecilia Rouse. "Orchestrating Impartiality: The Impact of 'Blind' Auditions on Female Musicians." *American Economic Review* 90, no. 4 (2000): 715–41.

Greenwald, Anthony G., and Thomas F. Pettigrew. "With Malice Toward None and Charity for Some: Ingroup Favoritism Enables Discrimination." *American Psychologist* 69, no. 7 (2014): 669–84.

Harvard. T. H. Chan School of Public Health. "Poll Finds a Majority of White Americans Say Discrimination Against Whites Exists in America Today." News release, November 7, 2017. Accessed October 1, 2018. www.hsph.harvard.edu/news/press-releases/poll-white-americans-discrimination/.

"High GPA Could Work Against Young Women Job Hunters." *Ohio State News,* March 22, 2018. Accessed October 1, 2018. news.osu.edu/high-gpa-could-work-against-young-women-job-hunters/.

Hughes, Brent L., and Jamil Zaki. "The Neuroscience of Motivated Cognition." *Trends in Cognitive Sciences* 19, no. 2 (2015): 62–64.

Hughes, Brent L., Jamil Zaki, and Nalini Ambady. "Motivation Alters Impression Formation and Related Neural Systems." *Social Cognitive and Affective Neuroscience* 12, no. 1 (2017): 49–60.

Hughes, Brent L., Nalini Ambady, and Jamil Zaki. "Trusting Outgroup, but Not Ingroup Members, Requires Control: Neural and Behavioral Evidence." *Social Cognitive and Affective Neuroscience* 12, no. 3 (2017): 372–81.

Kang, Sonia K., Katherine A. DeCelles, András Tilcsik, and Sora Jun. "Whitened Résumés: Race and Self-Presentation in the Labor Market." *Administrative Science Quarterly* 61, no. 3 (March 17, 2016): 469–502.

Livingston, Robert W., and Nicholas A. Pearce. "The Teddy-Bear Effect: Does Having a Baby Face Benefit Black Chief Executive Officers?" *Psychological Science* 20, no. 10 (2009): 1229–36.

Oreopoulos, Philip. "Why Do Skilled Immigrants Struggle in the Labor Market? A Field Experiment with Thirteen Thousand Resumes." *American Economic Journal: Economic Policy* 3, no. 4 (2011): 148–71. doi:10.1257/pol.3.4.148.

Quadlin, Natasha. "The Mark of a Woman's Record: Gender and Academic Performance in Hiring." *American Sociological Review* 83, no. 2 (2018): 331–60.

Quillian, Lincoln, Devah Pager, Ole Hexel, and Arnfinn H. Midtbøen. "Meta-analysis of Field Experiments Shows No Change in Racial Discrimination in Hiring over Time." *Proceedings of the National Academy of Sciences* 114, no. 41 (2017): 10870–75.

U.S. Department of Labor, Bureau of Labor Statistics. *Employment and Unemployment Among Youth—Summer 2018.* August 16, 2018. Accessed October 1, 2018. www.bls.gov/news.release/youth.nr0.htm.

Wolgast, Sima, Fredrik Björklund, and Martin Bäckström. "Applicant Ethnicity

Affects Which Questions Are Asked in a Job Interview." *Journal of Personnel Psychology* 17, no. 2 (2018): 66–74.

THE TRAINING IMPULSE

Crandall, Christian S., Amy Eshleman, and Laurie O'Brien. "Social Norms and the Expression and Suppression of Prejudice: The Struggle for Internalization." *Journal of Personality and Social Psychology* 82, no. 3 (2002): 359–78.

Frey, William H. *The Millennial Generation: A Demographic Bridge to America's Diverse Future.* Report. Brookings Institution, January 2018. Accessed October 1, 2018. www.brookings.edu/research/millennials/.

Haag, Matthew. "Oakland Residents Reported a Black Firefighter for Doing His Job." *New York Times*, June 26, 2018. Accessed October 11, 2018. www.nytimes .com/2018/06/26/us/oakland-black-firefighter-bias.html.

Kay, Aaron C., Danielle Gaucher, Jennifer M. Peach, Kristin Laurin, Justin Friesen, Mark P. Zanna, and Steven J. Spencer. "Inequality, Discrimination, and the Power of the Status Quo: Direct Evidence for a Motivation to See the Way Things Are as the Way They Should Be." *Journal of Personality and Social Psychology* 97, no. 3 (2009): 421–34.

Monin, Benoît, and Dale T. Miller. "Moral Credentials and the Expression of Prejudice." *Journal of Personality and Social Psychology* 81, no. 1 (2001): 33–43.

Ormiston, Margaret E., and Elaine M. Wong. "License to Ill: The Effects of Corporate Social Responsibility and CEO Moral Identity on Corporate Social Irresponsibility." *Personnel Psychology* 66, no. 4 (2013): 861–93.

Pager, Devah, and Hana Shepherd. "The Sociology of Discrimination: Racial Discrimination in Employment, Housing, Credit, and Consumer Markets." *Annual Review of Sociology* 34, no. 1 (2008): 181–209.

Paluck, Elizabeth Levy, and Donald P. Green. "Prejudice Reduction: What Works? A Review and Assessment of Research and Practice." *Annual Review of Psychology* 60, no. 1 (2009): 339–67.

Prentice, Deborah A., and Dale T. Miller. "Pluralistic Ignorance and Alcohol Use on Campus: Some Consequences of Misperceiving the Social Norm." *Journal of Personality and Social Psychology* 64, no. 2 (1993): 243–56.

Veklerov, Kimberly. "Black Firefighter on Inspection Duty in Oakland Hills Gets Videotaped, Reported to Police." *San Francisco Chronicle*, June 24, 2018. Accessed October 11, 2018. www.sfchronicle.com/bayarea/article/Black-firefighter-on -inspection-duty-in-Oakland-13021084.php.

BEYOND TRAINING

Associated Press. "Papa John's Founder Resigns After He Used a Racist Slur." PBS, July 12, 2018. Accessed October 1, 2018. www.pbs.org/newshour/nation/papa -johns-founder-resigns-after-he-used-a-racist-slur.

The Grim Reality of Being a Female Job Seeker. Report. Accessed September 27, 2018. fairygodboss.com/research/job-seeker-appearance.

Jackson, Amy Elisa. "This Is Exactly What Hiring Managers & Recruiters Look for When Scanning Resumes." *Glassdoor,* August 2, 2017. Accessed September 27, 2018. www.glassdoor.com/blog/scanning-resumes/.

Koblin, John. "After Racist Tweet, Roseanne Barr's Show Is Canceled by ABC." *New York Times*, May 29, 2018. Accessed October 1, 2018. www.nytimes.com/2018/05/29/business/media/roseanne-barr-offensive-tweets.html.

"A Letter from Howard Schultz to Starbucks Partners Regarding Race Together." Starbucks Newsroom, March 22, 2015. Accessed October 1, 2018. news.starbucks.com/news/a-letter-from-howard-schultz-to-starbucks-partners-regarding-race-together.

Lopez, Michael J., and Brian M. Mills. "Opportunistic Shirking Behavior During Unpaid Overtime." *Applied Economics Letters* (2018). https://www.tandfonline.com/doi/abs/10.1080/13504851.2018.1488048?journalCode=rael20.

Madell, Robin. "Here's Exactly What Hiring Managers Look for in a Resume." *U.S. News & World Report,* March 7, 2016. Accessed September 27, 2018. money.usnews.com/money/blogs/outside-voices-careers/articles/2016-03-07/heres-exactly-what-hiring-managers-look-for-in-a-resume.

Parsons, Christopher A., Johan Sulaeman, Michael C. Yates, and Daniel S. Hamermesh. "Strike Three: Discrimination, Incentives, and Evaluation." *American Economic Review* 101, no. 4 (2011): 1410–35.

Pettigrew, Thomas F., and Linda R. Tropp. "A Meta-analytic Test of Intergroup Contact Theory." *Journal of Personality and Social Psychology* 90, no. 5 (2006): 751–83.

Phillips, Katherine W. "How Diversity Makes Us Smarter." *Scientific American,* October 1, 2014. Accessed December 17, 2018. https://www.scientificamerican.com/article/how-diversity-makes-us-smarter/.

Sanburn, Josh. "How to Make Your Resume Last Longer Than 6 Seconds." *Time,* April 13, 2012. Accessed September 27, 2018. business.time.com/2012/04/13/how-to-make-your-resume-last-longer-than-6-seconds/.

Wolgast, Sima, Fredrik Björklund, and Martin Bäckström. "Applicant Ethnicity Affects Which Questions Are Asked in a Job Interview." *Journal of Personnel Psychology* 17, no. 2 (2018): 66–74.

ILLUSTRATION CREDITS

Page 25: Otto H. MacLin and Roy S. Malpass. "Racial Categorization of Faces: The Ambiguous Race Face Effect." *Psychology, Public Policy, and Law* 7, no. 1 (2001): 98–118. Published by the American Psychological Association. Reprinted with permission.

Page 28: Jennifer L. Eberhardt, Nilanjana Dasgupta, and Tracy L. Banaszynski. "Believing Is Seeing: The Effects of Racial Labels and Implicit Beliefs on Face Perception." *Personality and Social Psychology Bulletin* 29, no. 3 (2003): 360–70. Published by the American Psychological Association. Reprinted with permission.

Page 59: By the author.

Page 65: Jennifer L. Eberhardt, Phillip Atiba Goff, Valerie J. Purdie, and Paul G. Davies. "Seeing Black: Race, Crime, and Visual Processing." *Journal of Personality and Social Psychology* 87, no. 6 (2004): 876–93. Published by the American Psychological Association. Reprinted with permission.

Page 67: Joshua Correll, Bernadette Park, Charles M. Judd, and Bernd Wittenbrink. "The Police Officer's Dilemma: Using Ethnicity to Disambiguate Potentially Threatening Individuals." *Journal of Personality and Social Psychology* 83, no. 6 (2002): 1314–29. Published by the American Psychological Association. Reprinted with permission.

Page 86: Figure provided by Daniel Simons. D. J. Simons and C. F. Chabris. "Gorillas in Our Midst: Sustained Inattentional Blindness for Dynamic Events." *Perception* 28 (1999), 1059–74.

Page 130: By the author.

Pages 137, 139: Josiah Clark Nott and George R. Gliddon. *Types of Mankind*. Philadelphia: Lippincott, Grambo, 1854.

Page 161: Courtney M. Bonam, Hilary B. Bergsieker, and Jennifer L. Eberhardt. "Polluting Black Space." *Journal of Experimental Psychology: General* 145, no. 11 (2016), 1561–82. Published by the American Psychological Association. Reprinted with permission.

INDEX

Note: Page numbers in *italics* refer to illustrations.